£5,00

Professional
Practices

Tony Becher

Professional Practices

Commitment & Capability in a Changing Environment

Transaction Publishers
New Brunswick (U.S.A.) and London (U.K.)

This book is printed on acid-free paper that meets the American National Standard for Permanence of Paper for Printed Library Materials.

Library of Congress Catalog Number: 99-20883
ISBN: 1-56000-414-2
Printed in the United States of America

Library of Congress Cataloging-in-Publication Data

Becher, Tony.
    Professional practices : commitment and capability in a changing environment / Tony Becher.
        p. cm.
    Includes bibliographical references and index.
    ISBN 1-56000-414-2 (alk. paper)
    1. Professions. 2. Professional employees. I. Title.
HD8038.A1B43   1999
331.7'12—dc21
                                                            99-20883
                                                               CIP

To Susan

My close companion and partner

and

to my 190 respondents

Contents

Preface

By well-established tradition, a preface licenses the author not only to acknowledge indebtedness to others, but to indulge in anecdote and autobiography to a degree not always appropriate in the body of the text. I propose to take advantage of this useful convention. The anecdote takes the form of a sketch map of the intellectual journey that led to the writing of this book; the autobiography explains briefly why I have adopted one particular approach to the subject matter in preference to others. The acknowledgments, as is customary, occupy the concluding section.

My fascination with the professions, as a phenomenon in their own right, has a history stretching over nearly two decades. It was in 1980 that I first embarked on an exploration of the cultures of academic disciplines which culminated in the publication in 1989 of my *Academic Tribes and Territories*. Early in the course of the research, I became conscious that the three professionally oriented subject areas among the twelve I studied in their university settings—law, mechanical engineering, and pharmacy—seemed less well-documented and less easy to characterize than their "pure" counterparts, such as history and physics. At the time, I set this aside as an intriguing but not directly relevant puzzle.

A new dimension was added when I was given the opportunity with two highly congenial colleagues, Ron Barnett and Morwenna Cork, to undertake a small-scale comparative study in 1985 of the nature of professional training in nursing, pharmacy, and teaching (reported in Barnett, Becher, and Cork, 1987 and Becher, 1990). For the next few years I continued to be involved primarily in research into various aspects of higher education, but in the academic year 1992–93 I decided it was time to resume my interest in the professions. The present study is based on a research proposal I put to the Economic and Social Research Council in late 1992, which was awarded a grant in 1993 for the subsequent three-year period (later extended for another year). During the early stages of the fieldwork I was also involved in convening a conference for the Society for Research into Higher Education, on a bridging subject between my earlier and my more recent concerns. The theme, governments and professional education, was also the title of the accompanying background volume (Becher, 1994). A number of the ideas that arose from this involvement have proved helpful to my understanding of the pressures to which professions are subject.

The way in which I have chosen to tackle the present enquiry derives—as far as I can determine—mainly from my academic rearing as a student of philosophy at Cambridge in the 1950s. That was a period in which Wittgenstein's influence reigned supreme, when it was held to be intellectually degenerate to engage in any form of metaphysics. Doubtless, it is my loss, as others have often pointed out, that I have never been able fully to abandon that firmly instituted conviction. My way of thinking therefore lacks the grand sweep of theory, confining itself instead to a close analysis of specific pieces of data, which I examine to find significant but circumscribed patterns and interconnections. The outcome is a style more characteristic of a painstaking craftsman than of an inventive artist; of a tactician rather than a strategist in the ceaseless battle to understand and explain the world of human affairs.

The reader should accordingly be forewarned to expect no wide-ranging insights, nor even much reference to the all-embracing hypotheses advanced by others. At best, I offer what aspires to be a sensitive, if selective, glimpse into the working contexts and particular attitudes and ways of life of members of six occupational groups, drawing out some of their mutual similarities and differences, their common and idiosyncratic concerns. My own particular interest, which I hope others may share, lies in the recognition that those who live in worlds with which I am unfamiliar do not *au fond* behave very differently from other people: that strangers are not after all as strange as might be imagined, but turn out to have many of the same basic motivations and emotions as those to which the rest of humanity are subject.

But the book also has a further and more practical purpose than to contribute to the better understanding of professionalism. The achievement of that understanding, I argue, is essential to the important business of helping professionals keep up with the frequent changes that affect their work and that threaten to diminish their competence. The provision of what is nowadays commonly called continuing professional development—or in its acronymic version CPD—has become a quite sizeable industry, although, according to the professionals themselves, much of it suffers from a failure to appreciate what their main needs are and how they can best be met. The same holds true for much initial training. If this study helps to bridge some of the differences in mutual understanding and perception between practitioners and pedagogues, and leads to a more enlightened appreciation of professionals' learning needs, it will have achieved everything it sets out to do.

In carrying out the research, I must record a substantial debt, personal and pecuniary, to my financial sponsors, the Economic and Social Research Council, both in funding the field research and in allowing me to use some of the unspent balances to conduct a literature search based on the University of California at Berkeley, whose Center for Studies in Higher Education gave me a welcome base while I mined the university's massive library.

There are many old friends, close colleagues, and brief acquaintances who helped in one way or another in the process of bringing this study to completion: here, I single out for mention those who have made a significant contribution. Over the five-year period from 1993 to 1998, Pat Bone, Hayley Kirby, Margaret Ralph, and Penny Searls skilfully word-processed the interview notes and transcriptions and the successive drafts of the book. I am indebted to my son, Will Becher, for his skill in laying out and presenting the four figures in the text. Heather Nicholas in Sussex and Barbara Glendenning in Berkeley were a major help in my attempts to track down references on a broad theme that could not be found in any established bibliographical index. I am grateful to the officers of the various professional bodies who enabled me to check the relevant statistical and factual information, but particularly to Bill Cole, Research Officer of the Law Society, whose help went well beyond this to provide an informed commentary on the section on law in chapter 2.

A number of colleagues have also read and helpfully critiqued various sections of the text: notably Roger France, Marion Kumar, Anne Mandy, and Geoffrey Squires. I was lucky enough to persuade Michael Black, a senior publisher's editor and friend of many years' standing, to read the whole of the contents, which he reviewed with characteristic perceptiveness and clarity. To Susan Petri—to whom I owe a massive debt for her tireless readings and rereadings of every draft and for her countless constructive ideas and suggestions—a share in the dedication is inadequate recompense. The other share must rightly go to my 190 respondents, for their frank and often very entertaining interviews, and for providing the data without which this book would never even have existed.

Sussex, July 1998   Tony Becher

Part 1

Prospect

1

Introduction

What this Book is About

A title, unless inordinately long, generally fails to convey with any accuracy what its subject is about: and where it is deliberately ambiguous, the problem is further compounded. The term "professional practices" is here meant to allow for three related but distinct interpretations: the common activities, or established practices, of professionals; their working organizations—that is, their firms or practices; and their processes of developing and reinforcing professional skills, in the sense that "practice makes perfect." Bringing these together by way of simplification, it may be helpful to remark that the chapters that follow deal in one way or another with the working lives of professionals. But this statement needs to be qualified by acknowledging, first, that only certain aspects of those lives are referred to, and second, that only a limited range of professionals is taken into account.

The research on which this work is based adopted as its twin starting-points the contentions that studies of professional values could be given a clearer focus if viewed against a background of change: and that the strategies involved to cope with such change would throw light on the process of maintaining professional knowledge and capability. In line with this approach, after a brief review of each of the six professions chosen as subjects for inquiry (chapter 2), an account of the major influences to which the professions in question have recently been subject (chapter 3) is followed by an examination of related patterns of change in professional careers (chapters 4 and 5). The most substantial chapters in terms of length and content deal, respectively, with formal mid-career learning (chapter 6) and its informal counterpart (chapter 7). Problems directly related to establishing professional competence are examined in chapter 8, which leads into a concluding chapter reviewing some of the main issues arising from the study.

The choice of which professions to study, while it may appear at first glance to be arbitrary, was in actuality the product of a number of calculated trade-offs. In the first place, taking account of previous experience with a somewhat comparable study (Becher, 1989), I decided that a comparative enquiry was likely to prove more fruitful than one based on a single subject. But given a requirement to tackle more than one profession, the question arose of how many would provide a manageable yet reasonably substantial database. In principle, it might seem that the more different groupings the investigation could cover, the more convincing and comprehensive the findings would be. As against this, however, there lurked the risk of superficiality of treatment and the complication of a heavily overloaded database. Given a concern to explore each constituent profession in adequate depth, and the limits of the time available to do so, I decided that six would be a sensible target to aim at. In the event, this turned out to set a realistic limit on what could be achieved.

A further consideration related to the notion of professionalism. In colloquial parlance, the term is a very broad one. One might for example refer to "a professional gambler" or "a professional con-man": a more generous application of the concept than I was inclined to adopt. It seemed important in undertaking an exploratory enquiry of this kind to focus on professions with a clear-cut and unequivocal attribution. This in effect ruled out groups with uncertain boundaries and ambiguous status, which could prove difficult to handle and might invoke issues on the margins of professionalism, if not outside it altogether. Another obvious desideratum was that the practitioners concerned should be publicly recognizable and accessible in both geographical and dispositional terms. That would disqualify, for example, actuaries—a well-established but little-known and numerically limited occupational group, clustered mainly in the financial center of London, and equally those concerned with confidential activities, such as military attachés and certain categories of civil servant.

With these various considerations in mind, medicine, law, and architecture were readily identified each as recognized professions of long standing which appeared to offer interesting mutual similarities and contrasts. In choosing the other three, there promised to be some advantage in selecting cognate groups which would constitute matching pairs—in the sense that each pair shared some overlapping functional concerns. This could be expected to—and in the event did—yield useful information about the interactions between partially competing professions. The pairs chosen, again using the general criteria enumerated above, were pharmacy (of which I had some knowledge from previous research) as a subsidiary partner to medicine; accountancy as an opposite number to law; and structural engineering as closely related to architecture.

Who the Book is For

It is the practitioners in these professions—medicine, pharmacy, law, accountancy, architecture, and structural engineering—who provide the substance of the book. The findings need not, however, be seen as narrowly confined to the six, in that they also represent wider aspects of professions as a whole. It is not a contentious issue that in any field, the less established members tend to select the more fully established as their models, and that some of the characteristic features of the latter can be identified in the former. So while, for example, people engaged in teaching and social work do not enjoy as many of the privileges of professionality as those in medicine or the law, they nevertheless adopt a number of the same values and attitudes. It would be for such professionals outside the fields here covered to judge the relevance of the findings to their situations: but that there can be no relevance at all is certainly a false assumption.

With this said, the main audience for the book lies in more specific directions. Its primary focus is on those who, in one way or another, are concerned with or responsible for the education and training of professionals in general. For the now quite sizeable category of trainers, the contents should serve first and foremost to advance their greater understanding of those whose mid-career learning they seek to promote. Few of them would, given current views of the nature of continuing education, contest the importance of a close awareness of the frames of reference and attitudes towards acquiring new knowledge of their clientele. It is primarily such insights that they should be able to gain from the following chapters. For the related but distinct group of those concerned with the initial training of professionals, the text may be expected to bear a somewhat different emphasis. The charge often laid against them (see the postscript) is that they pay insufficient attention to the demands made on practicing professionals, and are ill-informed about what their current students need to know of the problems and possibilities of their future lives. Such issues, again, are subject to detailed enquiry in what follows.

A further potential audience consists of members of the six professions in question, who may well find it of interest to learn, not only how their immediate colleagues view the current scene, but what differences there are between their own activities and concerns and those of other professional groups. To judge by the interest expressed in hearing about the eventual findings by those I interviewed, this possible source of readership cannot be discounted. Such may also be the case with a number of those contemplating a professional career and wondering about the commitments involved.

There is, in addition, a smaller category of those with a scholarly involvement in professionalism and in those sectors of higher and adult education that touch on the professional world. They may find in the following pages ideas and data relevant to their own research concerns. It should, however, be emphasized that this study, although sharing an ethnographic approach characteristic of anthropology and some of the many rival schools of sociology, is not itself an anthropological or sociological work, in that it does not owe allegiance to any established theories or doctrines in those fields.

Finally, for a wider and more general readership, an insight into the working lives of the professionals with whom they come into contact, and an understanding of the ideas they embrace, may be of more than passing interest.

Previous Accounts of Professions

The study of professional activity has long existed as a field of enquiry, particularly among sociologists. Weber was an early forerunner; Carr-Saunders and Wilson (1933) provided the first main landmark. From then on, successive waves of theorizing, in tune with the intellectual fashions of the day, beat against the shifting shores of practice. Before World War II, the emphasis was on the ennobling aspects of the professions, and especially their ethical values and their altruistic traditions. The 1950s and early 1960s saw a growing interest in their defining properties, which subsequently gave way during the later 1960s and the 1970s to a highly critical account of their inequities, including their claims to status and their assumptions of privilege. It is only in more recent years that attention has turned to their individual and collective characteristics as particular forms of occupation.

There are abundant definitions of what a profession comprises. One of the most comprehensive is worth reproducing here, even though in its very comprehensiveness it lacks anything approaching universal application. Under the heading "Some defining characteristics of a profession," the Monopolies Commission (1970) enumerates seven criteria:

1. Practitioners apply a specialist skill enabling them to offer a specialized service;
2. The skill has been acquired by intellectual and practical training in a well-defined area of study;
3. The service calls for a high degree of detachment and integrity on the part of the practitioner in exercising his [*sic*] personal judgement on behalf of his client;
4. The service involves direct, personal and fiduciary relations with the client;
5. The practitioners collectively have a particular sense of responsibility for maintaining the competence and integrity of the occupation as a whole;
6. The practitioners tend or are required to avoid certain methods of attracting business;
7. The practitioners are organised in bodies which, with or without state intervention, are concerned to provide machinery for testing competence and regulating standards of competence and conduct.

For all their wide sweep, these attributes omit a number of the features emphasized by other more recent commentators, including the exclusive character of the professions (Abbott, 1988; Burrage et al., 1990); the enjoyment of autonomy (Burrage et al., 1990; Crompton, 1987; Eraut, 1994); the control of a particular market (Cervero, 1988); and the recognized entitlement to material rewards and a high level of status (Crompton, 1987).

The reader will find, in the account which follows, many instances of individual and collective failures to meet all of these lofty requirements, though some of them certainly obtain. Rather than attempt a rival depiction of a field so complex and various as to defy any simple summary, it may be more to the point to refer to what Becker (1970) describes as a "folk concept" of a profession—namely a down-to-earth and commonsense view based on knowledge by acquaintance rather than knowledge by definition—and to note his contention that what may be labelled the symbolic attributes of a profession are not adequately reflected in the realities of occupational life. The following chapters in large part comprise an attempt to portray those realities.

The Specifics of the Present Study

This enquiry is in certain respects an oddity. The way in which it relates to other writings on the professions and on professional education can best be explained in terms of the metaphor of an island, part of a small archipelago, sandwiched between two land masses. The largest land mass contains two related sets of inhabitants, focused on discussions of the professions in general and accounts of individual professions in particular. Examples of the first of these include works by Abbott (1988), Burrage and Torstendahl (1990), Freidson (1994), Johnson (1972), Larson (1977), and many others. A feature of the majority is a tendency to regard professions and professionalization as a unitary phenomenon, making few if any distinctions between fields as diverse as medicine and architecture. The homogenization derives from a concentration on sociological factors at a macro level, invoking concepts such as the exploitation of power and the creation of monopolistic markets for professional services.

The other group of contributions, although related, is more specific, concentrating on individual professions: among relatively recent cases would be found the diverse contributions by Addis (1990) on structural engineering; Crinson and Lubbock (1994) on architecture; Hafferty and McKinlay (1993) on medicine; Morison and Leith (1992) on the bar; and Roslender (1992) on accountancy. One noticeable feature of most publications in this genre is that, in portraying—often in close detail—the nature and functions of the professions concerned, they totally ignore the fact that professional capability depends not merely on gaining an initial level of competence but on being able to go on learning one's trade throughout one's professional career. This omission of what—as will be seen—constitutes a key professional activity weakens their claim to provide a comprehensive treatment of their subject matter.

The second land mass—somewhat smaller than the first—also houses two loosely connected groups, one dealing with the provision of continuing professional education and the other with studies of learning processes among professional practitioners. The doyen of the former is Houle (1980), with Cervero (1988), Curry et al. (1993), Madden and Mitchell (1993), and Vaughan (1991), among others, following in his wake. There is again a tendency among these authors to treat all professions as identical in their needs for continuing education: thus Houle (1980) argues that

> Certain dominant ideas guide all of them [the professions] as they turn to the task of educating their members…they tend to use essentially the same kinds of facilities, techniques and thought processes (p. 15).

The evidence from the present study (see in particular chapters 6 and 7) shows such a view to be a considerable over-simplification.

The close neighbors to the group of studies focusing on continuing professional education, with a certain amount of overlap of membership, comprise a variety of explorations of professionals' learning processes. The counterpart doyen to Houle here is Schön (1983 and 1987), whose style of enquiry has influenced several subsequent writers. Among others working in the same general territory—some of whom are critical of Schön's approach—are Eraut (1994), Marsick (1987), Marsick and Watkins (1990), and—specifically in relation to medicine—Boreham (1989). The same general tendency to homogenize is evident among the authors of these publications: the assumption, as with Houle, is that professions "tend to use essentially the same...thought processes."

Insofar as psychologically oriented studies in the one territory adopt a micro-level approach, and sociologically oriented enquiries in the other are carried out at a macro level, the inhabitants of the archipelago, located somewhere between the two land masses, could appropriately be described as operating at an intermediate meso level. They rely predominantly on ethnographic data, focusing on learning strategies rather than learning processes or issues of social or educational policy. Besides the present enquiry, the two neighboring islands of the archipelago are occupied respectively by the recent writings of Eraut et al. (1998) and Gear et al. (1994). Both are akin to this work in their general approach, but adopt somewhat different emphases. Gear et al. (1994) explore the nature of informal learning projects and their relationship to continuing professional development among a group of professions closely similar to those covered (though with nurses and social workers taking the place of pharmacists and accountants); Eraut et al. (1998) focus on patterns of on-the-job training across a broader range of occupational sectors (business, engineering and health care). Both rely extensively on interview data, each drawing on roughly the same sized sample as my own (150 in the case of Gear et al. and 120, plus 88 follow-up interviews, in the Eraut et al. study).

This account by no means exhausts the literature on the professions, being intended merely to represent those publications which are most usefully compared and contrasted with the present one. To summarize, the solitary inhabitant of this particular island is concerned with the portrayal of aspects of professional cultures through the exploration of how their practitioners set about maintaining the necessary level of capability in the context of the changes which impinge on them. The way in which this issue is tackled will be briefly explained in the next section.

The Method of Enquiry

The stance adopted in carrying out this research derived from the view that a careful and extensive analysis of what people actually say can illuminate their worlds in a contrasting way from one predicated on a predetermined theoretical position, and can help towards achieving a closely grounded understanding of why they act as they do. As suggested above, this seems to be a relatively novel approach to the study of the professions.

Be that as it may, any attempt to understand how and why people behave in particular ways must depend on some kind of empirical investigation: the exercise of deriving conclusions logically from first premises yields an altogether different set of results. And if one is after empirical data, there are four main ways of acquiring it. The first, over which the enquirer has least control, is to collect, analyze and interpret the empirical findings of others; the second, to conduct some form of questionnaire-based survey; the third, to base one's research on interviews; and the fourth, to engage in participant observation.

Of these, I decided to rule out the second and the fourth. Surveys are an appropriate means of gathering information of a general kind, allowing for broad-brush indications of people's opinions but leaving no scope for matters of finer detail: their credibility, moreover, depends on the acquisition of large numbers of responses. Participant observation has the opposite qualities: it is in some respects an ideal way of getting to understand how a particular group of people think and behave, but it is extremely time-consuming, runs the risk of being over-specific in its findings, and can present considerable problems in negotiating the necessary permission to carry it out. The third approach, interviewing, was accordingly my preferred option, which I decided to supplement with the first, the collection of findings from other relevant research.

Those who might consider it helpful to know in more detail how the interviews were carried out, and what issues they sought to cover, are referred to the brief appendix on methodological issues. Here, it may suffice to say that I set out to interview 30 respondents in each of the six professions,[1] between them covering as many different settings as possible. Age and seniority were obvious considerations: so, clearly, was gender. But it also seemed important to embrace a variety of working contexts. The practitioner's degree of specialization could be seen to impose its own demands and characteristics; so, too, could the size and nature of the organization in which each individual worked. Geographical factors —whether the practice was rural, suburban, or metropolitan—might also be expected to prove a significant variable.

This set of considerations represented a deliberate attempt to gain some understanding of the range of experience across each profession as a whole, rather than concentrating on one particular sub-group. The obvious limitation is that the numbers in each of the numerous sub-categories were very small, suggesting a difficulty in the generalizability and representativeness of the information each yielded. In the event, however, the variations in the characteristics and situations of respondents turned out to make relatively little difference to their fundamental representations of their values and their practice. There were, predictably, internal divergences between individuals in each field, but these were clearly outweighed by the similarities within each main professional sub-group—hospital doctors as against general practitioners, chartered accountants as against management accountants, and so on. The contrasts between the professions themselves, as one might expect, were in some respects very marked.

Rather than choosing potential respondents by some kind of random procedure—taking every thousandth name, say, out of a list of licensed practitioners—I elected to gather my sample by the so-called snowball technique (somewhat analogous with a chain letter): I began by interviewing the person I best knew in each profession, and asking him or her then to suggest two or three other possible interviewees. The process was repeated in all subsequent interviews. As the sequence went on, it was possible to spot obvious gaps in the coverage—not enough people in large firms, say, or too few women interviewees—and to ask for specific suggestions in these categories. It would be stretching matters to suggest that this procedure yielded anything like a statistically representative sample of the membership of each profession, but it did within the limits of practical possibility seem to result in a reasonably wide and varied coverage.

The interviews themselves were conducted on a semi-structured basis—that is, I based them on a broad agenda sent to respondents in advance, but let the latter take the lead in deciding what they particularly wanted to talk about. Although the focus of the study, as noted earlier, was on professionals' experience of change, their strategies for coping with it, and their views in general about their needs for continuing to learn, many of them also raised other issues—for example, concerning their careers or the new demands on them to demonstrate the quality of their work. These contextual topics, of interest in their own right as well as in relation to the main theme, are the subject of separate chapters in the book.

It was not until the interview data had been analyzed that I embarked on a systematic review of the relevant findings of other researchers. This served two functions. First, as intended, it gave an indication of where my accounts diverged from those fellow-enquirers—and thus needed to be flagged as open to question—and showed where they were independently corroborated by related investigations. The second function was unanticipated, but important in relation to the applicability of my results. It soon became apparent that a very large majority of the research literature I was able to track down was North American in origin, but that even so its contents closely matched what I had found. Perhaps, in the event, it is not altogether surprising that people engaged in very similar activities, even when the contexts of those activities are discernably different, share many features in common.[2] The fact that legal practitioners in the US are designated as attorneys, without the distinction made on the other side of the Atlantic between barristers and solicitors, does not mean that they must have quite distinctive views about the nature and values of their profession, or quite different ways of ensuring that they continue to exercise proper capability in its practice.

In virtue of the convergence of my collective conclusions with many of the specific outcomes of US investigations, it seems reasonable to claim that, although the fieldwork was carried out exclusively in Britain, the findings are of general relevance to the counterpart professions in Canada and the US. They would also appear, though on the basis of less extensive evidence, to be applicable to the Australian scene. What is quite clear, however, is that they can only have a very indirect bearing on Continental Europe, in that, as Torstendahl (1990) points out, the historic origins and contemporary ethos of the professions there deviate considerably from those of their Anglo-Saxon counterparts. As he usefully sums it up, the environment in which professional activities have developed

> has been determined in continental and Scandinavian Europe primarily by the state and in the Anglo-American world primarily by private sector enterprise...knowledge-based groups behave in some specific ways in the most different social settings, but...they are, at the same time, very dependent on the crucial variables of these social settings (p. 8).

The Limitations of the Approach

It is sound policy to acknowledge, at the outset of any account of research findings, the main limitations of the approach adopted. While this may not necessarily disarm criticism, it will at least confirm a recognition that alternative approaches might have been more satisfactory in some respects, if in their turn deficient in others. There are, as I see it, two main problems in the study reported here, one to do with its lack of a critical stance and the other related to its absence of a general theoretical framework.

Those viewing the professions from an externalist perspective have, at various times, come up with a wide range of negative comments. One often-quoted view, advanced by Shaw (1932/1911) claims that "all professions...are...conspiracies against the laity" (p. 11). In much the same vein, Illich (1977) contends that "The disabling of the citizen through professional dominance is completed through the power of illusion" (p. 27). Johnson (1972) sees professionalism as a form of occupational control, in which the exercise of power looms large; Larson (1977) presents a Marxist account according to which professionals collectively set out to constitute and control a market for their expertise, to translate their special skills into economic and social rewards, and to erect professionalism into an ideology. These, along with many other negative portrayals of the professions[3], mostly by sociologists, have led some of their number to protest that

> There is a highly critical tone in much of the current literature on the professions, which often seeks to debunk the moral claims of the professions, and to show that their behaviour falls short of their proclaimed ideals, while the critics themselves, by implication at least, assert the superiority of their own moral positions, in pointing out the excessive power and privileges that the professions enjoy, that their ethical codes are bogus and a cover for the pursuit of their material interests, and so on (Burrage et al., 1990, p. 223).

Academics, often writing from a left-wing standpoint, are not the only sources of generalized hostility towards the professional world. Burrage (1992) has cogently reviewed the impact and ironies of Margaret Thatcher's eleven-year confrontation with the professions. As he points out, much of the activity of the progressively right-wing administrations under her leadership was directed at weakening the position of professional bodies and practitioners. Along with the trade unions, they were demonized as constituting a state within a state, whose exclusionary and monopolistic practices had to give way to the greater glories of a market economy. Fired at from all directions at once, it is not surprising that, by the early 1990s, the professions found themselves in a vulnerable way, and showed a general concern to give a positive demonstration of their contributions to society and the worth of their activities.

The absence of a critical account in the following pages of what professionals do and what professions stand for is a direct artifact of the method of enquiry on which this study was based. It is a characteristic of ethnographic investigation that the researcher is concerned to enter as fully as possible into the frame of reference of the subjects of the research, and attempts subsequently to portray the world as they see it. To step outside this internal vantage point, and to view the scene once more as an outsider, is both to blunt the impact of the findings and to generate an awkward sense of double vision. Accordingly, the more sceptical readers may well conclude that what is being offered is a partial and partisan view of the subject matter. It is of course proper that they should supply their own correctives where they consider it necessary. The only point I would wish to emphasize is that, as far as I was able to tell, the large majority of my respondents for a large part of the time were speaking frankly according to their beliefs (if they were not, then they managed remarkably well to tell the same stories without an opportunity to collude one with another). Most of their key views and attitudes, and their accounts of their activities, were independently corroborated by one or more fellow-professionals; where this was not the case, the differences have been acknowledged in the text.

The second limitation again stems from the choice of research stance. To start an enquiry as far as possible without presuppositions is arguably to allow the data preeminence over an imposed and inevitably narrowing set of constraints. The tenets of what Glaser and Strauss (1967) originally defined as grounded theory require the investigator to work, so to speak, from the bottom up, as against adopting the top down approach characteristic of theoretically derived research. While the latter starts with a particular set of suppositions or expectations and seeks to validate them against the data, the former starts with the body of research findings and searches for patterns within them which promise to provide a starting point for more general propositions. Ideally, this can lead to what Merton (1967) has termed middle-range theories, that is, conclusions which, though not too remote from the particular to account for what is observed, constitute limited sets of assumptions from which specific hypotheses can be derived. What is very rare is to move directly from a single set of observations to an all-embracing grand theory, such as might be characterized in natural science by Darwin's and Einstein's contributions, and in social science by those of Marx and Keynes. In the present case, only a limited number of relatively low-level generalizations have been put forward, in that it has proved particularly difficult to discern clear regularities, despite several attempts to cross-correlate findings both within and across the research data. My conclusion is that this is a consequence of the number of variables involved—itself a result of the deliberately wide brief for the study as a whole.[4] What is offered instead is an insight into the working lives of a variety of professional groupings and of the pattern of interactions between them, set within an overview of their occupational contexts. Both the insight and the overview are supported by a more general contention: namely, that a key element in the motivation of practitioners is the concern to establish and maintain a personal reputation and a collective professional status.

Classifying and Characterizing the Professions

Professional groups have been characterized by previous writers in numerous different ways. Johnson (1972) offers one such taxonomy, based on forms of control. The first of them is designated as patronage, either oligarchic (wealthy individual patrons), corporate (large employing organizations), or communal (domination by members of the general public); the next is mediation (control mainly by state agencies); and the third, true professionalism (based on self-regulation and autonomy). Another broader distinction, first put forward by Etzioni (1969) and subsequently taken up by Glazer (1974), is drawn in terms of status. Those groups relatively deficient in certain key traits of professionalism, such as a substantial degree of higher education or independence in decision-making, are distinguished as "semi-professions" or "minor professions," as against major ones. Examples of the former would include nursing, teaching and social work; of the latter, medicine and the law. A quite different approach, based on psychological rather than sociological considerations, originates in Jung's Theory of Types, as elaborated in the so-called Myers-Briggs Type Indicator (MBTI): see Myers (1980). It sets out to identify individual scores along combinations of four different dimensions—sensing, feeling, thinking, and intuition—and to relate these to occupational characteristics. Despite the fact that the results are seldom clear-cut and can in some cases be mutually contradictory, the MBTI approach has spawned a modest industry, with disciples applying it to a variety of different professional fields.

At one stage, the MBTI framework seemed a possible one to adopt in relation to my own data, at least in an inverse direction: rather than attempting to match respondents' characteristics to their professions, an attempt was made to characterize the professions themselves as requiring particular types of thought and action. This move did not in the event prove fruitful, but one derived from it seemed to draw some useful, if not particularly original, distinctions between the six professional groups. What emerged was a general classificatory framework that divided the professions which seemed to be predominantly dependent on technical or scientific knowledge from those predominantly independent of a body of such knowledge; and which mapped this pair of contrasts against another, between those professions which could be described as procedural, or dependent on the relatively straightforward application of principles, and those which, in contrast, were processual, in the sense of being dependent on a mastery of processes.[5]

As in the case of MBTI, these categories are neither self-evident nor clear-cut, but they do offer a workable way of conceptualizing some of the main differences between the six professions. The group of technically based professions comprise medicine, pharmacy, and engineering; the remaining ones—law, accountancy, and architecture—could reasonably be said to be non-technical in contrast. The procedural professions—those which are largely rule-governed—embrace pharmacy, law, and accountancy, with the remainder—medicine, architecture and engineering—depending mainly on a mastery of process. Taken together, the distinctions can be summarized in a straightforward two-by-two matrix:

	Technical	Non-technical
Procedural	Pharmacy	Law, Accountancy
Processual	Medicine, Engineering	Architecture

Other, more localized distinctions are marked and explained in the body of the text, but two which have some general significance may be mentioned here. First, some aspects of professional activity can best be explained in social terms, as consequent on the values held at a given time by the community of practitioners concerned; others yield more readily to considerations derived from the nature of the relevant existing body of specialist knowledge. Thus, for example, along the social dimension, barristers are particularly resistant to demands for compulsory continuing education, in that they have in large part managed to maintain their role as self-governing professionals and are unprepared for this kind of inroad into their independent status; while along the cognitive dimension, surgeons have a predominant concern with "learning on the job" rather than learning from spoken or written sources, because of the practice-related nature of the work they do. Second, as an aspect of the cognitive dimension, it will prove useful at various points in the discussion to differentiate those professions—medicine and pharmacy—whose primary subject matter consists of people from those—law and accountancy—whose basic concern is with written or other symbolic materials, and again from those—architects and structural engineers—whose job is focused on artifacts.

The Conventions Adopted

In line with standard practice in research-based writings, references to and quotations from other authors are signalled in the text and cited in the collective list of references. However, in a study of the present kind, depending very strongly on the testimony of interviewees—and wherever appropriate quoting them verbatim—it is important for the reader to have access, if he or she wishes, to information about the individual referred to or quoted. Because a promise of anonymity was made to each interviewee, such information has to be given in general, non-identifiable terms: but it must, nevertheless, be pertinent to question whether or not such-and-such a person was speaking from a position of authority, whether the context was a large firm or a small practice, and so on.

Accordingly, each reference to interview data is cited as systematically as are references to published research, though in a different form. The procedure adopted aims to be uncomplicated. All the interviews in each professional group have been numbered chronologically, and the relevant number is used to identify the interviewee. The profession to which he or she belongs is designated by its initial letter —or in the case of accountancy and architecture the first three—to avoid confusion. Thus M/24 signifies the twenty-fourth interviewee in medicine, and Arc/2 the second interviewee in architecture. The one exception relates to the pilot interviews carried out before the main sequence began, many of which turned out to contain useful material. These are numbered 0, or in the cases of a second pilot, 0'. The counterpart to the list of research references is the collected set of notes on respondents cited, which gives in relation to each entry an indication of gender, type of professional activity, career stage, and working context. As it happens, but not by deliberate policy, nearly every informant has been cited at least once.

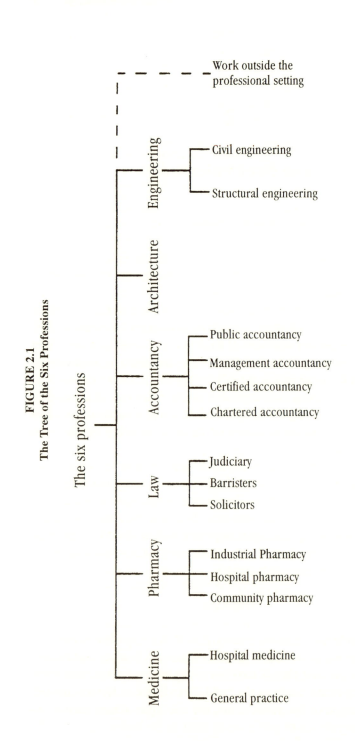

FIGURE 2.1
The Tree of the Six Professions

The six professions

Engineering
- Civil engineering
- Structural engineering

Architecture

Accountancy
- Public accountancy
- Management accountancy
- Certified accountancy
- Chartered accountancy

Law
- Judiciary
- Barristers
- Solicitors

Pharmacy
- Industrial Pharmacy
- Hospital pharmacy
- Community pharmacy

Medicine
- Hospital medicine
- General practice

Work outside the professional setting

various aspects are in consequence more fully documented than those of the other five areas of practice. Its primacy will be reflected in the high proportion of references to aspects of medicine and medical activity in the chapters that follow: the relevant literature is vast in comparison with that on any other profession.

The number of practitioners on the register of the U.K. General Medical Council in the later 1990s was slightly over 185,000. Over 35,000 of them were GPs, some 18,000 of whom were members of the Royal College of General Practitioners. The rest were divided among 14 groups of specialisms represented by the other Royal Colleges. A sizeable proportion—of the order of more than 10 percent—of consultants currently have some academic responsibilities. A small minority of qualified doctors work in the Public Health Service, and another minority occupy administrative positions in the National Health Service. Overall, the medical profession far outnumbers all others except accountancy in the size of its membership.

The structure of organized medicine is complex. Bucher and Strauss (1961) are at pains to emphasize "the great diversity of enterprise and endeavor that mark the profession; the cleavages that exist along with the division of labor; and the intellectual and specialist movements that occur" (p. 326). The most familiar division from the point of view of a potential client is that between the community medicine dispensed by general practitioners and the hospital medicine administered by a variety of more specialized professionals.[2] There is, however, another commonly recognized distinction, namely that between physicians and surgeons—a division that goes back a long way in history.

While medics as a whole enjoy high social and professional status, there are more-or-less implicit internal differentiations of rank. General practitioners, in particular, tend to defer to consultants, with whom they may have only quite limited contact.[3] Owen et al. (1989) illustrate the point by noting that nearly one in three of the 96 GPs interviewed in their survey would have wished for closer links with hospital doctors. One of my respondents, a woman GP (M/5), described medicine as "a network of old boys who tend to close ranks" and remarked that "relationships with consultants are sometimes difficult—should they be there to ask, or should they take over the patient?" Among GPs themselves, there are differences between sole practitioners—of which only a relatively few remain—and those who work in group practices. One of the former (M/12) acknowledged that he was professionally isolated and that his practice was expensive to operate and problematic in terms of out-of-hours patient care; but, on the other hand, with a relatively small list he could know all his patients and have total control of what was happening. He was nonetheless in the process of looking for a partner to join the practice.

A medically qualified interviewee currently working for a professional body (M/17) commented that hospital doctors work in a more structured and hierarchical framework than GPs, who have more freedom of maneuver, combined with the advantage of seeing their patients within their social context. There was, she said, less internal commonality among hospital doctors and less contact with outside society. There were also, in her contention, some clear internal differences between the consultants themselves. Some of them provide services on their own, while others function in groups and hence are more familiar with teamwork. Anesthetists, for example, engage in joint activity but surgeons tend to be more insular. While denying this general contention—"some juniors may have inadequate experience of teamwork, but this isn't true of consultants"—another respondent (M/19) commented that the relative power of physicians had diminished in relation to that of surgeons over the past decade, attributing this to a combination of medical advances leading to less need for continued treatment and the advent of better informed and qualified GPs. He related a familiar apophthegm within the trade, illustrative of its wide variety of occupations: "physicians know everything but do nothing; surgeons know nothing but do everything; psychologists *think* they know everything; pathologists know everything too late".

One indirect but indicative measure of status is the salary earned in a particular occupation. An academic in a medical school (M/22) commented on the large differential between practicing professionals and those in medical teaching. He estimated that a successful GP would earn more than twice the salary of a university professor, and that while (in 1995) an academic surgeon might earn sixty thousand pounds a year, one in private practice would be more likely to have an income of two hundred thousand. Even allowing that the figures may have been exaggerated for emphasis, it seems evident that academic medicine is not currently an attractive option or an occupation which enjoys particularly high standing.

Nonetheless, the profession as a whole is strongly research-oriented. It has been a common expectation that aspiring consultants will study for a research degree in the course of their early careers. The opportunity to do so has been reduced in the process of streamlining and abbreviating the previously lengthy professional education of doctors, as advocated in the 1993 Calman Report. Nevertheless, one of the working groups set up to consider the implementation of its findings recommended unequivocally that "doctors should be encouraged to undertake research during the period of specialist training" (Department of Health, 1995, § 22, p. 9). The unparalleled number of journals devoted to the publication and promulgation of research findings is itself a clear indication of how strongly professional practice is underpinned by systematic empirical enquiry.

There is also a well-established tradition of self-reflection and self-examination in medicine. Alongside the development of new techniques and treatments, there is a sizeable number of studies which set out to examine and evaluate aspects of existing practice. As will be seen in later chapters, and particularly chapters 6 and 7, how and what doctors learn, and how effective or otherwise their professional development activities are, form the subject matter of numerous publications which complement and parallel the more narrowly technical literature. In such enquiries reflective of practice, a strong tendency can be discerned to deploy the quantitative methods which have generally proved successful in medical research per se. This policy is at best debatable, in that— as in all more or less large-scale surveys offering statistically attested findings—there is little opportunity to identify causal connections or to offer more than shallow and superficial accounts of the phenomena under investigation.

The urge for quantification which characterizes both technical and reflective investigation can result in narrow scientism rather than genuine science; in a reductionism which isolates particular phenomena and treats them as independent of and unconnected to the contexts in which they occur. A consultant urologist in my sample (M/9) commented that "doctors are not proper scientists" and that some of them (herself included) "are forced to do research by people who aren't proper scientists either." A senior member of the medical establishment somewhat surprisingly expressed the view that medicine "is not remotely scientific," and that much medical education, particularly at the undergraduate level

is presented around the fact, the accumulation of fact, often presented with a scientific base which may or may not be spurious, and while the quality of the science is dubious, this pecking order of—at least science is hard, fresh, respectable, clean; and all these other things are soft, woolly and not quite respectable—that's built in very early on. If you become a psychiatrist or something, you're a little odd probably, but we accept that psychiatrists are a bit odd...qualitative research makes doctors very uneasy, and of course in the training all the soft communication, understanding, listening tends to get squeezed out because it lacks status. If it can't be quantitative, it's fuzzy. A lot of medical students,...have this I think built in very very deeply, so they may be talking science, but they're not very good scientists (M/30).

The same respondent went on to discuss the current advocacy of "evidence-based medicine"—that is, the notion that all aspects of practice should derive from a systematic review of previous successes and failures of treatment. He conceded that it was useful to look at why evidence was or was not used, and to define situations in which it was sensible to apply it. However, he saw a danger in adopting a dogmatic solution in complex and difficult areas, such as the treatment of back pain. Evidence-based medicine should not therefore be practiced uncritically, not only because it could preclude experimentation and improvement, but also because its application was liable to discount important individual features of a case. The risk was that it could create a straitjacket, again perpetuating the tendency of medical practice to ignore contextual considerations.[4] Following up these remarks, it might be noted that the attraction of the various forms of alternative medicine is attributable at least in part to their holistic approach, in contrast to the atomistic style often projected by their mainstream counterparts.

Pharmacy

Pharmacists are at a disadvantage in existing under the shadow of the much more established and august profession of medicine: a number of them will indeed have been unsuccessful applicants to medical schools. As a result, they tend to lack assurance, to have low visibility as a professional group and to enjoy limited political power. In my interviews, they emerged as generally more prosaic, and less given to surprising insights, than members of the other five professions. This slightly harsh judgment must be tempered by the acknowledgment that they appeared in general—like medical practitioners—to be highly committed and prepared to work long hours. In discussion during the interviews, they were as frank and open-minded as my other respondents.

The assertions about the status of pharmacy in then research literature are scarcely flattering. A distinguished sociologist, writing nearly half a century ago, implied that they were pretending to a grandeur to which they were not entitled: "The chief stock in trade...of pharmacists as small businessmen is their status, however anomalous, as professional men" (Mills, 1951, p. 139). In a later generation, Crompton and Sanderson (1989) put the point more delicately:

> it would probably be true to say that...pharmacy has historically fallen short of the top rank of professional esteem. The close association with 'trade' fell short of the gentlemanly ideal which predominated at the time the professions were crystallising as identifiable occupations...pharmacy would still probably not be ranked at the top of the 'first division' professions (p. 73).

In contrast, Turner (1987) is uncompromisingly blunt: "The professionalization of pharmacy has been limited by the petty bourgeois image of retail pharmacy and the inadequate apprenticeship system of training" (p. 141).[5] He goes on to comment that pharmacy is underdeveloped as a profession, and is accordingly seen in sociological literature as marginal and limited.

The total population of pharmacists in the U.K. is relatively small in comparison with that of medicine, law, and accountancy. The Royal Pharmaceutical Society, the registration as well as the professional body, had approximately 35,000 members in the mid-nineties—less than a quarter of the number of qualified doctors. A small scattering of some 400 were in academic posts in schools or departments of pharmacy; a larger minority—about 1600—were industrial pharmacists; some 5,500 were engaged in hospital pharmacy; and approximately 21,000 were community pharmacists. The remainder, though registered, were either retired or not practicing in the U.K.. A respondent (P/29) pointed out that as a largely self-employed profession, community pharmacy suffers less from discrimination than many professional groups. For that reason among others, it tends to attract large numbers of women and a high proportion of Asians. In the crude calculus by which occupational status is assigned, neither consideration helps to raise the standing of pharmacists in contemporary society.

The large preponderance of community pharmacists dominates the common perception of the professional group as a whole, particularly as many members of the public are familiar with chemists' shops but few have any involvement with the other contexts in which pharmacists work. Community or, as it is sometimes dubbed, retail pharmacy is itself divided into multiple or chain firms and single outlets. There appears to be not much love lost between the two, with numerous accusations that the former adopt aggressive and predatory policies towards the latter. In Canada, the trend towards multiples and away from singles is seen by Muzzin et al. (1994) to promise a release for community pharmacists from administrative and business activities, but to threaten both a reduction in service in less populated areas and a reinforcement of the image of the pharmacist as being little more grand than a grocer.

Currently, community pharmacists in Britain operate with the support of a subsidy from the National Health Service, which is intended to compensate for the reduced charges made on prescribed items. The universal view among single pharmacists is that this is not nearly sufficient, and that profits are being squeezed to an unmanageable degree. One (P/17) argued that the constant shaving of margins was a plot by the Thatcher/Major government to "get rid of small pharmacies," and to do so in a way that avoided compensation payments. An academic pharmacist (P/23) was, however, scathing about such pleas of poverty, remarking that in the mid-1990s, new graduates could easily pick up a job in retail pharmacy at a starting salary of £20,000 a year. Nonetheless, the economics of community pharmacy are precarious, in that an outlet with more than one qualified pharmacist appears to be unviable except in a heavily populated area where the turnover is very large, or in a branch of a chain pharmacy which can afford to offer numerous other services. The insularity of the single practitioner creates a number of problems, the most obvious of which is the need—since prescriptions cannot be dispensed by an unqualified member of staff—to be on call throughout the day (and often, when duty pharmacist in an area, into weekday evenings and part of Sundays as well).

A number of my respondents referred wistfully to the possibility of running what they variously termed "ethical" or "professional" pharmacies—that is, ones which do not need to survive on sales of non-pharmaceutical products. The pharmacies in a number of other European countries are run on this basis. There was, in fact, a campaign in the 1960s, backed by a sizeable majority of community pharmacists, to achieve ethical status. This became "a fight between the individuals and the multiples" (P/10), reaching the House of Lords before the multiples had their way. A pharmacist on the staff of the Royal Pharmaceutical Society commented that the National Health Service was highly unlikely in the present context to subsidize pharmacies to the extent that would be necessary, even though the move would be welcomed by the many community pharmacists who had had no training as professional retailers.

The permeability of the boundaries between the various branches of the profession was a matter of debate. Some respondents argued that, since all pharmacists had a common training and shared the same scientific knowledge base, transfer from one branch to another was relatively easy. Others claimed that specialization had now greatly reduced this possibility. A number of my interviewees had in the course of their careers made such a move; indeed, one (P/9) had started as a hospital pharmacist, stepped sideways into industry, and was at the time of the interview working as a community pharmacist. Others employed in hospitals or industry had taken on temporary part-time jobs as locums in community pharmacies, to earn extra money or "to keep in touch with the public." There were however no cases, at least in my relatively small sample of 31, of a transfer out of community pharmacy into either of the other branches. This is not altogether surprising, in that the technical demands of posts in hospitals and in the pharmaceutical industry are discernably higher than those in high street shops. It is in relation to the latter that the comment by Eaton and Webb (1979) is most apposite, although they were actually writing about hospital pharmacists: "overtrained for what they do and under-utilised in what they know."

Hospital and industrial pharmacy, for other reasons besides their more heavily scientific content, are seen within the profession as the more elite groups. Industrial pharmacists tend to have relatively little contact with the rest of the pharmaceutical community. The majority work in massive international concerns, in which they are outnumbered by people from many other disciplines—particularly in the biological and biomedical sciences. Their whole experience as salaried employees in large, hierarchical organizations contrasts sharply with that of their self-employed fellow-professionals in small, more or less insular enterprises. Hospital pharmacists, "unlike their counterparts in France" (P/21) tend to be seen as service personnel to the medical staff, but are steadily working to improve their standing. Recent organizational changes have pitched many of them into managerial or advisory posts, marking another contrast with community pharmacists outside large multiples.

In the mid-1990s, the Pharmaceutical Society orchestrated a campaign to improve the image of the profession and enhance its range of responsibilities. The movement, entitled "Pharmacy in a New Age," was widely supported within the membership and was thought to have made some impact on the medical profession, if not on the public at large. One of the main office-holders responsible for its initiation (P/20) acknowledged that pharmacists had a lower profile than doctors and were less politically successful as a group. This, she suggested, was in part because they were fewer in number and had a less public role: the campaign was designed to bring the profession more into the open.

Law[6]

The legal profession, like the medical, has its origins in antiquity, but is not accorded the same degree of public recognition. This is a natural consequence of its mission, which is to establish innocence or guilt in relation to breaches in the law and to arbitrate in disputes of various kinds; a less glamorous prospectus than healing the sick and promoting public health. The members of the profession have successfully protected their hegemony in legal matters. Even if among the general public they enjoy only a somewhat grudging respect, they qualify on most counts as belonging to a firmly established profession with a social standing second only to medicine.

It is a measure of a litigious society that the number of qualified lawyers has increased to a dramatic extent over the past generation. There was, in 1966, a total of 21,672 practicing solicitors in England and Wales. The corresponding figure for 1997 was 71,637; a leap of more than 230 percent. The growth in the sub-profession of barristers has been even more dramatic, though starting from a much smaller base: between 1966 and the beginning of 1998, the number of those in independent practice exploded from 2,239 to 9,613.[7] The size of the judiciary is not comparably documented, but it is safe to say that in comparison with these figures it has remained relatively static, though the number of legally qualified chairpersons and members of tribunals has also risen substantially in consequence of the deliberate shift—mainly on grounds of cost—of litigation from the courts to the tribunals.

The law, then, is a relatively sizeable profession with a status appropriate to its long history, the perceived complexity of its knowledge base, and the substantial income of most of its practitioners. Its branches, as indicated by the figures quoted above, are unequal in size as well as in internal prestige. Judges are at the top of the pyramid, being in all cases selectively recruited from the ranks of the more able practitioners.

There is a complex but clearly articulated hierarchy of the courts. At the apex is the House of Lords, which is the ultimate recourse to appeal in the British legal system. Below it comes the court of appeal, formed of two divisions: the civil division deals with civil law cases from the high court and county courts; and the criminal division deals with appeals on criminal law cases from the crown court. The third layer, the high court of justice, has three divisions (the Queen's Bench, dealing with contracts and similar issues; Chancery, concerned with property and wills; and the Family Division, covering divorce, wardship and the like). On the criminal side, the crown court tries major crimes such as murder and substantial theft. Both the high court and the crown court are presided over by circuit as well as high court judges (there are about 150 high court and 500 circuit judges). Below this three-tier structure—collectively designated the Supreme Court of Legislature—come the county courts, in which nearly every legal action starts. They are presided over by circuit judges and district judges (the latter mainly former solicitors). The fifth and lowest stratum comprises the magistrates' courts, which hear minor cases. Many magistrates have no professional legal training.

Within this elaborate framework, the professional standing of a judge is directly related to his or her level of activity, though, as a respondent explained (L/16), there is also a more subtle distinction between those dealing respectively with civil and criminal law cases: the criminal courts have a greater volume of work and are seen as the senior branch. At the upper end of the hierarchy, the members of the judiciary are by tradition appointed mainly from among the Queen's Counsel—barristers who are singled out for particular merit and permitted to appear in high court cases—though solicitors are also eligible in principle. At the lower end, there is a standard promotion pattern: the aspirant starts as an assistant recorder, then becomes a recorder, and may finally be appointed as a circuit judge. In all cases except those of the Justices of Appeal, judges are required to undergo a short but intensive induction course on first appointment and to attend five yearly refresher courses, together with an annual seminar on sentencing policy. A similar provision is made for tribunal chairs and magistrates. The responsible agency, the Judicial Studies Board, first embarked on a systematic training program in 1987: by 1991 it was catering for as many as 52,000 candidates a year, most of them magistrates and tribunal chairpersons (Partington, 1994).

Barristers are next in line of succession to judges. They represent—with the possible exception of a limited number of medical consultants and GPs in private practice —the only remaining group of leading professionals operating in a traditional style. That is to say, they function as single practitioners, remain staunchly independent and individualistic, actively retain their rituals and traditions, and are resistant to attempts to bring them more into keeping with contemporary professional values and practices. They have no direct dealings with members of the public: individual and corporate clients have to reach them through an intermediary who has been granted the right of access: normally a solicitor, though other professionals, including accountants and surveyors, may also have dealings with them. Their political credibility has suffered from the considerable reluctance they have shown to submit to external pressure for a compulsory scheme of continuing professional development (Lord Chancellor's Advisory Committee, 1997).

There is an implicit distinction, in terms of professional status, between those barristers who are members of one of the London-based Inns of Court and those, mainly in provincial towns, whose work lies in one of the six regional circuits: and even the Inns themselves and their constituent chambers (much as in the case of Oxbridge colleges) are tacitly graded in order of their ages and the degree of distinction of their members. The organization of the profession reflects these idiosyncrasies. After a minimum period of a year's pupillage, an intending barrister has to be accepted as a member of one of the existing sets of chambers, where he or she builds up a case list over time. Although all the members are financially and professionally autonomous, there is a good deal of informal interaction between them. The Head of Chambers, usually a high-ranking member of the profession, is responsible for bringing the members together for discussions—in most cases handled collegially—on housekeeping matters and decisions on substantial policy issues. However, there is no parallel here to the more formal partnership arrangements in other professions, including that of solicitors: and the only prospects of promotional mobility are to Queen's Counsel or to some level in the judiciary.[8] The barristers' representative body is the Bar Council, which remains determinedly democratic in its constitution and practice, and is small enough to avoid undue bureaucracy.

Roughly speaking, solicitors relate to barristers as GPs to consultants.[9] That is to say, the solicitors are generalists who are in direct contact with the public, and who deal with clients' problems up to the point at which they need to call on more authoritative advice, or decide to pass on to a specialist the responsibility for the conduct of the case in a court of law.[10] The main internal distinction within the sub-profession lies in the size of the partnership concerned. Although the policies of the Law Society, which is both the regulatory and the representative body for solicitors, tend to discourage sole practices (insofar as these offer a greater temptation to be negligent or to misappropriate clients' funds), there still remains a sizeable tail of single-partner firms: in 1997 there were just over 4,700 sole practitioners in private practice, accounting for 8 percent of the total professional population.[11] "The average firm," one respondent (L/9) volunteered, "has only about three partners." At the other extreme, some London firms contain hundreds of employees: the largest, in 1995, had nearly 300 partners, leaving aside more junior solicitors and support staff. The rate of growth has been rapid. Before the regulations governing partnerships were amended in 1967, no firm had more than 20 partners: in 1992, the corresponding figure stood at 230 (Davies, 1994). The 1995 edition of an annual rating exercise (Pritchard, 1995) predicted that the top ten in order of magnitude were likely to remain in a dominant position, but were increasingly open to challenge from some firms in large provincial cities.

There is a certain amount of mobility between the two main branches of the profession, in that barristers may switch to becoming solicitors, having for the purpose to pass only the appropriate transfer test, while solicitors can qualify—after similarly appropriate assessment—for "rights of audience" (i.e., a license to practice) in the higher courts. Solicitors have a number of other career options, including the acquisition of further qualifications in areas such as insolvency, taxation and financial services, or employment outside the legal system in public service organizations and commerce and industry.

Although legal expertise depends in large measure on the ability to handle a complex volume of documentary material, in the form of published records of previous legal decisions, there are other equally important components. A closely related requirement is the ability to master the background information relevant to the understanding of a nonroutine case: one instance cited by a respondent (L/9) concerned the operation of gear-boxes in lifts. Another desideratum is verbal dexterity, particularly in the conduct of advocacy in the courts (a skill which is by some attributed to natural talent and is by others seen as needing careful training). Yet another is the general intellectual capability of marshalling and deploying an argument. As one respondent (a barrister) put it, "You're always trying to see principles or invent them...the courts like you to present a conceptual basis for your argument, not just to quote rules" (L/32).

Accountancy

A succinct definition of accountancy, attributed to the American Accountancy Association, is quoted in Roslender (1992): "the process

of identifying, measuring and communicating economic information
to permit informed judgments and decisions by users of this information" (p. 2). Its standing as a profession is moderated by the fact that,
unlike medicine, pharmacy, or the law, it is non-exclusive: there is no
prohibition on people who are not technically qualified from performing accountancy tasks (though formal auditing is an exception). In the
1980s, following financial deregulation and the so-called 'big bang' in
the City of London, the image of accountancy in the U.K. was at its
zenith, enabling it to offer high starting salaries and to attract an un-
precedented proportion of well-qualified graduates from other disciplines (including a significant number with doctorates in physics, who
were at the time confronted with a dearth of academic jobs). The position has changed since, to the extent that the profession has collectively
backed away from the possibility, once seriously entertained, of re-
cruiting an all-graduate entry. The status of accountancy has been further modified by a series of major scandals relating to fraudulent dealings by large enterprises—of which the Maxwell and BCCI affairs and
the near-collapse of Barings Bank were notorious examples—in which
major and otherwise reputable accountancy firms were involved.[12] All
in all, accountancy may be said, in the words of a senior staff member
of one of its professional bodies, to be "aware of its lower status [in
relation particularly to law] but eager to establish its own claim in corporate affairs" (Skordaki, 1997, p. 79).

One of the salient features of the U.K. accountancy profession, which
limits its political credibility and influence, is its fragmentary nature.
While medicine, despite its proliferation of specialist Royal Colleges,
manages to project a reasonably coherent image through the British
Medical Association, there is no such unity among accountants, who
are divided into no less than six separate professional bodies. In 1997,
the largest and longest-established was the Institute of Chartered Accountants in England and Wales (ICAEW, or more shortly ICA) which
received its Royal Charter in 1880. In descending order of size, the rest
were the Chartered Institute of Management Accountants (CIMA), the
Chartered Association of Certified Accountants (ACCA),[13] the Institute of Chartered Accountants of Scotland (ICAS), the Chartered Institute of Public Finance and Accountancy (CIPFA), and the Institute of
Chartered Accountants in Ireland. Separate bodies cover related specialist activities such as taxation (two rival associations), insolvency,
securities, venture capital, futures and options, and compliance. There
have been various attempts, mostly initiated by the ICA, to gain greater

strength against state and European Union interference by reducing this organizational profusion. When an earlier effort to combine forces with ICAS failed, a merger of ICA and CIPFA was mooted; subsequently a link with ACCA seemed on the cards but was eventually aborted by the latter body. By the time of my interviews in 1995, the mutual overtures then being made between ICA and CIMA were regarded with some disdain by respondents who were members of the former body: one (Acc/29) commented that management accountants were "not blue chip—they're commercial rather than professional."

As this last remark implies, chartered accountants regard themselves as being "a cut above the rest" (Acc/22). Certified accountants—that is, the members of ACCA—are next in order of precedence, in that they are qualified to conduct audits, whereas management accountants are not. CIPFA stands aside from the internal status ladder, being both small in membership, specialized, and generally isolated from the rest. There is very little mobility between the different sectors of the profession.

The total U.K. population of accountants on register in the late 1990s was approximately 200,000, some 81,000 of whom were currently in practice. Of these, over 36,000 were members of the ICA. The structure of the profession ranges from gargantuan firms, half a dozen of which have more than 6,000 employees (the largest ran to some nine and a half thousand in 1995) to small single partnerships. It was typical of interviewees to describe their organizations in terms of their rankings of size and turnover, both being precisely tabulated by an annual survey in one of the main professional journals. Frequent reference was made to "the big six" or "the big ten," according to taste.

The sheer scale of activity in the larger firms serves to promote a significant degree of specialization. The different areas of activity, sometimes grandly denoted as "disciplines," are labelled in various ways: one typical categorization distinguishes between audit, accounting, consultancy, corporate finance, financial management, taxation, insolvency, and information technology. Consultancy is a relatively recent development, limited mainly to the larger firms. It, along with insolvency practice, calls for a more entrepreneurial set of skills than those required by traditional accountancy functions such as audit. It was said that consultancy and accounting represent two very different cultures, providing a good example of opposites that can support one another. Management accountants typically work within commercial or industrial organizations, rather than in accountancy firms: their task is to provide their employers with information for management activities such as decision-making, planning, and financial control. In contrast, those working in the field of finance cover a wider range of activities, depending as much on a knowledge of economics as on competence in accountancy. It should also be remarked that large numbers of qualified accountants are not engaged in accountancy as such (misleadingly termed "public practice," since most of it entails working for private organizations): in 1992, it was reported that over half the ICA membership was "involved in management positions of some sort" (Swinson, 1991, p. 19).

From an outside perspective, one of the surprising aspects of accountancy is its engagement in quasi-philosophical issues and in systematic research. Far from being remorselessly pragmatic, or having an exclusive concern with monetary transactions, there is an extensive literature, symbolized in, but not confined to, the journal *Accounting Organizations and Society*, focused on the social context of the profession and the implications of different ideologies, "rooted in the different positions individuals occupy in the business environment" (Burchell et al., 1985, p. 389 fn. 1). All three of the largest professional institutes, ICA, CIMA and ACCA, support active research departments, and CIMA in particular sponsors a wide range of investigations by both academics and practitioners into themes such as risk management and performance measures.

Architecture

Si monumentum requiris, circumspice (if you want a memorial, look around you) is the famous epitaph to Sir Christopher Wren in St. Paul's Cathedral. Even lesser architects are in the business of designing their own memorials: architecture is the most public and visible of professions, and hence one which attracts comment and criticism from the least as well as the most informed observer. It has attracted poets for its artistry. Goethe described architecture as frozen music, and Longfellow wrote of it as surpassing painting and sculpture as substance surpasses shadow. It has a long history, dating back well into remote antiquity, before the famous treatise on the subject by Vitruvius in the first century BC. And despite the bewilderment, veering to outrage, which has greeted some modern works—exceeded only by the lay response to modern art—it remains a well-regarded activity. Architects as a group share that largely positive image. Some indeed become well-known public figures: architecture, as Symes et al.(1995) point out, operates a star system analogous with that among actors, so that at any one time there are a few household names, some hundreds of aspirants waiting in the wings, and a large supporting cast reconciled to a lesser role.

The profession, like that of accountants, is regulated but not exclusive. That is to say, anyone can set himself or herself up to design a building, but only formally qualified persons can use the term architect. The registration body in the U.K. is the Architects Registration Board (formerly Council);[14] the main professional organization is the Royal Institute of British Architects (RIBA). There are a number of much smaller associations, such as the Architectural Association and the Architects and Surveyors Institute; neighboring bodies include the Royal Town Planning Institute, and the Society of Chartered Designers and Architects in Commerce and Industry. The RIBA, however, occupies the central role in professional activities, partly at least because— unlike the other professions so far considered—there is virtually no fragmentation into specialist sub-groups. This is perhaps a reflection of the fact that the population of architects is relatively small, at under 31,000 members on register in 1996—only the number of qualified structural engineers is lesser among the six professions.

As one informant (Arc/8) explained, architecture is simultaneously art, technology, and business. If there is a division within the profession, it lies between those who invest their efforts strongly in the aesthetics of design and those who stress the importance of practical and functional considerations. The latter accuse the former of betraying the profession by creating buildings which look pretty but fail to work; the former complain that the latter are mere functionaries who fail to uphold the best traditions of Western architecture. Neither group considers itself much good at business,[15] which helps to explain why the profession has lost out in the recent power struggles within the construction industry—a matter to be discussed more fully later in this chapter, and in chapter 3.

Specialization is exceptional: most architects find a virtue in working in a wide variety of different fields, from private housing and office building to the design of schools and hospitals, and along another dimension in refurbishment and conversion, especially of housing estates. The design of airports and airport buildings is seen as characterizing the more esoteric lines of activity, as is work in the field of classical architecture and historic buildings. At one time there was a sizeable body of architects in the public sector, but the remorseless privatization during the long Conservative administration from 1979 to 1997 resulted in a virtual elimination of local authority architects' departments, which had previously been entrusted with much of the public building work.

On a smaller scale, commensurate with their smaller numbers, architects' firms, like those of solicitors and accountants, have shown a tendency towards obesity. In 1996, the May issue of the *Architects Journal* recorded the four largest practices as having, respectively, 268, 191, 145, and 100 qualified architects. Eight practices jointly took 93rd place (making up the top 100 firms) with 17 partners each. There remain, however, large numbers of very small firms—according to one estimate in 1995, seventy percent were being run by six or less people (Symes et al., 1995).

The architects I interviewed shared a sense that the profession has lost out in a number of directions—an understandable concern, with an under-employment/unemployment level of some 38 percent in 1992. A few suggested that there were still too many architects in practice nonetheless, and commented that though architectural education was in "a dilapidated state" (Arc/29), the architecture schools were producing many more to swell the ranks of those already out of work. Despite this, the respondents appeared to have retained their sense of dignity and place at the apex of the construction industry: one spoke delicately of there being "a bit us and them" in architects' relationships with builders, though they were closer to structural engineers. Most saw themselves as "the rightful leaders of the building team" (Arc/4).

In many ways, the profession has had a battering experience over the past decade or so. The interviewees shared the view that they had been deliberately undermined by government policies, and that the quality of their relationships with clients had changed for the worse. They were aware of growing public alienation from some of the more conspicuous modern architectural products, and stung by the recurrent "bashing in the press" (Arc/22). It was not thought helpful to the collective image that the heir to the throne had taken on himself the task of commenting in an *ex cathedra* manner on various aspects of the profession's work—among his more widely-quoted remarks being his description of a planned extension to the National Gallery as "a monstrous carbuncle" and his dictum that "architects tend to design houses for the approval of their fellow-architects and critics, not for the tenants."

Structural Engineering

One of my respondents (E/1) observed ruefully that "in Britain—

though not in the rest of Europe—engineering isn't seen as a profession." That is perhaps one source of its relative invisibility. As in the case of pharmacy, structural engineering seems to lack a clear public image, not quite managing to make it as a professional pursuit. In some respects, moreover, it is subservient to a better-known profession: saddled with a relation to architecture which echoes that of pharmacy to medicine.

To compound its status problems, it also has a larger and more powerful sibling, with which it has to share its territory. There is in practice a considerable overlap between civil and structural engineering. Although the two have separate professional institutions, quite a few of those in the field are members of both. The differences between them are mainly in terms of scale of operation. While civil engineers may engage in the design and assembly of large structures such as highways, bridges, and dams, their structural engineering counterparts are more typically involved with buildings of many different kinds—hence their close connection with architects ("the structural engineer's job is to create the skeleton inside the body"—E/21), ensuring that the architectural conception will not collapse during or after its rendering into physical form. But civils and structurals can often be found straying into each other's territory, because they share the same basic professional knowledge and principles.

In the late 1990s, there were less than 8,500 qualified structural engineers in practice in the U.K., making it the smallest by some way among the six professions. However, if civil engineers were to be added to the roll call, the number would swell by another 63,600 or so. Only a relatively small number of these, of course, would at any one time be working on buildings as such: the far larger proportion would be engaged in labor-intensive civil engineering projects.

The tendency to create large professional firms is more marked than in architecture or law. Some of them almost approach the massive accountancy organizations in scale. The most sizeable partnership concerned predominantly with structural engineering has nearly 3,000 staff, though some of these have other professional qualifications related to the construction industry. There are even more gargantuan contracting firms—one with over 24,000 staff worldwide—which concentrate on large civil engineering projects and have relatively little involvement in structural activities as such. As in other professions, however, the overall pattern varies between large, medium, and very small partnerships, with only relatively few sole practitioners in this particular case.

The profession of structural engineering has no clear internal divisions, though a distinction is commonly drawn between consulting and contracting engineers. The consultants are the designers and specifiers who provide the final drawings for the building and lay down what needs to be done; the contractors' task is to implement the specifications and to take responsibility for the provision of the building itself. People can fairly readily move between the two activities, though the former is seen as superior in status, having closer links with architects and more distant ones with builders; contracting engineers are saddled with "a muddy boots image" (E/21). Beyond this functional division, there is little in the way of a subsidiary layer of specialized roles. Most structural engineers, following the pattern in architecture, see themselves as general practitioners, needing a wide knowledge rather than a specific expertise. But, again as in architecture, there are a few areas—the restoration of historic buildings is one—which call for unusual techniques and unfamiliar materials, and so encourage a measure of specialization.

As a form of applied science, engineering in general and structural engineering in particular is predominantly quantitative, offering less scope for creative invention than its paired profession of architecture. Addis (1990), writing as an academic rather than a practicing professional, questions the idea that its practice gives rise to determinate solutions, though Rice (1994) as a reflective practitioner argues that this is the natural way for structural engineers to operate ("the solution to the problem will often come fully worked out.... It is characteristic of the way engineers think: because they are working with objective parameters these lead to only one conclusion," p. 78). Both, however, comment on the general tendency to neglect design as a central element, and to treat aesthetic issues as subservient to technical ones. Even in my relatively small interview sample, a clearly discernible minority of respondents resolved this dilemma in favor of design, showing many of the same attributes and attitudes as architects, with whom they were concerned to work very closely.

One of the most striking features of the structural engineering profession is its dearth of women members. A review of the role of women in the professions remains to be undertaken in chapter 5: here it is sufficient to note that the proportion in this field is by far the lowest of the six (1 in 85 in the late 1990s). Various explanations were offered by my respondents, including the heavy mathematical content in engineering degrees and the standard image of the engineer as a male having to use brute strength. One interviewee (E/21) suggested wryly that most women were too sensible to get involved in construction, "a rock bottom industry, where there can be a lot of rough and tumble and a fair bit of discrimination on site."

Relations between the Professions

These brief portrayals of the professions under review can provide no more than the distant likeness of a series of passport photographs, presenting a fixed and static image of their subjects. But professions are no more fixed and static than people: so the next stage must be to give some indication of their mobility, offering a metaphorical videotape in place of a still photographic display. One of the main sources of their changing characters lies in their interactions with other professions, which are—as will be argued—themselves subject to constant change.

The interactions within and between professional groups were usefully identified and explored over a generation ago by Bucher and Strauss (1961) in their exploration of the complex, constantly changing structures within the field of medicine. In alluding to "relations with neighboring and allied occupations," they wrote:

> One branch of a profession may have more in common with elements of a neighboring occupation than with their own fellow professionals. For example, experimentally minded pathologists consult and collaborate with biochemists and other basic scientists, while pathologists oriented toward practice make common cause with clinicians of various specialties (p 330).

Hanlon (1997), taking the analysis further, concedes that specialization does indeed lead to interdependence, but postulates that the interdependence is more evident between professions than it is within them. Abbott (1988), in his finely crafted and scholarly work *The System of Professions*, makes the point even more trenchantly: "Books on individual professions spend much of their time on interprofessional relations, but none draws the obvious moral that interprofessional relations are potentially the central feature of professional development" (p. 18).

The data from my interviews illustrate not only what these relationships have been, but also how they are being modified over time. Taking the pairs of cognate professions, medicine and pharmacy emerged as being linked hierarchically. The medics rarely made much mention of the pharmacists; the latter implied that they had always been kept at a distance, but that this was changing in hospital medicine ("there's a lot of contact now between consultants and pharmacists"—P/16). In community pharmacy, one respondent (P/17) claimed that there had been only slow progress over the past ten years in linking up with GPs, though another (P/20) pointed out that a number of GPs have pharmacists working in their practices, developing formularies (lists of recommended drugs with descriptions of their properties), and giving advice on prescriptions.

Between law and accountancy, the relationship seemed to be complementary.[16] There was little direct overlap, though practitioners in each might have occasional recourse to the others, and clearly recognized them as occupying neighboring territory. Traditionally, however, accountants had what one barrister (L/24) described as "a quite unjustified awe of lawyers." In recent years, as new specialisms have developed in areas such as tax advice, compliance activities, and insolvency practice, the two professions have found themselves engaged in active competition.

For different reasons, connected with the crisis in the U.K. building industry in the late 1980s and early 1990s, architects are no longer able to sustain their established roles as leaders in the construction process, and their dominance over structural engineers has declined to a significant degree. Nevertheless, their working relationships with engineers have remained symbiotic: "Engineers and architects come from opposite ends of the spectrum, but have to come together in designing buildings" (E/26). "Designs and structures go hand in hand—you can't develop an architectural design without recourse to structural engineering" (E/9). However, as Addis (1994) observes,

> the relationship between structural engineer and architect is not symmetrical...there are as many types of architect/engineer relationships as there are types of married couple. Likewise there are no more guidelines for a successful design than there are recipes for a successful marriage...there is always a difficulty when two people with different skills work together (p. 17).

Working relationships of the type discussed have given rise, in the cases of law and accountancy and of architecture and engineering, to combined organizations, now commonly designated as multidisciplinary practices. The development of such practices was first given tentative official encouragement by the report of the Monopolies Commission, in 1970, on "the general effect on the public interest of certain restrictive practices so far as they prevail in relation to the supply of professional services," which came out in favor of a limited move towards interprofessional partnerships, particularly between lawyers and accountants (§§ 184–195).

It was, in fact, architects and engineers who moved most readily in this direction. One engineer I interviewed (E/26) worked in a firm established in the early 1960s, now one of the largest in the field, with a total of 26 professions represented on its staff. An architect in a medium-sized firm (Arc/15), remarking that his partnership included planners, landscape architects, and quantity surveyors, but no engineers, referred to another large partnership which had merged with an engineering firm that was now dominating the practice. The view of engineers as predators, occupied in buying up medium-sized architectural partnerships to form large design corporations, was advanced by another architect (Arc/3) who considered his firm vulnerable to attack. There were other instances, however, of long-established cohabitations in which architects and engineers worked amicably and equitably together, or in company with other professions in the construction industry.

The formation of joint partnerships between lawyers and accountants is a more recent phenomenon, following a relaxation by the Law Society of the firm prohibition against participation in multidisciplinary practices (MDPs). An initial move was the acquisition, in the early 1990s, of a prestigious English solicitor's firm by a massive American accountancy practice, though the two remained at the time organizationally separate. An accountant (Acc/17), referring to this, added that there were also some specialist tax practices, recently established, which involved both accountants and lawyers; and an academic in the profession (Acc/0) noted the emergence of a number of joint law and accountancy degrees yielding a new specialism, forensic accounting. The reaction of two lawyer respondents was less sanguine. One (L/0') acknowledged that the profession was moving towards an involvement in multidisciplinary practices, but remarked that there was a fear of being overwhelmed by accountants in the process. The other (L/23) took a similar view: he saw the recent takeover as pointing the way to the future, but held that "It looks like a significant and threatening development. It will be detrimental to solicitors because they'll get swamped—the big solicitors' firms are much smaller than the big accountants' firms. So far the two professions have coexisted quite happily, feeding off each other." An earlier comment on "the implications of allowing multi-disciplinary practice for lawyers in England," was advanced by James (1991), in a conference paper colorfully entitled "Whistling against the wind." He observed that

> The legal profession has traditionally seen [the] difficulties as insuperable...the lawyers ask "why" whilst the accountants ask "why not". My concern is that by the time these issues have been debated and decided on, the accountancy profession, not for the first time, will have stolen a march on the lawyers and will have MDPs in place and up and running in the U.K. (p. 35).

It was not to be long before his prophecy was fulfilled.

Because in large part neither hospital nor community medicine are run on a commercial basis in Britain, there is less of a tendency to echo the U.S. pattern of very sizeable health management organizations, and hence doctors have little incentive or opportunity to develop massive interprofessional partnerships with pharmacists. However, as noted earlier in this section, there is now more joint activity than before, albeit on a modest scale: and the politically driven tendency towards amalgamations into larger units in the hospital service and towards the formation of bigger general practices may see a gradual emergence of the multidisciplinary pattern clearly discernible among engineers and architects and among lawyers and accountants. Indeed, some foreshadowing of this could be seen at the time of the interviews in the references to the concept of a practice team, calling for closer professional interaction between GPs, practice nurses, midwives, and health visitors. In the hospital service, a consultant (M/13) commented that he expected interprofessional relationships to evolve—"but I don't see that as a threatening issue."

It is debatable whether organizational subservience at the socio-political level is less or more tolerable than usurpation at the cognitive-functional level. The former has its main impact on the profession as a collectivity, while the latter has a direct bearing on the day-to-day work of the individual practitioner. What is at stake in such a case is the loss, whether total or partial, to a rival professional group of a previously protected role. A change or loss of role may happen as a result of deliberate action on the part of the rival group; or it may be occasioned through some independent contextual event, enabling such a group to exploit a new opportunity.

The first kind of relinquishment of function is clearly evident in the interaction between doctors and pharmacists. This offers a particular instance of the claim, by Hopkins et al. (1996), that "the nature of the work undertaken by different health professionals and interprofessional boundaries are constantly shifting" (p. 364). As Hughes (1994) explains, "European pharmacists are in the process of changing their professional profiles even more than other professions" (p. 81). She cites the shift of emphasis among community pharmacists from dispensers to counsellors and diagnosticians; among hospital pharmacists towards prescribing drugs in competition with doctors; and among industrial pharmacists in having to adjust to new manufacturing techniques. Eaton and Webb (1979) are concerned to discount the notion that pharmacists are engaged in a process of encroachment on medical preserves, suggesting that their acquisition of new responsibilities is a consequence of delegation rather than surrender. However, that was not the impression given by my respondents, one of whom (P/17) referred explicitly to the suspicion and hostility evinced by some GPs towards his current provision of pregnancy tests and his planned introduction of blood pressure testing and checking for diabetes. Another interviewee (P/23) mentioned that he was now offering to measure cholesterol levels, while a third (P/10) spoke confidently of the arrival of a time when doctors would confine themselves to diagnosis while pharmacists took on the task of prescribing. None of the doctors in my sample expressed any concern about such developments. One GP (M/12) commented that he had not noticed any change of relationship with pharmacists, and certainly not any change in relative status; a hospital consultant (M/13) observed that "the pharmacist contributes rather than leads—in the end the clinician can always wield a big stick."

As far as the professional interactions between lawyers and accountants are concerned, there was little indication in the interview data of a takeover in role, other than —as noted earlier—in the provision of tax advice and the conduct of insolvency practice, where both professions have a stake. One respondent (L/30) implied that the accountants had won out in the latter field, commenting that "Even those lawyers who are appropriately qualified often don't exercise their expertise." However, a contributor to a 1996 conference on legal education and training (Lord Chancellor's Advisory Committee, 1996b) warned that barristers and solicitors were likely to face increasing future competition from non-qualified legal advisers, and Freedman and Power (1992), in more general terms, argue that "territorial issues between accountants and lawyers...are far from fixed. Indeed, they are in a process of continual change and negotiation at significant points of contact in their environments."

The situation in respect of architects and structural engineers is not as clear-cut as that arising in medicine and pharmacy. It is not so much that the engineers have deliberately set themselves to take over aspects of the architects' traditional tasks as that the architects have more or less consciously abandoned one of their main roles and that the engineers, among others, have moved in to fill the vacuum. One might classify this as an intermediate case between intentional colonization and the accidents of external circumstance. The origin of the change, on which respondents in both architecture and engineering were agreed, lay in the drastic effects of the recession at the turn of the decade—that is, between the late 1980s and early 1990s—on the construction industry as a whole.

In a buyer's market, many of the larger clients became critical of the managerial competence of architects (who as a profession had at the time swung heavily in the direction of emphasizing their design function at the expense of attending to the effective cost control and management of the construction process as a whole). A new fashion accordingly developed for what was termed "design and build" arrangements, in which a contractor, acting on behalf of a client, specified an outline design which was then put out to tender. The architects who were engaged found themselves constrained by the initial specifications and unable to interact directly with the client: their task was limited to a filling-out of the design requirements. The supervision of the building process was left in the hands of a project manager, working for the contractors, who might or might not be professionally knowledgeable about design matters or building problems. When design and build projects were first initiated, the project managers were often quantity surveyors, but according to a number of respondents they were seen to be inadequate to the task because of a lack of necessary technical experience. Structural engineers, at least in the estimation of many of them, were better suited to the role and became favored candidates for it. However, the system did not prove popular within the construction industry, and one or two interviewees suggested that it was in the process of being abandoned.

With few exceptions the architects in my sample blamed themselves for failing to meet the challenge of coping with the increasing managerial complexity of contemporary building schemes, and seemed understandably concerned to restore their reputations and their professional status. Whether they would be able to wrest back the responsibility for the oversight of the total building process from the structural engineers and others in the zoo of construction industry professions remained to be seen.

Further instances in which roles have been lost through external circumstance call for only a passing mention. In pharmacy, Birenbaum (1982) notes, automation in drug supply and stock control has virtually eliminated the dispensing role. A barrister (L/14) argued that the incidence of civil law cases has declined as a result of changes in the legal aid regulations, covering subsidized provision for low-income litigants. The auditing function in accountancy has steadily reduced, particularly because of legislative changes exempting small enterprises. Johnson and Kaplan (1987) refer to the growing obsolescence of management accounting in the light of computerization, changed industrial production techniques and deregulation—a view supported by one respondent (Acc/21) but contested by another (Acc/22).

These examples of organizational contest, role incursion, and role evaporation clearly support the prediction by Freedman and Power (1992) that "Territorial disputes will shift; priorities will change; new 'professions' may arise...as some barriers break down, others go up and there will be new disputes and conceptual debates" (p. 23). Abbott's thesis, in his *System of Professions* (1988), goes further in suggesting the central importance of competition between the professions:

> interprofessional conflict over work is not simply a peripheral phenomenon, providing detail to the general outline of professionalization.... By understanding where work comes from, who does it, and how they keep it to themselves, we can understand why professions evolve as they do (Abbott, 1988, p. 279).

One more point remains to be made in concluding this exploration of interprofessional relationships. It bears on the proposition introduced in chapter 1, that a key element influencing professional practice is the quest for individual reputation and collective status. A striking feature of the tussles between paired professions for organizational dominance and for usurpation of function is that it appears invariably to be the lower-status partner that takes the aggressor's role. One does not find general practitioners attempting to purvey the medicines they prescribe, or solicitors offering to audit their clients' accounts. The same phenomenon is, incidentally, to be found in divided professions, in which (for example) GPs currently carry out minor surgery and solicitors can acquire qualifications to act as advocates in the courts.

The explanation that suggests itself is that a high-status profession or sub-profession may be willing to shed or share some of its more routine and less glamorous tasks, taking the view that in the process it will enhance its standing. A low-status profession or subprofession, in taking on these tasks, will consider that it too will earn a higher status by association with work previously done by its perceived superiors. There is something like that contention in the complex analysis in Abbott (1981); and Hopkins et al. (1996) explicitly refer to less powerful groups of health professionals "trading up" to tasks previously undertaken by more powerful groups (p. 367). There seems otherwise little reason for initiating the complicated process of takeover or amalgamation of partnerships in another field, or for deliberately taking on additional obligations when one's existing responsibilities are demanding enough.

As noted earlier, those who find their working territories invaded are not always sanguine about losing tasks to, or sharing them with, others. Here too, questions of status will be involved—but of maintenance rather than enhancement. In circumstances calling for concerted resistance to encroachment, the relevant professional bodies are often brought into play. It is their functions, and the perceptions of them by their members, that will now be explored.

Professional Bodies and Commercial Agencies

Besides their interactions with members of their own and related professions, practitioners are liable to find themselves in contact with three main groups. The first and most obvious comprises their clients, to whom further consideration will be given in chapter 3. The second and third are, respectively, the professional bodies to which they belong and the variety of other agencies with whom they interact—usually reflecting some mutually satisfactory commercial connection with the profession concerned.

Professional bodies can be roughly categorized (though the divisions are not sharp, and there are some overlaps between them) into three groups, which may be labelled as professional institutions, professional associations, and interest groups. The first are in many respects the most significant, in the sense that they are seen, both internally and externally, as in some sense representing the relevant profession's interests. Some but not all act, among their other functions, as registration bodies—that is to say, they are responsible for formally admitting new entrants to the profession and for deleting individuals' names from the list of members when they cease to be active, or—rarely— when they are "struck off" for serious professional misconduct. The performance of the latter role can at times conflict with the other activities of the institution.

These other activities normally include functioning as a learned society, serving as a trade union for their members, and acting as a public relations organization for the profession as a whole. In their learned society function, the institutions will typically provide resources such as libraries, research units, conferences, symposia, and lecture programs: they may also offer specialist advice and information. When acting as surrogates for trade unions, they will concern themselves with such issues as fee levels, the preservation of monopolistic activities and other considerations relating to the working conditions and remuneration of their members. Their public relations role—which has assumed increasing importance since the Thatcher government's concerted assault on the professions in the 1980s—includes acting as a political lobby to further or defend the membership's corporate interests and promoting a public perception of quality assurance through increasingly rigorous requirements for entry; through imposing similarly demanding conditions for continuing membership; and through the specification of needs for continuing professional development. Many of the institutions covering the six professions under review provide, at least in part, the formal training programs required to help meet the current continuing professional development targets which they have set (see chapter 6).

Particularly among the larger institutions, some form of subsidiary grouping may be adopted. In some cases this may be done on a geographical basis, with regional branches located across the country. For example, both the Royal Institute of British Architects and the Institution of Structural Engineers operate in this way, with much of the regional responsibility resting on the members themselves rather than on the institution's professional staff. In contrast, many of the Law Society's directly professional activities—that is, its functions as a learned body—are conducted through nationally organized groups (for example, those concerned with commerce and industry or with local government); while the Institute of Chartered Accountants is subdivided centrally into "faculties" covering topics such as finance and management and audit.[17]

Professional associations may be broadly distinguished from professional institutions by their more *ad hoc*, voluntary character. They lack the formal apparatus of royal charters or legitimating acts of parliament, and are usually run on a self-help basis rather than by a corps of central administrative staff. They are established to explore and promote shared professional interests of a more or less specialized kind, and are in that sense more true examples of learned societies than are the professional institutions. Illustrative examples include The Concrete Society in structural engineering, the International Taxation Group in accountancy, and the British Association of Pediatric Urologists in medicine. Most associations publish their own journals and run their own conferences, but offer little more in the way of membership facilities. They are varied in size and scope: some are large enough to contemplate a metamorphosis into professional institutions in their own right; some are international in their coverage; others are too specialized in their interests to have any ambitions beyond surviving as relatively small-scale coteries.

What may be termed interest groups are in another case again. Their focus tends to be social rather than cognitive in that they are usually based on, and concerned to promote, some particular contextual activity rather than an area of technical knowledge as such. Some examples may help to clarify the distinction from professional institutions and associations. The National Pharmaceutical Association, for instance, operates mainly as a trade organization for community pharmacists, and is in that respect clearly differentiated from the Royal Pharmaceutical Society—though in addition to its promotion and representation functions, it aims to enhance its members' business skills and management competence and to provide other advisory and support services. In some respects, the British Medical Association could be said to fall into this category, though it is long enough established and well enough endowed to go beyond a run-of-the-mill interest group. The British Association for Management in Medicine is a clearer case in point, in that its main rationale is to raise the level of managerial competence of the medical profession not only by providing appropriate training but by changing the prevailing climate of professional opinion in a more positive direction.

As in the case of many apparently straightforward factual accounts, this leaves out an important element, namely that concerned with the underlying political issues. Bucher and Strauss (1961) make the point in general terms, remarking that

> Professional identity may be thought of as analogous to the ideology of a political movement; in this sense segments [i.e., the groupings which emerge within a profession] have ideology ....They also tend to develop a brotherhood of colleagues, leadership, organizational forms and vehicles, and tactics for implementing their position (pp. 332–33).

Wilmott (1986) refers more specifically to professional organizations in accountancy as inescapably political bodies whose power derives from their organizational capacity to continuously secure from the market and the state the right to control and regulate the supply of, and influence the demand for, accounting labour (p. 574).

But the politics of the profession have an internal as well as an external dimension. To quote Bucher and Strauss (1961) again:

associations must be regarded in terms of just whose fateful interests within the profession are served. Associations are not everybody's association but represent one segment or a particular alliance of segments...established associations become battlegrounds as different emerging sections compete for control.

A clear illustration of this conflict of interests is given by Swinson (1991), in his capacity as an official of the Institute of Chartered Accountants. Referring to the "ten very large, very substantial firms" in which a significant proportion of the Institute's membership works, he notes that

Those ten train something over 90% of all students who wish to become chartered accountants, so that they have a whip hand over our plan for Education and Training. We cannot change if they do not wish us to go in a particular direction. But more importantly, if they wish to go in a particular direction, then sooner or later the Institute will change...But even they are held back if the members, and we have 90,000 of them [the figure for 1991], do not wish the changes to take place (p. 18).

Here, then, is a professional institution having uneasily to pursue its policies in the face of a pincer movement comprising the few large but influential corporate member firms as one prong and its numerous small partnerships as the other. The Royal Pharmaceutical Society in its turn has a particularly difficult task in maintaining any reasonable balance between its own mass membership of single-practice community pharmacists and the considerably smaller representations of industrial and hospital pharmacists: consequently, as one respondent (P/14) commented, "some people see it as playing a weak part in policy formation." The inertia which can result from balancing acts of this kind is presented by Wilmott (1986) in dramatic terms:

Anything more than cosmetic changes in the organization of the [accountancy] profession and its stewardship of the public interest are likely to occur only when the interests of influential individuals or organized sections of the membership are frustrated, when the state threatens to withdraw the privilege of self-regulation and/or when self-interested procrastination over the deep-seated political and organisational problems of the profession weakens the profession's standing and capability.

In practice, exit presents an option aside from voice and loyalty.[18]

That is to say, while some members of the institution may remain loyally in defense of the *status quo*, and others may raise their voices in attempt to bring about reform, others again may express their dissidence in defection, either espousing a rival group or setting up one of their own. Insolvency provides a good example. Both lawyers and accountants have a stake in insolvency practice. A number of respondents in each profession who had joined or who contemplated joining the established professional body, the Insolvency Practitioners Association, came to the view that it was "a cartel, a little club...very cliquey and unproductive" (Acc/6), and accordingly seceded to a recently formed breakaway group, the Society of Practitioners of Insolvency, which was seen as trying to usurp it.

All in all, professional institutions—and particularly the major ones representing their professions as a whole or their main subprofessions—have a difficult time of it. Much as the average citizen will on the one hand complain that the government of the day is providing seriously inadequate welfare services, and on the other protest that it is demanding an excessive level of taxation, so too professionals are inclined to condemn their institutions for charging excessive membership fees while expecting them to offer every desirable service at the highest possible level.

My interview data yielded a surprising degree of criticism from practitioners about their parent bodies, stemming from respondents in almost every profession with the exception of medicine.[19] The complaints ranged widely, to include charges of bureaucracy; neglect of particular sectional concerns; failure adequately to represent the interests or enhance the status of the profession; generally conservative attitudes; and uncertainty of purpose. The language in which many of these judgments were couched reflects the blend of articulate and critical styles of thinking characteristic of many of my respondents. Because they also give some insight into the particular internal problems of the professions concerned, some of the observations made are worth repetition here.

The pharmacists who commented adversely on the Royal Pharmaceutical Society seemed in general concerned with its lack of political power and its absence of clear vision. It was said to do "little for community pharmacists" (P/26) though they form by far its largest constituency; and its elected officers were, in general, branded as dogmatic and old-fashioned. The respondent already quoted (P/26) claimed that "it's seen as a laughing stock; it doesn't give a realistic lead to the profession."

The Law Society was undergoing a certain degree of internal turmoil during the latter part of the interview program, resulting from the election of a maverick president who was soon at odds with the permanent staff. Although the dispute was sufficiently acrimonious to attract some hubristic attention from the media, no direct mention was made of it by respondents. Nor was any complaint voiced about the Society's uncompromising stand on the imposition of compulsory requirements for continuing professional development. In fact the only adverse comment, other than one or two about membership fee levels, was made by a solicitor in a small provincial partnership. It seemed devastating enough to drown the silence of all the other respondents: "The Law Society is the only practice union that works against the interests of its members" (L/10).

Among the various accountancy bodies, it was only the Institute of Chartered Accountants that came in for slating. A respondent in one of the top ten firms (Acc/30) saw it as "confused in its role—not a great body." Another (Acc/2), acknowledging that "it hasn't served its members particularly well," added in exoneration that it had had to cope, and help its members to cope, with "numerous changes in taxation and the law, year on year" (as an aside, he commented that the annual subscription was "a bit of a protection racket"). A third malcontent (Acc/22) represented the ICA as being "run for the benefit of the big firms;...its activities are distorted by the ambitions of would-be presidents."

In their characteristically anarchic way, the architects were the most explicit in their criticisms of their professional institution—the Royal Institute of British Architects—though there were also a number of more positive comments. In all, just over one in three interviewees spontaneously offered their views on the Association—more than twice as many as in any of the other professional groups. The RIBA's tendency to exclusivity was subject to various comments: "It's a club for rich private practices" (Arc/3); "it went through a cliquey period, looking after established practitioners, not necessarily of high quality" (Arc/15); "it's unrepresentative—you need to be a household name to get anywhere" (Arc/6). There were also doubts about its clarity of purpose: "There's been some improvement lately, but its goals remain unclear—should it promote architecture or promote architects?" (Arc/13). "The profession is torn between professionalism and commercialism...it has even been suggested that the RIBA should be divided, with one part hiving off to become a learned society, and the other a trade organization" (Arc/29).

The voices raised in defense were less numerous and more muted: "it's changing a lot as an institution—people in the regions don't realize how much it actually does for them" (Arc/15); "It's not as good as it should be, but it's getting better, even though the professional members don't contribute much time and effort." A respondent (Arc/2) who had recently held high office in the Institute observed that it was "very abused—some criticisms are valid, but many are overdone." He was joined by others in extolling the excellence of the RIBA library. But as if to demonstrate the contention by one interviewee (Arc/15) that "architects don't feel disloyal in slanging the RIBA," two others threw moderation to the winds: "It's morally bankrupt and corrupt—it does nothing to support individual members; it only cares about the top brass" (Arc/27); "The RIBA has marginalized itself through its foolish policies. It fills me with despair, but it has a good bookshop" (Arc/30).

In comparison, the engineers' comments—though voicing similar criticism— seemed tame to the point of docility. "The profession," said one respondent (E/27), "has a questioning attitude at present, and there is much debate about the professional institutions." A second (E/1) saw them as "luddite-like," especially in their dogged preservation of traditional styles of education. As in the case of the RIBA, the Institution of Structural Engineers was seen as "very cliquey—it doesn't do enough to promote the profession" (E/11). A recently elected committee member of the Institution of Civil Engineers (E/6) referred to its "unbelievable bureaucracy and inordinately long time scales." Another interviewee (E/13) saw the Institution of Structural Engineers as having "good and bad points—it represents the profession's interests in discussions with public bodies, but it seems ineffective in improving the status and salaries of structural engineers." He went on nonetheless to commend the worthwhile research and development it promoted, the properly demanding standards it required for professional qualification and the good quality of its provision for continuing professional development.

So much for how the professional bodies impinge on the attitudes and practices of their members. Another set of organizations which have some—though considerably more marginal—influence on professional practitioners was mentioned in the introductory remarks to this section, namely the commercial agencies who make available one kind of service or another to individual firms. There is a good deal of differentiation here between the different pairs of professions. The practitioners in medicine and pharmacy interact mainly with drug companies, while manufacturers specializing in medical equipment are of most relevance to hospital doctors, of some to GPs, and of virtually none to pharmacists. Architects and structural engineers have a direct interest in the conventional materials supplied, and the new materials developed, by the manufacturing side of the construction industry. Because their professions are not directly concerned with artifacts, lawyers and accountants have less involvement with purveyors of products, except in the tangential sense of office equipment, information technology, and the like. However, there are other services that are relevant to all professions, such as the provision of background data, the delivery of training programs, and the furnishing of advice of various kinds. Most of these are provided by specialist agencies, some catering to the professions as a whole and others specializing in one to the exclusion of others.

The references to specialist agencies on the part of my engineering and architectural respondents were somewhat desultory. One sole practitioner in structural engineering (E/11) spoke of a problem which involved his contacting a soil mechanics expert, and a second respondent in a medium-sized firm (E/25) spoke of hiring a consultant on acoustics and soil analysis. Others spoke more generally about using outside specialists. One interviewee (E/7) had himself become a specialist in testing building materials and tackling structural problems. Among the architects in the sample, one (Arc/7) had had recourse to a consultant specializing in theater design, and another (Arc/11) had tracked down an expert in mosaics by seeking advice from the British Museum. A practitioner in a two-partner firm (Arc/10) referred to the value of seeking comments on materials from manufacturers' representatives and technical advisers, while another mentioned the seminars organized by manufacturers on such topics as damp-proof treatment ("a cross between sales talk and technical advice").

The pharmacists referred to their contracts with drug companies in generally positive terms. Several noted the role that representatives played in the dissemination of information on new drugs, including the distribution of non-promotional material. One interviewee (P/8) noted, however, that "only a very small percentage of new products end up in general use," and another (P/2) commented that "representatives from drug companies aren't usually qualified pharmacists these days—all they do is pass on the medical information from their firms." A second main benefit deriving from the larger pharmaceutical manufacturers was their provision of "talks, demonstrations and film and video presentations" (P/1), their support of training courses and their sponsorship of meetings in the form of "paying for the speaker, the course literature and the refreshments" (P/3).

The faint air of wistful reverence towards pharmaceutical companies purveyed by some of the community pharmacists in my sample is understandable in terms of the impact of external visitors on otherwise largely isolated practitioners. There was no such respect shown by the members of the medical profession in their interview contributions. Most of them, both consultants and general practitioners, displayed—or possibly considered it appropriate to display—a marked lack of enthusiasm about their contacts with drug company representatives. Some typical GP responses were: "All of us have our own criteria for seeing representatives—for me, they aren't of much benefit. They reinforce what I already know, or maybe introduce a new drug, but they don't influence my prescribing" (M/5); "They come round to discuss new drugs, but that usually turns out to be a waste of time" (M/2). For the consultants similarly: "Developments in drug treatments happen all the time: that gives the pharmaceutical companies scope to promote their wares. They are quite successful at passing on information but they don't constitute an important source of knowledge" (M/10). Yet Davis et al. (1994) confidently assert that "One example of an external influence on professionals' learning, perhaps to a greater extent than acknowledged, is the pharmaceutical representative" (p. 155), while Owen et al. (1989), on the basis of interviews with nearly a hundred GPs, note that a significant number of them (37) were in practices that had recently arranged one or more meetings in which the main content was provided by drug companies.

Various interviewees touched on the issue of sponsorship by pharmaceutical firms of training sessions—often without a direct commercial interest—and of general information sources and research. One consultant described her involvement in the development of a particular drug, which she had tentatively prescribed during its trial stage:

> The drug company then started...to promote the drug, and I went on a conference sponsored by the company. One must beware of that—of the fact that they have a vested interest in selling this drug —but where they will invite in acknowledged experts, you become aware of it that way, then you become aware of it because the trials are appearing in the journals. I've now used it in two other cases (M/2).

An academic raised the issue of how the development of appropriate equipment had transformed a particular surgical technique, adding that

> Partnership with industry is a key element. When the appropriate equipment ex-

ists, the scientific literature grows and then the new development becomes a band waggon ....Sometimes the equipment manufacturers provide much of the training in how to use it. Of course progress will be tempered by critical peer review, but it's important not to underestimate the importance of commercial involvement. Medicine is a very practical activity—very often it's the pharmaceutical and equipment companies who create the new developments (M/0).

This introductory overview has been concerned primarily with the characteristics of the six professions that form the subject of this study, their interactions with one another, the professional bodies which attempt, as best they can, to serve their diverse interests, and the other agencies which provide them with services of various kinds. Having looked at some of the internal issues, the next set of questions to be considered relate to the extrinsic pressures with which professionals individually and professions collectively find themselves having to contend.

Notes

1. As will shortly be evident, these commentaries are illustrative rather than comprehensive. For a more systematic source of factual information on most of the professions dealt with here, and on several more besides, the reader is referred to Allaker and Shapland (1995).
2. The distinction does not exist in the U.S., where qualified medical personnel are referred to generically as physicians, and the locations in which they work as HMOs (health management organizations).
3. The balance of power between GPs and hospital doctors may change over time, in consequence of the policy decision within the National Health Service that resources and priorities should begin in the 1990s to shift from secondary (hospital) to primary (community) care.
4. In another context, he parodied the prevalent attitude to evidence-based medicine as "something that everyone else should be doing—I, on the other hand, need clinical discretion."
5. The comment about an apprenticeship system is now considerably out-of-date. Entrance to the profession has since the early 1960s required the successful completion of a three-year degree course, which was extended in 1997 to four years.
6. The coverage of this section does not include Scotland or Northern Ireland, which have separate legal systems and professional bodies.
7. The statistics are derived from the Second Report of the Lord Chancellor's Advisory Committee (1997), Appendix G, pp. 99 and 101; and from the Research and Policy Planning Unit of the Law Society and the Records Office of the Bar Council.
8. An entertaining and readable account of the realities of a practicing barrister's life is to be found in Morison and Leith (1992).
9. As in the case of medicine, there is no comparable distinction in the United States, where all lawyers share the attribution of attorneys.
10. This is actually an over-simplified picture, since a significant number of individual solicitors and some solicitors' firms are themselves specialists, and some barristers deal with a fairly wide range of cases.
11. See note 7.

12. It became clear in the course of my interviews that the failure of the accountants to uncover the irregularities in question was due less to inefficiency than to the combined fear of punitive litigation if they proved to be mistaken and the risk of losing a lucrative client.

13. Excluding its very large overseas membership, which, if included, would bring it well above CIMA in the ranking.

14. The Council was not established until 1931—a much later date than one might have expected. Solicitors were the earliest profession to be registered, in 1843; the registration body for "pharmaceutical chemists" was established in 1852; registration for medical practitioners came later than both, in 1858.

15. The only non-professional I interviewed (under a misapprehension about his status), a businessman brought in to put a failing firm to rights (Arc/25), complained that his architect colleagues were untaught in economic costing; failed to see the importance of making a profit and were obsessed with producing "the best product"; did not understand the concept of a return on investment; accepted technological developments only grudgingly; saw information technology as producing status and quality rather than generating a product and productivity; and wrongly assumed that sponsors chose firms by the merits of their design instead of by the extent to which they met their needs.

16. A barrister and a chartered accountant gave, respectively, a brief insight into the cognitive differences between their professions. Perhaps surprisingly, the barrister credited accountants with the greater degree of judgment and intuition:

> It is not unusual for a solicitor to ask a question of the accountant, who on hearing the question answers a different question, and for neither of them to know that this is happening....some solicitors have a very good feel for the way in which the accountants think and some accountants have a very good feel for the way in which lawyers think: but there is a difference of approach. The accountants, particularly on the accounting side, are not overly concerned with precision....auditing is concerned with establishing that the accounts are not materially incorrect, and immaterial errors, provided one's assured that they are not cumulatively material, are not a problem...whereas a lawyer doesn't come to it with that approach at all. The lawyer comes to most problems, or very often the lawyer comes to problems with the idea that he's faced with the problem of classification, something is this or it's that, it's just a question of finding out what's going on and putting it into its box and being precise about it. Whereas the accountant thinks in different ways, in some ways more artistically and less mechanistically.... (L/32)

whereas the accountant envied the lawyers their greater precision:

> Certainly in tax and in law, precedents, legislation and so on are far more important elements of analysing a problem than intuition and common sense, which tend to be much more common in accounting. But I think there is a dramatic difference—why I think a lot of accountants think they are good tax people and they're not very good is because they still operate in a mind set which is disinclined to go back and look at the law or the cases. If you've got a problem in tax, what you should do is go back and research the legal precedent, the tax law and so on and look for a solution in that, not say, well that must be sensible to do that, because very often it isn't (Acc/30).

17. A more extensive, if somewhat bland and simplistic, account of what has here been termed professional institutions is to be found in Watkins et al. (1996). It is a measure of the confused nature of the terminology that they refer to associations rather than institutions—a term which is here given a different denotation.

18. The trilogy of terms derives from the study by Hirschman (1970) of "responses to decline in firms, organizations, and states," but has subsequently been applied in other contexts as a useful labelling of client attitudes to provision which is in some respect unsatisfactory.

19. A speculative explanation, unsubstantiated by any direct evidence, may lie in the particular organization of medicine into several separate Royal Colleges, each (apart from the Royal College of General Practitioners) with a relatively small, relatively homogeneous membership, constituted along largely democratic lines, and representing predominantly individual rather than corporate interests. The separation of the trade union function, generally seen to be efficiently performed by the British Medical Association, may also be a relevant factor. Alternatively, the absence of complaints could perhaps have been due to a collective reluctance by medics to wash their dirty linen in the presence of an outsider—though my respondents showed no hesitation in doing so on other scores.

Part 2
Change

3

Pressures for Change

The Sources of Change

Sam Goldwyn, famous for his aphorisms as for his role as a Hollywood producer, once observed that "nostalgia ain't what it used to be." Whether or not he was right to detect a deterioration in its quality over time, a number of my older respondents displayed it in high degree when looking back to their early careers. Contemporary professional life was seen to be less enjoyable and less rewarding (not only financially but socially and psychologically) than in the past. The causes of decline were represented as multifarious: at the risk of oversimplification they can be grouped in various broad categories, which will be reviewed in this chapter.

Before coming to the specific issues raised in the interview data, it may be useful to rehearse some general shifts in the social climate within which professionals have now to carry out their work. Perhaps the most evident is a diminished readiness by society at large to see the professions as predominantly concerned to serve the public good, as against satisfying their own vested interests. In effect, the claim to altruism—to a commitment beyond the merely contractual—is no longer generally believed. This may, in part, be a consequence of the fairly consistent negative image projected by academic critics, particularly in the 1960s and 1970s (see chapter 1), but it must also be attributed to the irresponsible and occasionally dishonest behavior of some practitioners. A related phenomenon is the extent to which professional misconduct, once discreetly dealt with inside the profession itself, can now attract widespread media attention. Thus it is that errors in hospital operations, failures by accountants to spot financial irregularities and the like, can fall victim to trial by tabloid and television rather than be more comfortably subject to peer review. The aura of mystique in which professionals were once able to cloak themselves has also yielded to a generally more scep-

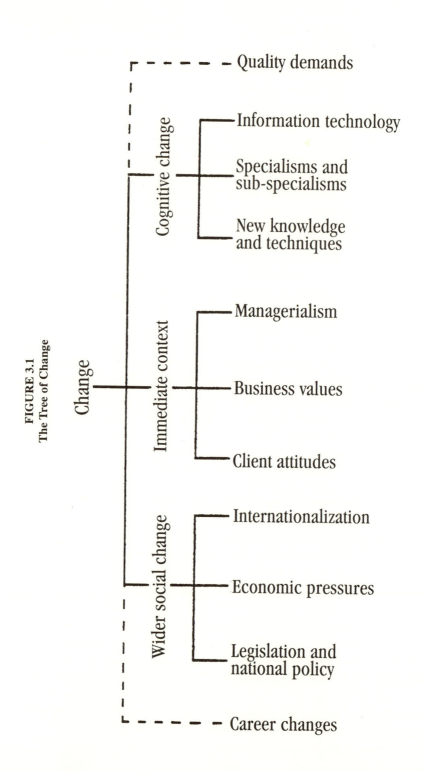

FIGURE 3.1
The Tree of Change

tical and better-informed populace, and its gradual evaporation has been accompanied by a clear diminution in status and esteem.

In addition to these broad changes in their social environment, the practitioners in the six professions which form the subject of this enquiry have encountered a number of more specific sources of variation in the quality of their working lives. Those identified in my interviews can be roughly classified into nine main categories—namely the effects of legislation and national policy; economic pressures; internationalism; changes in client attitudes; the adoption of business values; the rise of managerialism; the development of new knowledge and techniques; specialization and subspecialization; and the impact of information technology. Each of these factors—shortly to be discussed in more detail—calls for some adjustment in the established pattern of professional activity, and entails the need to develop some means of coping with the consequent change. For the most part, as will be seen in chapters 6 and 7, that coping mechanism takes the shape of formal or informal learning activities, or both.

Even those professionals who, in their interviews, represented such changes as being largely for the worse were nevertheless emphatic that they would not wish to resign from practice: their sense of commitment remained strong. It might seem, in any case, that the golden past was not without its tribulations. No less acute an observer of the social scene than Jane Austen was able as long ago as 1818, when *Persuasion* was published, to represent the hardships of professional life through the voice of the egregious Mrs. Clay:

> ...even in the quieter professions, there is a toil and a labour of the mind, if not of the body, which seldom leaves a man's looks to the natural effect of time. The lawyer plods, quite care-worn; the physician is up at all hours, and travelling in all weather...though every profession is necessary and honourable in its turn, it is only the lot of those not obliged to follow any, who can live in a regular way (Ch. 3).

The Effects of Legislation and National Policy

It would be a considerable exaggeration to suggest that, in the 1980s and early 1990s, every act of deregulation by a government dedicated to "rolling back the frontiers of the state" was matched by a compensating act of regulation. However, while many long-standing aspects of professional exclusivity were being opened up to the vagaries of the market, many others were simultaneously being constrained by new legislative demands or policy requirements.

Of the six professional groups under review, it would seem that medics, and to a lesser extent lawyers, were least subject to external interference. One might conjecture that this was in part a consequence of their established position in British society, and of the comparatively high status level they managed to sustain. In the case of medicine, at least, it could also be attributed to the speed and efficiency with which the profession has been able to demonstrate its capacity to respond to potential criticisms. A good example is offered by the advent of laparoscopic, or "keyhole," surgery techniques, which were over-enthusiastically adopted by a number of practitioners who lacked the necessary skills. After a limited number of disasters, the General Medical Council, as the central regulatory body, moved swiftly to ensure that no one could be permitted to adopt the relevant approach without suitably thorough training, with the result that the problem abated before the advent of any major public outcry.[1] Not all professions are however as adept at preventive self-regulation.

The interviews with pharmacists gave rise to a number of complaints about the unreliable behavior of the Department of Health, described by one respondent (P/5) as "whimsical and irrational, imposing lots of unnecessary rules." Another community pharmacist (P/17) complained about the inconsistencies between different Family Service Health Authorities, resulting in more discriminatory decisions in some areas than in others. On the whole, it clearly suited the government of the time to control the activities of the pharmaceutical profession through tight financial regulation and through the demand for internally generated quality control rather than through more direct legislative measures.

One might expect lawyers to gain benefit from most changes in legislation, in the sense that they would be the profession best placed to interpret and implement them. This did, indeed, appear from the interview data to be the case: while practitioners were often required to master new areas or aspects of the law, they commonly found it beneficial to rise to the challenge. Among the examples cited of this phenomenon were the change in divorce law from a fault to no-fault basis and the amendments in family law and children's law. However, as Thomas (1992) points out, the profession itself was subject to the provisions of the 1990 Courts and Legal Services Act, one of whose consequences was that "40 percent of legal aid solicitors had given up offering criminal legal aid and 28 percent...matrimonial legal aid." So far, however, the lawyers have escaped the root-and-branch reforms proposed for their Australian counterparts. There, a wide-ranging report of the Australian Trade Practices Commission in the early 1990s recommended applying the Trade Practices Act to legal practitioners, reducing or eliminating their monopoly in many areas, ending the division between barristers and solicitors, removing restrictive practices among barristers, ending restrictions on advertising, and introducing new fee arrangements. Even though lawyers in Britain have not been threatened to this extent, one of the judges I interviewed (L/8) observed that "There have been several recent challenges in the law—one might say that it is going through a major upheaval. The question is how best to deal with them. It's an exciting time." Thomas (1992) reaches a similar conclusion: "Her [Margaret Thatcher's] legacy for the profession is that of turmoil, change, uncertainty and opportunity."

As a whole, the accountants in my sample accepted that the recent legislative demands placed on them had been "designed to protect the public" (Acc/1). The basic standards of practice laid down by the profession's watchdog body, the Accounting Standards Board, are supplemented by procedural requirements initiated by the various professional bodies for auditing and for planning, carrying out, and documenting work. A number of respondents commented on the burdensome level of form-filling and the complexity of the guidelines which had to be followed. Aside from the frequent but sporadic changes imposed by new and revised procedures and standards, there were also major legislative reforms to contend with. The Companies Act was extensively updated after the series of financial scandals in the late 1980s and early 1990s, while the passing of the Insolvency Act in 1980 was said to have brought about "massive changes in professional practice" (Acc/10). Inevitably, such changes gave rise to new demands for updating and new efforts to interpret the legislative requirements. To cite one among a number of examples, it took the management accountants in a relatively small industrial company two weeks to work out how to put a particular set of new standards into effect. An academic (Acc/22), reviewing the issue of keeping up with changes in legislation, commented that the main burden fell on the smaller firms, since they were not easily able to accommodate the extra training that was often called for.

It was the architects who appeared to have suffered the most from changes in national policy during the decade before the interviews took place. "Deregulation," remarked one respondent (Arc/10), "has had a devastating effect." He went on to explain that it came into operation at a time when there was a considerable oversupply of architectural services, so that "prices shot down by around one-third." The abolition of agreed terms of appointment, linked with a recommended fee scale, meant the end of standard contracts, and an increase, often exacerbated by the involvement of solicitors, in time and money for both architect and client. The introduction of compulsory competitive tendering, which was a governmental requirement for all public sector work, further depressed profit margins. It also had the effect, together with curbs on local authority expenditure, of severely reducing some council architecture departments and eliminating others altogether.

A different set of pressures derived from the opposite pull of regulation. New planning laws were imposed which—like the legislative demands on accountants—were ambiguous enough to require the architects' attendance at special courses and in some cases to put clients in need of legal advice. The European Union's demand that tenders for any project estimated as costing more than a specified sum should be submitted in writing was seen by one respondent (Arc/18) as yet another imposition. Building regulations had proliferated over the years: a sole practitioner in late career (Arc/28) looked back to the time when "they used to be a quarter of an inch thick and cost seven shillings and six pence—now they're more than six inches thick and cost £45." At the time of the interviews, a new complication had arisen, in the form of Construction Design and Maintenance (CDM) regulations—an optional requirement emanating from Brussels in response to which, as one interviewee bitterly observed, "the British government immediately went to town—even went overboard—where other EU countries, including Germany, have not." Most respondents remained uncertain at the time about the precise implications, though aware that they were concerned with enhancing health and safety procedures throughout the construction process and subsequent to it, and involved clients in appointing planning supervisors to ensure conformity. Failure to comply with core CDM requirements would carry criminal liability for negligence, so it was not surprising that several of those interviewed had attended courses of up to three days, together in one case (Arc/22) with a series of in-house seminars.

CDM was also seen by structural engineers as at best "a bit of a burden" (E/26) and at worst "a handicap to the profession" (E/30). However, there was less reference in the interview data to other regulatory demands, or to the impact of central policies. The only issue aside from CDM about which any significant concern was expressed was the constant updating of professional codes of practice: but since such codes emanate from within the profession itself, they can scarcely be categorized as products of governmental imposition.

Overall, it seems reasonable to conclude that in most professions, with the exception of architecture, and to a lesser extent, pharmacy, national policy and central legislation have had an irritant rather than a seriously debilitating effect. More numerous and more complex rules of procedure have called, in the cases of accountancy and the construction industry, for greater vigilance and additional learning; lawyers have had to meet the challenges occasioned by change and uncertainty; doctors have preempted external involvement by internal vigilance. The effects of economic pressures, however, have been in some respects more far-reaching.

Economic Pressures

The turn of the decade between the 1980s and the 1990s saw the advent of a worldwide economic recession. In the U.K., its impact was long and deep, affecting all sectors of the community. Medicine and pharmacy, the two professions (among others outside my sample) affiliated to the public sector, were subject to tight governmental controls on expenditure. Hospital medicine was badly hit, with enforced contractions in staffing and consequent reductions in ward capacity. A gynecologist in a provincial hospital (M/25) gave a detailed account of the strictly limited time available for operations and consultancies, resulting in unacceptably long waiting lists. The decision by the Department of Health to make a gradual shift of resources from the hospital sector to general practice made matters even worse. One demoralized respondent (M/10) saw hospital medicine as "rapidly becoming a second-class system"; another (M/24) described it as "a high volume, low quality service." None of the GPs interviewed voiced comparable concerns.

The hospital pharmacists presented a muted version of their medical counterparts. The use of expensive drugs was closely scrutinized, and there was considerable emphasis on finding cheaper substitutes: staffing was also kept to a minimum level. Among pharmacists in the community, the main burden of complaint fell upon the Department of Health, whose zealous cost-cutting included reductions in the subsidies and allowances for dispensing prescriptions. One respondent (P/10) protested that "the DOH is constantly wanting more for less": he estimated that his profit margin on each item had fallen over the previous four years from 22 percent to 15 percent. A second (P/19) reported that an increase of 20 percent in the number of prescriptions had been matched by a decrease of 5 percent in profit. There was little reference to pharmacies going out of business, though it was said in passing that some small local ones had had to close in the face of increasing competition.

Redundancies, early retirements, and wholesale closures of firms were no more than a marginal phenomenon in law and accountancy, where there remained a reasonably steady demand for professional services. A number of less efficient partnerships went to the wall, and other small enterprises were unable to take on new members of staff as existing ones retired. In some instances problems arose from the insolvency of clients. However, the general volume of concern expressed by lawyers and accountants about the effects of the recession was discernably lower than that manifested in the health services or the construction industry.

As in the case of legislation and policy, it was the architectural and structural engineering professions which came off worst under recessionary pressures. According to Hughes (1994), "European architects...have been severely affected by the crisis in the building sector and the resulting unemployment." In the U.K., the consequences could be measured in terms of quite massive redundancies: according to one estimate—see chapter 2—nearly 40 percent of qualified architects were short of or out of work by the early 1990s. Large and small firms alike were subject to dramatic contraction. Numerous examples were given by respondents. The turnover of one medium-sized firm was said to have plummeted from £6 million to £2 million a year. A large organization had reduced its staff numbers from 350 to 100, and another even more dramatically from 650 to 90. Among the smaller architectural partnerships, the staffing in one had fallen from 36 to 5, but had recently risen again to 10; a second had suffered a lesser drop from 25 to 10, which had climbed back up to 13. Engineering had suffered less drastically: as a respondent (E/25) explained, "although there are now rather too many engineers, there are at least twice as many architects as society needs." Even so, the payroll of a structural engineering firm of some 75 people had fallen by one-third to 50 and that of another from 55 to 30 between 1989 and 1994.

A review of the research data yielded no consistent pattern of devastation. Indeed in some cases partnerships had managed, through a combination of neat footwork and good fortune, to survive intact, or even to expand slightly, during the period of the recession. A two-partner architectural practice was "cushioned by hospital projects"; another maintained its staffing level of 10 people by working a four-day week during a critical period. A medium-sized engineering firm managed to swim

strongly against the tide by expanding from 150 to 260 but its profit-
ability, according to one of its partners (E/12), had failed to keep pace
because of the very tight margins imposed by competitive tendering.

It may be observed that architects are unique among the six professions in having had to contend with a threefold series of misfortunes.
Their vicissitudes in terms of the draconian cuts in earnings and employment during the recession were compounded, as noted in the previous section, by the combined effects of deregulation and compulsory
competitive tendering, and further exacerbated by the reduction in their
status and their role as discussed in chapter 2. Only the last of these
could be attributed to their own failings in attending too much to design
and too little to the management of the construction process: the rest
were a consequence of free market dogma and the vagaries of the glo-
bal economy. Their survival, albeit in a leaner and necessarily more
efficient form than before, is a measure of the value still accorded by
society to the professional services they offer.

Taken as a whole, the effects of economic pressures have been erratic, imposing more debilitating effects on some professions than on
others. Some individuals, some partnerships and some sectors have
borne the brunt of financial stringencies while some have come off
relatively lightly. In the return to a period of growth, even the survivors
have emerged with a degree of wariness: "there is no time to sit back,
and no long-term certainty" (Arc/13). There is also a general sense that
people are expected to work harder, and to be more competitive, than
they were in the past.

The changes brought about, or at least triggered, by the recession
can be seen as predominantly social rather than cognitive in character:
they may have affected the lives and incomes of many professionals,
but they have not in any significant measure caused them to adapt existing skills and techniques or learn substantially new ones (except in
the non-trivial sense of becoming redundant and having to embark on
an entirely new career). That is not altogether true of the next source of
change to be considered.

Internationalism

Professions are international in the general sense that they exist in
recognisably similar forms in all advanced countries. In some cases
(see chapter 6), their practitioners cross national boundaries to meet in
specialist conferences, while most professional journals give some at-

tention at least to developments overseas. Significant new findings made in one country are rapidly disseminated to others; some research is conducted jointly between academic groups in different parts of the globe. Yet on the ground, there appears to have been surprisingly little involvement of the British professionals in my sample with activities outside their own country (architecture and engineering being again atypical of the rest). This is the case even in relation to the European Union, whose developing influence, and particularly its emphasis on the inter-European applicability of professional qualifications, might lead one to expect a significant level of interchange between Britain and other member countries.

In medicine, a small handful of those interviewed had had a brief early career experience working in developing countries, and one or two consultants had attended specialist courses in the U.S. However, none of the 32 respondents made any direct reference to the effects of EU membership on the profession. Nicholas (1994), writing from the perspective of the British Medical Association's European Committee, suggests that relatively few British doctors emigrate to Europe, but adds that "the U.K. imports a far greater number of doctors than it exports." In this respect at least there is some international activity within the profession, even though it cannot be said to constitute a significant source of change. There is a similar pattern in pharmacy: a sizeable number of Asian students are trained in pharmacy schools in U.K. universities, some of whom stay on to practice. There is again no evidence in my sample of any other form of international involvement.

When it comes to the law, one finds a surprising dearth of interest in mastering European law. Wood (1994) writes that "To many solicitors, the need to assimilate the European legal dimension…is a nightmare scenario"; Sherr's (1993) study of the needs for skills training among solicitors indirectly confirms its low priority by noting that EU law was only cited once among 16 responses. In the other main branch of the profession, the Lord Chancellor's Advisory Committee (1997) endorses the view that "EC law has remained largely the province of specialist EC practitioners, instead of becoming, as it should be, part of the armoury of every practicing barrister (§4.15)." Among my respondents, one (L/28) of the two solicitors currently practicing European and competition law (the topics are closely intertwined) remarked on the paucity of available courses, noting that the smaller firms do not offer posts in the subject. On a wider scale, international law is seen as a specialized theme, largely confined to major firms and university law departments.

The main impact of internationalism on the profession is the indirect one created by the emergence of a small number of worldwide practices with built-in scope for mobility of staff across national boundaries. The same is true of accountancy, where the major firms (see chapter 2) are even larger. The only direct reference, during accountancy interviews, to European Union activities came from a senior accountant on the staff of a local authority (Acc/12), who commented that although the international aspects of his job were "fairly pathetic," Brussels was beginning to make an impact in terms of grant funding for inter-regional collaboration.

One of the effects of deregulation and economic recession on the construction industry was to stimulate many firms to look overseas for work not available in the U.K.. One large architectural partnership had expanded into Belgium, France, Germany, Italy, and Poland, and was beginning to embark on new developments in China. Another had designed airports, business parks, and shopping centers in locations as diverse as Athens, Bologna, Lyon, Salonika, and Abu Dhabi: in the year preceding my interview with one of its partners (Arc/21) it had earned 20 percent of its income from overseas. Even some of the smaller firms had overseas ventures—one, for example, in Barbados, Japan, and Slovakia; another, more modestly, with an associate in France. As one respondent (Arc/17) noted, "the European Union is likely to have a major effect on the construction industry—already, most of the building products are integrated."

It was said (E/0) that the professions of structural and civil engineering are international and expose their members to different cultural norms; even so "it is difficult to relate to Europe." Certainly, many interviewees mentioned the involvement of their firms in countries outside the European Union, including China, Egypt, Hong Kong, India, Malaysia, Saudi Arabia, and the US; and as in accountancy, a number of very large firms now operate on a worldwide basis. Nevertheless, there also appeared to be a substantial amount of activity within continental Europe, notably a massive project involving a British, German, and Spanish consortium of contractors, as well as a medium-sized firm with one-fifth of its staff working on a major development in Berlin. As a number of respondents pointed out, codes of practice have progressively been Europeanised. An engineering respondent to Neale's (1994) questionnaire survey is quoted as remarking:

> we now have link offices in Madrid, Lisbon and Paris and we are talking to the Germans and we expect to have one shortly in Czechoslovakia...it could well be

that integration throughout Europe takes place in this sort of informal way. By permeation rather than by due process (p. 12).

It would appear, from this evidence, that the insularity traditionally attributed to an island race may be gradually breaking down. In the case of architecture and structural engineering, the change has been brought on by a crisis of major proportions, while in accountancy and law it has followed the wave of take-overs and amalgamations generated largely to dominate a competitive market. In medicine and pharmacy, less strongly driven by economic considerations, the phenomenon of internationalism has left both professions relatively unaffected.

Client Attitudes

Many of the more senior professionals I interviewed were inclined to hark back to a golden age in which their clients were deferential, biddable, and loyal. Nowadays, as one remarked nostalgically

> Client expectation has totally changed, and I think the older people in the profession really regret this...your client became your friend and you became the family adviser over the years ....It's now much more value based.... Now the old client trust and loyalty—it's a generalisation, there's obviously exceptions, in some exceptional cases it's not like this—has gone...and that I think has upset a lot of people. It's just not the profession they came into any more (Acc/19).

A community pharmacist (P/28) made the further point that "Members of the public have become more aggressive over the years...they show an increasing lack of respect for professionals." "Professionals," added an engineer (E/0) "have failed to persuade society of their differences from shopkeepers."

The fault, a number suggested, lay more with the professions than with the public. An architect (Arc/1) considered that he and his confreres had lost client trust by "passing the buck to sub-contractors"; a second (Arc/11) claimed that "modernism is largely to blame—it has encouraged architects to despise the public, and they have kicked back." A senior hospital pharmacist (P/16), accepting the validity of a patient's complaint that "the pharmacy treats you like second-class citizens," initiated a change from a product-oriented to a service-oriented quality system. In medicine, Betz et al. (1983) cite a relative lack of sensitivity to patients as one source of problems in the US; in the U.K., Elston (1991) refers to a variety of sources of consumer dissatisfaction, leading to an increasing interest in alternative approaches to health and illness.

It is a short step from expressing dissatisfaction to "becoming more insistent about one's rights" (P/28). A medical respondent (M/22) noted that "patients are becoming more demanding, looking for someone to blame when things go wrong and calling out doctors for quite trivial reasons." He ascribed this to general social change but also to the publication of the Patients' Charter (an official statement of the entitlements of those seeking medical help). The Marre Report (1988), in addressing itself to the future of the legal profession, argues that "Consumers need to know to whom they should complain about inadequate services and they need to be confident of effective redress in the event of a complaint being made" (p. 175). Nearly ten years later, Barnes (1997), the Legal Services Ombudsman, makes a similar point less tactfully "Solicitors would find their reputation as a profession greatly enhanced if they could bring themselves to adopt a response to complaints of poor service much more akin to that of major high street retailers." Many respondents confirmed their "increasing acceptance of client rights" (Burchell et al., 1985), though not necessarily for disinterested reasons: "the profession has shifted to client responsiveness as a survival strategy" (L/27); "Professionals are biased towards strong client relationships and client satisfaction—the extra work from deregulation is falling off and there's over-capacity among the big auditing firms" (Acc/15).

One significant change concerned the costs of professional services: "competition has driven the fees down—in the present culture, everything is measured by money" (E/30); "on the fees front, people try it on" (Acc/25); "the client nowadays will look at the price more than he will at the relationship" (Acc/14); architects are "chosen for the cheapness of their fees rather than the quality of their work" (Arc/7). Another change lies in the tendency towards litigation: "clients are litigation conscious, and want 100 percent cover for a 10 percent fee" (Arc/28). In medicine, by contrast, the prospect of legal action tends "to make doctors more defensive and specify more tests, so as to guard against accusations of incompetence" (M/22).

There are, it needs to be remembered, different categories of client.[2] Eraut (1994) makes a useful, if broad, distinction between "a relationship of patronage, by wealthy and powerful clients...; a commercial relationship;...and a welfare relationship" (p. 5). The traditional patron, though given substantial attention in Johnson's (1972) account of the rise of professionalism, has given way to increasingly influential corporate clients for whom—outside the health services—the larger firms compete. Individual clients tend to gravitate towards the smaller practices—though it is only in medicine, pharmacy, and to a much lesser extent law, that they are cast in anything approaching a welfare relationship.

Institutional clients were variously perceived. Powell (1985), writing about the different, but related, legal scene in the U.S., referred to "a greatly increased...legal sophistication of the corporate client" (p. 291). A British engineer (E/29) took a similar view: "It's easier to deal with large organizations, because their staff tend to be more sophisticated—they have a better understanding of the problems and aren't dealing directly with their own money." In contrast, one architect (Arc/5) complained that "The major clients are no longer experts nowadays"; a second architect (Arc/30) put forward the mediating view that "while they may be technically more educated, they are aesthetically less so—they don't know much about architecture as such." An engineer (E/30) saw "organizational clients" as "anxious to protect themselves by hiding behind routines." But if clients can be very demanding, an accountant (Acc/30) suggested, it is because often they too face demands and pressures: "I still enjoy working with them."

It was widely agreed that increased competition to attract both institutional and individual clients had—alongside the changing nature of the clients themselves—channelled the relationship away from a cozy personal interaction towards a more strictly functional arrangement. "Clients expect you to be businesslike—the days of the long liquid lunch have gone" (L/9). This shift has been accompanied by a virtual abandonment of the prohibition against actively seeking clients, and particularly those already involved with other professional firms. An accountant (Acc/25) welcomed the fact his firm "has taken clients away from the Big Six," especially because they had attempted to poach his clients during the recession. A barrister (L/32) neatly summed up the transition: "Once we were forbidden to tout—now we're encouraged to market." The change in client attitudes has thus begun to generate a countervailing change among professionals: as one of the informants in Symes et al. (1995) ruefully noted, "as soon as you are no longer treated as a gentleman you cease to behave like one" (p. 105).

But if the professions are increasingly seen—and see themselves—as commercial enterprises, the process of adaptation still remained incomplete in the mid 1990s. "Some people find it hard to adjust to a commercial ethos, and find their clients' monetary values disturbing" (Arc/12); "between exploiting the market and expressing a personal responsibility to society, architects have yet to find a comfortable role" (Arc/29). A lone voice (L/27) claimed that "some things are unchanging, such as the personal relationships you form with clients." Nevertheless, the adoption of a more businesslike ethos and approach seems inevitable.

The Business Ethos

Different professions have been affected in different ways by their apparently remorseless commercialization. A medical respondent in the study by Watkins et al. (1992) of professional life in the 1990s is reported as concluding that "Everything is becoming very financially oriented and there is this move away from looking after the patients to looking after the money. Everyone is very antagonistic ....It has demoralized the profession generally" (p. 45). Community pharmacists have always had to mediate between their need to earn a livelihood from their business and their concern to keep up with developments in pharmacy, but their "intensely competitive" (P/5) environment in recent years has made it hard to maintain their professionalism. In the mid-1990s, lawyers remained divided on the issue of "whether to submit to a market-led metamorphosis of their traditional image as non-commercial generalists...the reality of economic survival has turned many law firms into businesses that happen to practice law" (Wood, 1994, p. 69). The same ambivalence emerges in my interview data: "In a number of firms, there's a tension between profession and business—but it's a business" (L/4). The accountants in the sample showed less concern with the move towards commercialization, though according to Wilmott (1986) "accountants are under mounting pressure to allow their actions to be guided by market forces and naked self-interest, unbuffered by the gentlemanly ideals of professional conduct" (p. 576). In engineering, too, "Professional work is nowadays seen as a business, more concerned with money than with quality" (E/25).

Thomas (1992), in his wide-ranging review of the pressures on, and consequent changes to, the British legal profession during 1979 to 1990 (the "Thatcher years"), contrasts "the hallmarks of market forces" with

the ideology of altruism which for so long had underpinned lawyer/client relationships...; Firms increasingly identified themselves as 'collective entrepreneurs' in the business of making money by providing a service.... The commercial reality of large firms was that they increasingly saw and promoted themselves as competitive, efficient, business enterprises geared to providing a service for the client (pp. 7–8).[3]

The most tangible outcome of the espousal, however reluctant, of business values has been a recognition of the need for improved client relations and a greater emphasis on sales techniques. Solicitors, accountants and architects, as the respondent groups mainly concerned with attracting and maintaining a clientele,[4] showed a particular interest in courses on marketing, self-presentation and public speaking: further details of such courses are given in chapter 6. This move was sometimes met with resistance, as in the case of an architect (Arc/3) who complained about having to present himself "in a suburban way." On the whole, however, the new emphasis on "good customer care" (L/0) has been adopted with varying degrees of enthusiasm. An accountant in a small practice (Acc/25) had, for example, established a Family Business Club which held regular meetings to provide up-to-date financial advice as a means of attracting new clients.

Symes et al. (1995) suggest that "the majority of [architectural] firms are not organised to undertake direct marketing efforts" (p. 88). Their comment would seem to relate to the lack of an appropriate management structure. The evidence from my interviews suggests, however, that all six professions have begun to succumb to the pressures of managerialism—itself a predictable consequence of adopting business values.

The Rise of Managerialism

The idea that management skills and techniques form a significant component of professional life is not new: almost half a century ago, C. Wright Mills was able to assert that "most professionals are now salaried employees...successful professional men become more and more the managerial type" (Mills, 1951, p. 112). However, the major shift to a managerial culture can be linked closely to the advent of very large partnerships and their consequent incorporation into limited companies.

The simplest form of professional practice, run by a sole practitioner, calls for no elaborate machinery of decision-making or of financial control. By the time the practice expands to include five or six partners, the tradition has been to operate on a mainly consensual basis, giving every member some sense of control over his or her work. But for firms of around twenty or more, joint decision-making tends to become untenably cumbersome and time-consuming, and other structures have to be devised.

The solicitors in my sample showed some resistance to management, but adopted a variety of systems to cope with its demands.[5] For example in one medium-sized firm there were, among the salaried partners, eight equity partners who made all the financial decisions: the whole partnership voted on other policy issues (L/11). In a much larger firm, the managerial structure comprised a senior partner, a managing partner, and a deputy managing partner, together with an elected council The central group exercised overall control, but each of the branches operated more or less autonomously (L/21). Most barristers' chambers, in which independent practitioners share facilities, are small enough to be run collegially, though one informant (L/32) commented that the head of chambers—usually (as noted in chapter 2) a distinguished QC or high court judge—"owns the lease, licenses the members, and has the power to throw them out." Architects and structural engineers also show some reluctance to adopt a thoroughgoing managerial ethos: thus one highly successful architectural firm with about 20 professional staff was run as a cooperative in which all architects were appointed as partners after working in the firm for a year, and agreed the division of income together (Arc/7); while a firm of consulting engineers with over 250 staff had "a broadly consensual management, though the senior partner acts as managing director" (E/12).

Like it or not, however, most professions have had managerial demands thrust upon them, through a combination of increasing size and growing financial stringency. The former has been dominant in general practice and the latter in hospital medicine. GP partnerships have tended to expand under fund-holding arrangements, giving them greater discretion over their own budgets, to a point at which, one respondent (M/12) ruefully observed, "general practice is less about diagnosis nowadays than it is about management." In hospitals "every senior consultant has to be involved in management" (M/8), and indeed "there is growing pressure for some doctors to become full-time managers" (M/19), in a context in which resources are scarce and difficult questions of priority have to be decided. For a number of the hospital pharmacists interviewed, managerial responsibilities were welcomed as a means towards increased influence and status—"it's the way to get on" (P/16). An industrial pharmacist in mid-career (P/9) expressed some reluctance to take a management qualification, though other interviewees working in the same field (P/7, P/28) and in large retail chains (P/12, P/14) had abandoned professional practice at an early stage and had made successful careers as managers. For all their hesitations about the move from their professional roles, many architects and engineers had also been siphoned off into management: Symes et al. (1995) note that, over the past 30 years, the time spent in drawing by the principals of medium-sized architectural firms has dropped by nearly half. The accountants in the sample made few comments on the subject, giving the impression that it was not seen as a major deviation from existing technical activity or as a threat to established professional values.[6]

For those determined to avoid managerial responsibilities, there appear to be two main courses open. One is simply, as an individual, to refuse to take on administrative tasks. This seems to be a viable strategy among hospital consultants, whose careers will not be adversely affected: as one loftily remarked, "I do my best to keep out of administration—in medicine, we have to deal with imperatives" (M/10). Elsewhere, promotion is likely to be jeopardized: "I don't want to be involved in management, but I shall have to do it" (L/4). The second approach is collectively to appoint a suitably qualified manager—sometimes an accountant, but seldom a renegade member of one's own profession—to take on the task of practice management. This was an emergent or already-established pattern in several small-to-medium sized firms in general medical practice, architecture and structural engineering—all, it may be noted, processual professions in the terms specified in chapter 1. It was noticeably less marked in the data relating to pharmacy, law, and accountancy, where professional competence itself demands a familiarity with procedural activities, to which management is to some extent analogous.

Where professionals and managers coexist, tensions may well arise. Dawson (1994) offers an interesting comparative analysis of lawyers' and medics' attitudes to management in general and practice managers in particular, and discerns a trend in both professions towards greater hands-on involvement. Freidson (1986), writing in the U.S. context, notes a key contrast between hospital managers and professionals: "the emphasis of the practitioners in discussing their work is on quality, while...management's *de facto* emphasis is on what can be measured readily—cost and quantity" (p. 170). The move in hospital management to employing senior doctors, noted above, may be seen as an attempt to bypass this source of contention.

A clear structural indicator of the change of emphasis from profession to business, and the corresponding move from partnership to managerialism, lies in the increasing number of professional firms—mainly but not exclusively the largest—which have turned themselves into limited companies.[7] The perceived advantages of this move are varied. Most respondents pointed to the reduction in partners' liability, and the related fact that some of the more sizeable organizations have become "virtually uninsurable." Others commented on the increased ability to raise equity, the scope for improved pension fund arrangements, the greater flexibility in promoting and also in shedding staff, and—not least—the perception that the clients' image of the firm would be enhanced. Whatever the technical advantages, it seems evident that the incorporation of professional firms as companies signals a move from the traditional values of self-governing partnerships to the more overtly business-like, managerial, and customer-friendly world of commerce and industry, with its concomitant losses and gains.

Knowledge Development

Alongside the wider social changes in legislation and policy, the economy and internationalism, and the more immediately contextual effects of alterations in client attitudes, business values, and managerial practices, there is a third and equally important set of factors which have a direct impact on professional life. They can again be grouped in a triad, under the broad heading of cognitive changes: the accumulation of relevant professional knowledge; the consequent development of specialisms; and the far-reaching effects of information technology.

The first of these—the accelerating growth of new knowledge—is widely recognized as a twentieth-century phenomenon, and needs no special comment. In relation to the professions, it can be looked at in various ways. Abbott (1988) offers a characteristically well-argued analysis, distinguishing between "the addition of new knowledge" and "the replacement of old" (p. 175). In the former, detail increases while coverage remains the same; in the latter, old facts or methods are replaced by new ones: an important aspect is "the gradual changes of paradigm" (p. 178). "In the professions," he goes on to add

> incremental minor change seems more frequent than paradigm change. Laws and regulations change often; jurisprudence and accounting theory do not. Information on drugs and other medical treatment changes weekly; general approaches to medical care do not. (p. 179)

Scientific advances are cumulative and focused in a way that social changes are reiterative and scattered: they are also, in a generally competitive environment, rapid and frequent. So, as far as the replacement of knowledge is concerned, one might expect the technically based professions—medicine, pharmacy and engineering—to be affected more directly than the others in the sample. The data suggest that this is indeed the case in both medicine and pharmacy, fed as they are by a highly developed research base.

The pressure for replacing old knowledge does not, however, seem to be as strong in structural engineering: as in architecture, law and accountancy, the main emphasis is on addition rather than replacement. This may be ascribed in large part to the considerably lower levels of research investment.[8] One significant technical change was, however, mentioned by a respondent (E/13), namely the recent use of steel sheets for roofing or wall cladding, calling for a change of emphasis and a need to relearn design. The same interviewer mentioned limit state design as a new methodology involving "changes that are fundamental but fairly easily picked up."

In architecture, some interviewees were generally wary of "untested materials and innovative technologies—there is less demand for hi-tech approaches than for simple ones related to green thinking" (Arc/1); "there is a move towards natural ventilation and away from air conditioning" (Arc/3); "Architectural design is market-led, not technology-led. The claim that it's the duty of architects to experiment with new types of material is absurd in a one-off industry" (Arc/4). Others, emphasizing knowledge accretion (Arc/7, Arc/11), referred to the need to know about new materials and cited the problem of keeping pace with development.

Lawyers and accountants are also in general more concerned with the addition of new knowledge than with the replacement of old. However, the major changes in the legislative framework noted earlier in this chapter, together with the upheaval in employment legislation following the Industrial Relations Act and the restructuring of financial services resulting from radical deregulation, could reasonably be said to constitute a series of paradigm changes.

Abbott (1988) suggests that it is growth, rather than replacement, that leads to specialization, "in order to maintain at a constant level the amount of knowledge a given professional must know" (p. 179). This contention is not entirely borne out by my research, in that the replacement of old knowledge with new (which in Abbott's scheme instead "gives rise to abstraction"—p. 179) can also be seen to create powerful specialisms, as in the case of radically novel surgical techniques, such as laparoscopic surgery, and the experiments with low energy buildings currently promoted by the specialist members of the Earth Shelter Association. In any event, the emergence of new specialisms constitutes another significant element in the changes that confront the professions.

The Emergence of Specialisms

In *Myth and Meaning* (1978) Levi-Strauss points to a difference between pre-scientific thinking, which aims "to reach a general understanding of the universe and not only a general but a *total* understanding" and scientific thinking, which seeks "to divide the difficulty into as many parts as...necessary in order to solve it" (p. 17). The emergence of specialisms in professional life, as in the academic world, can in these terms be seen as a move from a pre-scientific to a scientific way of being.

Before exploring the issue further, a distinction may be drawn between specialisms and specialization. In rough and ready terms one might say that the notion of a specialism is cognitive—that is, it derives from a mapping of the knowledge base of a given field—while that of specialization is social, in that it reflects the choice of an individual to concentrate on one area of knowledge (that is, one specialism) and so to direct his or her attention away from others. That the two are interconnected is evident enough: one would not designate a particular area of knowledge as a specialism if no one were to specialise in it; and one would not be identified as a specialist without a recognisable and bounded area of knowledge to address. But for the purposes of a clearer analysis—albeit at the cost of some degree of artificiality attendant on the abstraction—the topic of specialisms as a cognitive issue will be reviewed in this section while the subject of specialization as a social phenomenon will be deferred until the next chapter, and discussed as an aspect of professional careers.

One can perhaps most usefully think of specialisms not as fixed lines of demarcation on the territory of professional knowledge, but rather as the cells in a biological culture, involved in constant movement, absorbing other cells or being absorbed by them, generating new entities and dying off as the context changes. Pursuing a similar metaphor, Bucher and Strauss (1961) observe that "Specialties frequently arise around the exploitation of a new method or technique, like radiology in medicine, but as time goes by they may segmentalize further along methodological perspectives" (p. 328). They add that "they tend to be more or less continually undergoing change" (p. 332). The research literature, in company with my interview data, contains numerous examples of specialist areas, though—because of the intervention of social factors—the catalogues often differ in significant or trivial respects. To cite only one among many cases in point, Gordon (1987) lists restoration, health care design, housing for the aged, sports facilities, and laboratory design as typical instances of specialisms in architecture, while Symes et al. (1995), addressing the same topic, cite housing, commercial/industrial design, institutional/public commissions, urban design, and work for individual clients.

More tightly structured professions, such as medicine, and to a lesser extent law, are less subject to such relativism: but even where the main divisions may be broadly agreed, what is to be designated as a specialism rather than a sub-division of the profession is not always clear: and there may also be disagreement over what is to count as a sub-specialism, or even a sub-sub-specialism. One of my respondents (M/28), a urologist, was of course a member of the sub-profession of hospital medicine, and within that a practitioner in the sub-sub-profession—or arguably the specialism—of surgery. Within surgery, one might say that his specialism—or arguably his sub-specialism—was urology. However, he had further decided to specialize in pediatric urology—or should one say sub-specialize, or sub-sub-specialize?[9]

The phenomenon of continual change can be illustrated in hospital pharmacy by the recent emergence of new specialisms in radio diagnostics and psychiatric pharmacy; or in law by professional indemnity as a specialist area of civil litigation and by VAT law as an aspect of tax law. The disappearance of a number of existing specialisms was noted by a senior medical administrator (M/30), especially as a result of changes in technology; a solicitor in a large city law firm (L/30) pointed to shipping law as a branch of professional work which was now virtually defunct.

A number of respondents, though themselves engaged in a specialist area, were clearly uncomfortable about the effects of the constant and accelerating increase in the number of specialisms within their profession. This was particularly the case in medicine, the most strongly research-based of the six professions, and hence the one with the most rapid knowledge growth. "The problem with hospital medicine," said one interviewee (M/10), "is that there are a great many specialisms and little sense of unity." Another (M/24) doubted whether a high level of specialism was good for patients, "because things get missed." Arguing along the same general lines, an architect (Arc/15) observed that "if all architects were to specialize, holistic decisions would be very difficult: the ideal solution is to build up a specialist area but avoid keeping within boundaries and learn to work in groups."

The idea of "tackling problems through interdisciplinary teams" was taken up by a senior accountant in one of the larger firms (Acc/11), who went on to note that it was "unusual to move from one discipline to another" (the term "discipline" being commonly used in accountancy to designate a broad specialist area, such as tax or corporate finance). But while there is a certain amount of interspecialism in accountancy and in structural engineering, and a tendency to avoid working in specialist areas in architecture, doctors, pharmacists, and lawyers, insofar as they are not general practitioners, tend to remain insulated within their own areas of specialist knowledge.

A phenomenon discerned by Bucher and Strauss (1961) was that "Methodological differences can cut across specialty—and even professional—lines with specialists sharing techniques with members of other specialties which they do not share with their fellows" (p. 328). It was noted in Chapter 2 that interprofessional activity is assuming greater prominence with the emergence of very large professional organizations. This tendency may represent a move—determined by the market rather than by concerns about the fragmentation of knowledge—towards the more holistic approach which characterized the professions before the advent of high specialization. But insofar as that is the case, the holism can be seen to rest on collective specialist activity rather than on the contributions of individual generalists. Despite the heroic rearguard actions of many architects and some structural engineers, there can be no putting the clock back to the days, now long past, when the body of knowledge within a given profession was sufficiently self-contained to allow for undifferentiated general practice to be seen as the norm.

The Impact of Information Technology

New technological developments—and, in particular, advances in computing—have in their turn made a significant impact on the professions. Indeed, it is fair to say that a knowledge of computer applications is fast becoming an essential ingredient in professional activity. As might be expected, that impact is variable, depending on the nature of the profession concerned. For reasons shortly to be explained, hospital medicine has been affected relatively little, and architecture to a very substantial extent.

Something of the recent history of the interactions between professionals and computers can be drawn from the research literature—characteristically, the large majority of it based on the U.S., and carried out in the 1980s. Early in that decade, Zoltan and Chapanis (1982) reported that accountants and pharmacists had the most favorable attitudes towards computers, and lawyers the least; doctors were intermediate between the two.[10] Some years later, Anderson (1986) reported that the hospital doctors in his investigation continued to be exercised by the legal and ethical implications of using computers in patient care, as well as by the possibilities of external control and by the threats to privacy in their own work.[11] Focusing on management accountants, Johnson and Kaplan (1987) argued that current professional practice demanded radical modernization in the light of computerization, alongside changed industrial production techniques and deregulation. By the end of the decade, Staudt (1989, reported in Bainbridge, 1991) was able to record that the percentage of U.S. lawyers using computers in 138 large firms had risen from 14 percent in 1986 to 30 percent in 1988.

My own data showed a very extensive use of computing and associated facilities by the mid-1990s. Much of this was for what might be described as routine office and administrative purposes—word processing, record keeping, inventory and stock control, accounting and invoicing, and preparing spreadsheets. More recently, e-mail and accessing data bases on CD and by modem have been added to the repertoire. Profession-specific uses include labelling prescriptions in community pharmacy, together with a special program which identifies potentially dangerous drug interactions; a program for solicitors to draw up wills ("not very useful"—L/10); desktop publishing for brochures and newsletters in accountancy firms; and computer graphics in architecture and engineering.

In general medical practice, computers have become reasonably well-established, particularly in relation to patient records. In hospital medicine, the picture is different, in large part for historical reasons. In the early days, computers were seen by hospital administrators as an important management tool: the costly and often cumbersome systems they introduced were not appropriate for use by the medical staff. The majority of the medics I interviewed had given up attempting to get even basic relevant information out of the central system, and individual departments had instead begun to set up their own small-scale local systems for record-keeping and patient data-analysis. This fragmentation is perhaps inevitable in large hospital trusts with something of the order of 50,000 outpatients a year and 150,000 people passing through (P/20): but because of the slow development of a grass-roots provision, hospital medicine has lagged behind other professions in its exploitation of computers, even if in many other respects it is technologically advanced.

The leading edge of information technology yields a more futuristic vision. General practitioners are inclined to toy with the notion of a "paperless practice" (M/3) in which all relevant patient information is held on disc, but are wary that transferring data about patients who move practices would "open up a medico-legal minefield" (M/5): in any case, as one (M/6) said, "there is a strong conceptual resistance to the idea." One GP reported using a computer program to "break down the stages in diagnosis" (M/11), but the notion of going further to "tap the symptoms into a computer and come out with a diagnosis" (M/8) was repudiated on the grounds that the large majority of cases are too complex to allow this—"computerized medicine is dangerous, because it doesn't allow for commonsense or the complexities of reality" (M/24). In the view of a staff member of one of the relevant professional bodies (M/20), "Clinical decision-making systems could transform medical practice—but there's a cultural problem to overcome first."

Developments in law and engineering include a sophisticated computer-based system for handling situations which involve very large numbers of documents ("document imaging"), and in hospital pharmacy a scheme which has been devised for "critical path dispensing." But in many respects the development of computer-assisted drafting and computer-assisted design in architecture and structural engineering represent the most far-reaching incursion of information technology into professional practice. These facilities allow for designs to be produced at a considerably more rapid rate, and also enable amendments and adjustments to be made with much more ease, than is possible by hand. A recent extension of this technology makes it feasible to share "drawings that no-one ever drew and virtual 3-D models" between architect, builder and client (Arc/17). Taking it even further, there were a number of experiments by the mid-1990s in "paperless construction"—a system of information storage and transfer which both automates and integrates the processes of commissioning, designing, and constructing even the most substantial building projects (E/27).

But however enthusiastic the proponents of information technology, no interviewee went so far as to present a science-fiction scenario in which professional activity could be taken over by a future generation of computers. For one thing, the acronym GIGO (Garbage In, Garbage Out) serves as a reminder that the initial data have in most cases to be supplied by human agency, and that any defect there would be reflected in the final output—a serious problem in hospital medicine if busy people failed to encode the necessary information (M/21), or if it were to be carelessly recorded (M/15). In any case, computers and their programs, alongside other hi-tech devices, are not infallible, and it is always wise to check their products by some independent means (M/24, E/16). In design applications, while—as elsewhere—the quality of the result depends strongly on the quality of the input, computers introduce "a loss of spontaneity" (Arc/12); they are "no good at expressiveness or indeterminacy" (Arc/3).

There is nonetheless no escape from the inexorable progress of this particular revolutionary movement, even where the initial costs of installation are substantial and there is a frequent need for replacement with the latest facility. How professionals themselves come to terms with the implementation of computerized systems will be considered further in chapters 4 and 6. At this point, all that remains to be said is that information technology has without question to be ranked among the many other pressures with which members of the professions have currently to contend.[12]

The Cumulation of Change

The various forms of extrinsic and intrinsic pressure which became apparent during the course of my research have clearly had a cumulative effect on professional life. As one senior lawyer (L/1) remarked, "legal practice is much harder, clients are less easily managed, fees are more competitive, and the law is more complicated than it used to be." Echoing that litany, the managing partner of a medium-sized architects' firm (Arc/12) observed that "the complexities are greater, the program time shorter, the clients more critical, the building regulations more exacting and the contractors' margins narrower than ever they were before." Even so, there were few respondents who complained that they were hard done by, or that their jobs had ceased to be worthwhile. In the large majority of cases, people had managed to find something positive in the process of having to meet the challenge of change.

Nevertheless, there were two general consequences of the upheavals in professional life over the decade or so preceding the interviews which were a source of general concern, to do respectively with time and money. A hospital pharmacist's comment was typical of many: "The main problem is time pressure—the amount of work you have to do and the need to do it at speed" (P/6); "Everything," said an engineer (E/13), "is nowadays more of a rush and more intense." As might be expected, financial pressures were felt particularly keenly in the National Health Service: "there's been a 10 percent increase in professional work since last year, but no increase in resources" (M/1); "Over the past eight years, the number of prescriptions I've dispensed has doubled, but in spite of that my income has dropped" (P/11). In the construction industry, too, the combined effects of competitive tendering and the recession have—as noted earlier—drastically reduced fee levels and made it difficult for firms to remain solvent.

These limitations of time and money have had various knock-on effects. One medical consultant (M/24), in a matter-of-fact rather than a complaining tone, said that in the previous (atypical) week he had worked 168 hours, and that over the preceding three-week period he had never got home in time to see his children. The terms "stress," "tension," and "pressure" appear in various interview records: for example, "As a consultant, you have to undergo quite a lot of stress and pressure—your home life suffers" (M/8); "It's important to monitor your own stress level, and watch the problems that can eat you away" (Arc/19). In depicting their overall reactions, two respondents independently used similar terms: "work used to be fun, but now there's a lot of pressure" (Acc/25); and "Thatcherism has permeated the professions, so that working in them isn't fun any more" (E/25).

But despite such vicissitudes, professional life goes on: there are no signs of a mass exodus into other forms of activity. The older professionals seem ready to cope with changed circumstances and the younger ones to take them as given. Following up this generational distinction, the different career stages can be seen to present their own particular challenges.

Notes

1. Since this was written, one such outcry was generated by the failure to deal satisfactorily with apparently fatal inadequacies in a team of brain surgeons in a large provincial children's hospital. The consequent proposal to set up a formal inspection process must modify the claim made here for the relative invulnerability of the medical profession.

2. Two of the six professions studied have no direct (lay) clients, but work through their related professions: namely, barristers and (except in design and build arrangements) structural engineers. However, this does not exempt them from many of the problems related to changes in the nature of institutional and individual clients.

3. "At the other end of the social spectrum, consumerism was far less successful.... Only 9 per cent of solicitors' firms now handle any legal aid work...access to justice, even second class justice, has been denied to an extra five and a half million households since 1979" (Thomas, 1992, pp. 8–9).

4. As noted above, barristers and structural engineers have mainly fellow professionals as clients; the relationships in medicine and pharmacy have less directly financial implications.

5. The different approaches, and the respective degrees to which they have been taken up in small and larger firms, are usefully tabulated in Jenkins (1994), on the basis of a Law Society survey carried out in 1992 (see table 2, p. 229).

6. It could be argued, by way of explanation, that a central element of management resides in efficient financial control, on which accountants by definition need little new expertise. However, as noted in chapter 6, they can be found among the participants in other forms of management training.

7. Analogous in the U.S. to corporations, and in France to sociétés anonymes.

8. The lack of emphasis on research is even more evident in architecture. A recent report on the research awards administered by the Architectural Research Council of the United Kingdom (ARCU.K.) shows a total expenditure in the quarter century from 1970 to 1995 of £312,541—a modest average of just over £12,500 per annum (Darke, 1996) for a professional population of about 30,000.

9. One's choice of answer might be conditioned by the respondent's comment that at the time of the interview there were only some ten to twelve others practicing in the same field in the U.K.

10. Their questionnaire survey was addressed to 521 CPAs (Certified Public Accountants), attorneys, pharmacists, and physicians in the Boston City area: the reported response rate was 27.7 percent.

11. The findings were based on a study of 644 medical staff in a single large teaching hospital in the U.S.

12. The pace of change in the field is exemplified by the rapid development, in the year since this test was written, of the Internet and the World Wide Web as a powerful means of communicating and deriving information.

Part 3

Commitment

4

Professional Careers

Career Patterns

Any attempt to offer a systematic, comprehensive, and statistically based set of observations about careers in the six professions would call for a quite different study from the one which was undertaken. However, though its purpose was not directly related to the question of careers, various aspects of professionals' life histories are relevant to the ways in which they adapt to new circumstances: and indeed, career changes are among the circumstances to which they have to adapt.

What needs first to be said on the subject is that few of those interviewed considered their careers to have been planned in any systematic way: one (L/1) considered that he had been "swept along by events." Many people started off in one direction, only to find themselves going in another. A doctor, (M/3) for example, had qualified as an anesthetist but, because her father became terminally ill, took a 9-to-5 job organizing clinical trials in a pharmaceutical company and then became a GP; a lawyer (L/9) had started out as a policeman, had become a barrister, but was now working in the litigation department of a small solicitor's firm; an accountant (Acc/14) had changed from working as a "financial psychiatrist" to strategic financial planning, and then to marketing. Some respondents—especially hospital doctors—had moved jobs several times; others had experienced major changes in the nature of their work within one and the same firm. There were those (for instance L/13) who felt that their current careers were not leading anywhere, and who were contemplating a change; and those who saw their past careers as "a series of poor decisions" (Acc/3). Among other research studies, Morison and Leith (1992) give an interesting and insightful account of the generally haphazard nature of barristers' careers; and Allen (1994) points out that in medicine only 60 percent of men and less than 50 percent of women remain in the same specialty four years after registration.

A fairly significant sub-category of professionally-qualified people end up working outside the boundaries of their professions: for example, in 1996, nearly 20 percent of qualified solicitors were in employment outside legal firms.[1] A deliberate attempt was therefore made to interview a sample of professionals working in other settings. As might be expected, some had carved out highly successful careers. One (M/26) had moved from hospital medicine to a firm of medical insurers, and was currently in a senior post with a national agency concerned with quality issues; another (Arc/24) had had an equally varied career, moving from a large architectural partnership to work for a local authority, and then for a leading supermarket chain, before becoming a management consultant. There were others who, in retrospect, regretted their earlier decisions to move out of their own professional contexts. A chartered accountant (Acc/17) working as a tax adviser in an industrial company felt that, as a technical specialist in the firm, his career had stagnated; a solicitor (L/27), after fifteen years spent working for a high street banking firm, considered himself "standing still in terms of non-professional development"; and an architect (Arc/27) in an oil company disliked the confrontational atmosphere and the sense that he was overworked and undervalued. In part, the problems seemed to lie in a conflict between commercial cultures and professional traditions; but there was also a concern that, outside the mainstream, one could get rapidly out of touch with changes in the profession itself and could thus cut off a possible escape route back into private practice.

Individual careers, one might say, are as different one from another as are the professions themselves. Some people seem to have a clearer idea where they are going than others, even when the directions they choose may be idiosyncratic rather than conformist. It is nonetheless possible to make some general comments about how professional careers are shaped. A useful starting-point is Brown's (1982) categorization of careers in general as entrepreneurial (giving scope for self-employment); organizational (taking place in bureaucratic settings); and occupational (allowing mobility through the possession of qualifications). To these, he added "careerless," as a means of including short-term occupations taken up without conscious planning.

It is easy enough to apply this taxonomy to the professions. Small partnerships can be labelled as entrepreneurial contexts, and large ones as organizational. Occupational careers would be those in other sectors, involving mobile individuals with appropriate qualifications. Professionals with only short-term contracts (as is currently the case with many architects) could be labelled careerless.

However, when one looks at career strategies, as against career types, Johnson's (1983) notions of contingencies and tradeoffs offer a useful framework. He writes specifically about the medical profession, where the concepts apply readily to hospital medicine. In my sample, a number of consultants and more junior doctors had found reason to move jobs or adjust specialisms to fit in with available or probable vacancies. But the same general consideration can be related to other entrepreneurial careers, such as the bar, where choices have to be made not only about one's initial membership of chambers but later in terms of whether or not to engage in the financial gamble of becoming a Queen's Counsel (and therefore demanding significantly higher fees) and perhaps subsequently of aiming for a judiciary appointment (with a gain in prestige offset, often, by a reduction in income). The element of gamble can in some cases be reduced by careful strategic planning at the outset, as in the case of a barrister (L/6) who remarked that "It's important to take the right options at university; and when you're working for the CPE [Common Professional Examination] you have to think about pupillage at a good set of chambers with high quality people and interesting work". Along similar lines, a structural engineer (E/25) observed that "In an engineering career, it matters where you go in the first five years."

The absence of a clearly defined career sequence has an important set of consequences which are spelled out by Bennett and Hotvedt (1989):

> The practice of medicine, unlike most other occupations, does not exist within a formal organization with a clear authority hierarchy, job descriptions, and lines of advancement. Job titles do not change as expertise, influence, and experience expand. Promotions, with new titles, are not directly acquired by an individual as an acclamation from his or her superiors. The cues for status are therefore different. In medicine, the role of peers is especially critical in determining one's place in the structure of the profession. The movement through career stages, as a result, may be subtle, and felt indirectly by feedback from peers and patients as well as by self-assessment (P. 76).

This analysis, though said not to apply to "most other occupations," can readily be adapted to most contexts which Brown (1982)—see above—would designate as entrepreneurial. It is when attention is turned to bureaucratic working environments that different considerations arise. Here, there is often a set of stages which an individual may be expected to negotiate. As a senior partner in a moderately large practice (Arc/30) put it, "It is common for architects to have six or seven years' training, followed by ten years of practice and then spend the rest of their careers in management". The pattern is more variable than this statement suggests, but it is nevertheless the case in the larger legal and accountancy firms as well as in structural engineering and in hospital pharmacy that a substantial period of professional training may be followed by a relatively short spell—not more than fifteen years or so—of using and developing one's professional skills before switching to a predominantly administrative and managerial role. The alternative is to cultivate a key specialism, and so to remain directly involved in professional activity. The problem with this option is that specialist expertise tends to have lower status than management: "If you are seen as a success, you're promoted to being a general manager" (E/16).

The Great and the Small

The size of the organization in which a professional decides to work makes a considerable difference to the nature of his or her career experience. It is therefore a crucial option whether to apply for work in a large enterprise as, essentially, a salaried worker in a hierarchical structure or whether to seek, in a small or single partnership, the right to a considerable degree of self-determination as a more or less self-employed individual.

Each option brings several other consequences in its wake. In a large firm, there will be opportunities to develop a high level of specialization; in a small one, while some measure of concentration may be possible, the main emphasis must be on general practice. The few exceptions are "small specialist consulting firms known in the financial press as 'boutiques'" which "complement the existing ranks of small general accounting practice firms" (Roslender, 1992, p. 47), together with similar counterparts in law and—more marginally—architecture and structural engineering. Career stages, as noted above, are more clearly mapped out in large than in small enterprises: in one legal firm, for example, the progression was from assistants to associates to equity partners, rising finally to a managing partnership (L/28).

Opportunities for enhancing one's professional expertise are—as might be expected—greater in the larger firms, many of which run their own training organizations and set up their own lecture programs. To maintain a competitive edge, some will be prepared to second staff members to client organizations, usefully extending in the process the range of expertise of the individuals concerned. In small organizations, there is necessarily a good deal less flexibility, even to the point of its becoming too time-consuming and expensive for partners to partici-pate in continuing professional development (see chapter 6): in par-ticular, "one-man bands find it very hard to keep in touch" (Arc/20).

The types of client and the kinds of task with which a firm deals are usually quite closely related to its size. Most single or small partner-ships in law and accountancy act for individual clients in fairly run-of-the-mill cases, referring more intractable or esoteric problems up the line to larger agencies. In architecture and structural engineering, indi-viduals and modest-sized practices concern themselves mainly with housing and other relatively low cost projects. The largest organiza-tions attract corporate clients of a comparable size with themselves and engage in large-scale, high-cost commissions. The negative aspect of interactions on this scale is that there is seldom any personal contact involved. Except perhaps at the senior executive level, "members of the firm have little contact with the client and are divorced from the overall picture" (Arc/23). Conversely, "some clients complain that in large partnerships they have to deal with a series of different minions." In smaller firms (as some of the comments on client attitudes in chapter 3 suggest), there is still a residual sense of personal involvement be-tween professional and client, however utilitarian that involvement may have become.

It might be supposed that the larger enterprises would have devel-oped a well-organized system of career progression for their profes-sional employees. This was certainly the case in some of the more size-able architectural and structural engineering firms in particular, but was less evident in the massive law and accountancy conglomerates. An accountant working as a financial controller in one leading legal part-nership (Acc/28) noted, as an established tradition, that "it makes no attempt to take care of people's careers, and sees its employees as re-sponsible for carving up a suitable role for themselves." As another respondent in a sizeable accountancy firm (Acc/23) explained, "staff development calls for a long-term investment—just letting people go on courses is the easy way out." It could be said that the result of this laissez-faire approach is to evade any accusation of paternalism, and to encourage a sense of personal responsibility among employees. But firms adopting this hands-off approach also find it easier to shed large numbers of staff without any evident sense of going back on an earlier implied commitment. Thus, for example, the partner in charge of "people development" in one of the big six accountants (Acc/15) remarked *en passant* that "100 partners were eliminated last year out of a total of 700, mostly by early retirement." Career prospects, though they may be less varied and less challenging in much smaller firms, are also a good deal less vulnerable; at the extreme, a sole practitioner would only abandon his or her career by personal choice.[2]

The compensation for working in a context in which the axe may be poised to fall at any moment is that the available resources are likely to be significantly greater than in partnerships of, say, up to half a dozen people. One respondent (Arc/17) estimated that "the leading [architecture] practices are currently [in 1994] pulling in about £100,000 annually per member, the middling firms about £50,000, and the small, relatively unknown ones £20,000." The differences are evident enough in the furnishings of the offices, the size and nature of the buildings and the initial impact on the visitor. Many of the leading enterprises in law and accountancy are housed in centrally located, purpose-built, architect-designed establishments with large, cool reception rooms bedecked with potted plants and peopled with well-spoken, carefully groomed receptionists; the professionals' offices are also light and airy, with large modern desks and comfortable chairs. The most modest counterparts are in rented premises in more or less salubrious districts (depending on the nature of the practice) with one or two upright visitors' chairs in a small reception area, leading into equally small and sparsely furnished offices. Not surprisingly, those who work at the opulent end of their professions tend to show a greater sense of the importance of their calling than those who work in humbler surroundings, even though they are employees subject to superior direction and to hiring and firing, rather than autonomous individuals able (within limits) to choose what they want to do.

That no mention has so far been made of medicine and pharmacy is because, in general, size has only a limited effect on career in these professions. It is of course true that working in a major teaching hospital is more prestigious than practicing in a small provincial one, but in each case people work their way up through the early career stages to a point at which they become largely self-directing. The only approximation to a sizeable professional firm is to be found in the large multiple retail pharmacies and the bigger industrial pharmaceutical companies. But even careers in the former are conducted in a series of comparatively modest-sized outlets, possibly culminating in a managerial post at the firm's headquarters: it is the latter, accounting for only a very small proportion of pharmacists, that can offer something approaching a corporate career. General medical practitioners, along with barristers, are subject to none of the contrasts of scale with which this discussion has been concerned.

Recruitment and Initial Training

The aspiration for any calling to qualify as a profession depends on the provision of special introductory training of an appropriate kind, in that no one could credibly claim to be a professional without such training. The form this takes, and the time it lasts, varies considerably from one profession to another. There is usually some ambiguity in the use of the term, particularly in those fields which require a preliminary period spent in higher education before taking the first formal steps towards registration. The degree course or its equivalent can be considered as initial training: but so can the subsequent period of supervised work in a professional setting before passing a further qualifying test to achieve full recognition. That is unlikely to mark the final stage of training, since—as will be seen in chapter 6—there may be a compulsory or semi-compulsory requirement to undergo some form of continuing education throughout one's career. The present discussion will, however, focus on the period before formal qualification, indicating where "training" applies to the phase before graduation and where it denotes the time spent as an unqualified probationer in practice.

A comparable distinction needs to be made in relation to recruitment, in that the term may be used to refer to the initial intake into professionally focused higher education or to the subsequent flow of graduates into different branches of the profession. Recruitment and training may be expected to be closely interlinked, since a training course which is seen as lively and interesting will attract recruits in a way in which one that is perceived as arduous or dull will fail to do. There are, however, other factors at work: for example, an academic engineer (E/1) lamented the fact that the number of applicants for engineering degrees had continued to decline, in part because "there's a greasy hands image of engineering," while a practitioner of long standing (E/23) pointed out that since the recession employment prospects in the profession had suffered a substantial decline.

The pattern of recruitment in any given profession is not easily predictable. To take a case in point, Lambert et al. (1996) report that in their survey,[3] 70.5 percent of those attaining a medical qualification in

1993 cited hospital medicine and only 25.8 percent general practice as their first preference, whereas the comparable figure for the latter choice in 1983 had been 47.7 percent. Given that by the time of the survey there was an explicit policy within the National Health Service to switch resources from hospital to community medicine, one might have expected a contrary trend. The continuing buoyancy of recruitment into architectural courses at a time of mass unemployment among architects is equally difficult to explain. Another phenomenon was reported in accountancy, where—as one respondent (Acc/16) claimed—10 percent of all U.K. graduates in the mid-1980s went into accounting, but where "the bubble burst" in 1989-90 and resulted in a drastic reduction in intake which had only begun to pick up by the middle of the subsequent decade.

Various devices are used by professional firms to attract able students from universities. In their quest for talent, some major City law firms were said to have aggressive recruitment policies and to produce their own recruitment videos (L/0). The smaller engineering partnerships tend to take on undergraduates for in-course periods of work experience in the hope of finding new potential recruits; the more sizeable ones appoint graduates in significantly larger numbers than they expect to need, with a view to retaining only the best. This was said also to be the case in a large multiple pharmacy (P/10), a major interdisciplinary building firm (Arc/17), and one of the big six accountants, which was prepared to take on 750 new graduates each year, of which 250 would be expected to remain four years later (Acc/5). An informant in the legal branch of a rival accountancy concern (L/24) speculated on whether her firm was justified in spending time and money in training those who did not stay on. The justification, according to an interviewee in a medium-sized engineering partnership (E/12), was partly the altruistic one of feeding smaller enterprises with trained people, and partly the self-interested one of re-employing some former recruits after they had acquired a wider background of experience in other parts of the industry. Adopting a different policy, a large legal partnership (L/25) selected its new intake with particular care, because they were expected to stay on after the substantial investment in their training.

Not all partnerships have the opportunity to take on trainees. In general medical practice, community pharmacy, and chartered accountancy, for example, training provision is strictly controlled by the relevant professional body, and designated agencies have to meet specified cri-

teria, including significant and validated requirements for the continuing professional development of trainers and a stipulated scale of activity. Those respondents whose firms had achieved the necessary status
clearly considered it a benefit to take on trainees, both because it gave
them a reliable means of identifying potential new recruits and because
it encouraged them to keep in touch with new developments both in the
mainstream profession and in the professional schools in the higher
education sector.

The latter were often the subject of critical comment by practitioners.
In particular, as Abbott (1988) points out,

> theoretical education in the dominant profession is often irrelevant to practice. The
> practicing physician has no use whatever for his fading knowledge of biochemis-
> try, any more than practicing lawyers have for theoretical training in constitutional
> law (p. 68).

Architects are notable for their complaints about the pattern of training
provision in their profession. One (Arc/16) thought that the existing
seven-year training period was too long; another (Arc/25) suggested
that "it ought to be more like doctors' training, with a generic initial
study of all the construction disciplines followed by learning a specialism."[4] In retrospect, a respondent (Arc/27) saw his own initial training
as "rather woolly" and argued that architects very seldom design grand
buildings, as they have to do in student projects; it was also remarked
(Arc/18) that schools of architecture remain relatively introverted—
"they are keen on ensuring that students do the wrong things." An academic engineer (E/1) accepted that the degree courses in his subject
were particularly demanding in terms of work, but attributed this to the
outdated requirements imposed by the Institutions of Structural and
Civil Engineers.

An over-abundance of theory is not always seen as a disadvantage.
The length of the pharmacy degree course was increased to four years
in 1997, even though there was evidence to suggest (Becher, 1990) that
there was already an excess of academic material in the three-year
course. However, the practitioners who commented on this saw it as an
indicator of higher status for the profession, rather than as introducing
further irrelevance. Medical training, in contrast, was held by some
respondents to be not theoretical enough: "it is a disgrace, and takes
experiential learning to the extreme" (M/21); "it's badly organized in
terms of teaching, and based too much on the apprenticeship system"
(M/9).[5] There were nonetheless those who staunchly defended the ex-

isting largely self-directed approach, often covering a wide range of topics. The medical interviews took place shortly after the publication of the Calman Report (1993), which recommended a significantly shorter, more structured training for hospital doctors, giving rise to some concern that it would produce "second-rate, narrowly specialized consultants" (M/25) and—like the U.S.system—eliminate individuality, to yield "a standard sausage" (M/28). Even so, at an estimated "112 hours a week over 11 years" (M/25) to produce a consultant, some degree of streamlining would seem reasonable enough.

One career in particular begins relatively late in life, so that its period of initial training comes long after the normal stage around one's twenties. An appointment as a judge or a tribunal chairperson follows several years of practice in the law (Paterson, 1983). Only in recent times has it required a compulsory training program, organized in England and Wales by the Judicial Studies Board (Partington, 1994). Unlike the initial Bar School course for intending barristers, this provision was generally referred to by my respondents in positive terms as well-planned and reasonably comprehensive, even if the course for judges might be too strongly geared towards the criminal courts. There was no evident support for Armytage's (1996) contention that, for judges in particular, "group learning...is inadequate and inappropriate as a comprehensive delivery strategy" (p. 152).

Specialization and Advanced Qualifications

A distinction was made in chapter 3 between specialisms, as the division of knowledge into subsidiary areas (a cognitive process) and specialization, as the choice of an individual to concentrate on one particular area (a social process). In looking at professional careers it is the latter which is primarily in question. The initial training in a profession will normally cover a broad canvas. In particular, degree courses aimed at a professional qualification mark no clear distinction between one branch of the field and another (engineering is an exception among the six professions, in that engineering degrees are differentiated at the outset between aeronautical, electrical, chemical, mechanical, and other branches of the subject). Where a specifically vocational degree qualification is not required—as in the case of law—the choice between a barrister's and a solicitor's training has to be made immediately after the Common Professional Examination; where a non-graduate intake is accepted—as in accountancy—the initial training is directly related to a particular qualification—chartered, certified, management, or public accountancy. For the rest, the choice of sub-profession, if one exists, is usually made after graduation, early in the professional career. That choice is not necessarily irrevocable—my sample, for instance, covered cases of a hospital doctor (M/3) becoming a GP, a pharmacist (P/ 9) who had worked in hospital, industrial, and community pharmacy, and a barrister who had become a solicitor (L/21).

Specialization is commonly taken to denote a level more specific than a sub-profession as such: one would not, for example, refer to work in community pharmacy or management accountancy as a specialized career. Many people, once having chosen their sub-profession, will elect to draw on their initial training to work as generalists; others will at some point make a subsequent career choice to specialize.[6] A number among my informants held that specialization was inexorably on the increase, a view supported by some of the relevant research literature. As far back as the early 1950s, Mills (1951) warned his readers that "intense and narrow specialization has replaced self-cultivation and wide knowledge" (p. 122). By 1978, Rothman (1984) records, over 40 percent of U.S. lawyers defined themselves as specialists, while in 1997 a survey by the Law Society in England and Wales indicated that 71 percent of respondents claimed specialist status, and over 50 percent did in fact undertake less than three types of casework. One of my informants (Arc/17) saw the trend as having emerged in the nineteenth century, with a social division between gentlemen and tradesmen being drawn to distinguish architects from other participants in the construction industry.

If specialization is held to have negative consequences—"specialists can't see the connections" (E/28)[7]—one respondent (Arc/24) suggested that the drawbacks were gradually being acknowledged: "There's currently a reaction against all specialized functions. In large companies it's becoming evident that a lot of problems are caused by departments dominated by specialist groups, because the needs of their own specialisms tend to come before the needs of the organization as a whole." Nonetheless, it is in the larger partnerships that specialization is rife. Roslender (1992) writes of the accountancy profession that "Increasingly life in one of the large firms, after qualification, is as a specialist" (p. 46). In structural engineering, "In very big practices people develop an expertise: even in an average-sized practice the whole organization may have a reputation for a particular specialism, such as in steelwork" (E/1). In law, too, in a sizeable firm, "Everyone has some specialist identity—in European law, construction and so on—there are no general practitioners" (L/20).

It seems a contradiction in terms for general practitioners to label themselves as specialists: yet in medicine the relevant Royal College, in the final paragraph of its *Priorities for the Future* (RCGP, 1990), was prepared to announce that "the College supports specialist registration for general practice at the end of vocational training." A similar trend can be discerned in other professions. Thus, "senior hospital pharmacists are usually specialists, and keep up to date in their own particular fields" (P/6); "some barristers are narrow specialists (L/14); "accountants used to be generalists, but there's a need for specialization now— it's a painful change for some" (Acc/23).

Becoming a specialist is sometimes a formal process. For example, tax advisers can acquire a separate qualification, as can insolvency practitioners. In large part, however, one gains a particular expertise by virtue of frequent practice rather than by systematic study leading to some form of examination. Thus, for example, a hospital doctor (M/4), having spent the first twelve years of his work as a consultant undertaking general surgery, had subsequently worked in a gastrointestinal team for four years, and had then begun increasingly to work on breast surgery on which he was now regarded an expert. He achieved this status by reading relevant journal articles, attending national meetings, but for the most part learning by experience—becoming, as another respondent (Acc/19) termed it, "a specialist by reputation." A solicitor (L/25) who decided to specialize in European Community Law worked with an experienced partner for eighteen months, but was given no time by his firm to study the field and similarly had to pick up the subject as he went along. And although specialism is uncommon among architects, one respondent (Arc/4) claimed to be recognized as an expert in classical architecture on the basis, not of formal training, but "from reading books and using my eyes." It fell to the accountants to raise concerns about the process of formalizing expertise. As Collier (1993) records, the main objections of members of the Institute of Chartered Accountants to proposals for the recognition of post-qualification specialization were: (1) the possible devaluation of the core qualification; (2) the effect of specialization on the role of general practitioners; (3) the cost of the proposals; and (4) the possible duplication of the training and qualifications already available.

The decision whether or not to specialize, and in what particular field, can be seen as a strategic career choice. "Specialization in a rare area," according to a senior member of a large accountancy firm (Acc/ 30), "is a fast route to a partnership." However, "the demand for expertise depends on circumstances—you have to respond to the pressure of need" (P/9). This implies some measure of adaptability from one topic to another, which depends in turn on "a sound general education," enabling people to "change their areas of specialism with greater ease" (Lord Chancellor's Advisory Committee 1996b, p. 17). Even so, the shift is not always easy to achieve, in that the fundamental knowledge required may be very different: "it would, for example, be a big jump to move from audit to tax" (Acc/19). The difficulty is compounded for more senior professionals, because "they are more expensive to release and to train" (L/9). In any case, "switching is risky, because companies prefer experienced people" (E/16). Especially in large law firms, only the fittest survive: "the policy is to throw out redundant experts, or push them into management" (L/23). It may be easier, in some professions, to move from being a specialist to becoming a general practitioner. Christakis et al. (1994), in a large-scale study in the U.S. investigating the readiness of "physicians who are currently specialists [to] become generalists," concluded (p. 669) that the "change from specialist to generalist is not uncommon," especially but not exclusively among those under 40, and that "many physicians already consider a generalist discipline to be a secondary emphasis of their practices."

As noted above, specialization does not necessarily depend on achieving further qualifications. Conversely, advanced qualifications do not necessarily promote specialist status, particularly where they are academic rather than practical in their emphasis. Nevertheless, they may often be acquired with a view to general career advancement. Something of the order of ten percent of my interviewees had been awarded an advanced degree, either as part of their initial training or after they had become established in their profession.[8]

A number of hospital doctors had, en route to consultant status, undertaken a research-based master's degree in the form of an MChir or MD: one (M/14) had subsequently taken an MA in Medical Law and Ethics which raised her profile as a consultant involved in the ethical aspects of her specialism. A smaller number, engaged in hospital management, had acquired a Master of Business Administration (MBA) qualification on a part-time basis. Pharmacists were another group showing a high incidence of advanced study: in their case the main motivation appeared to be the acquisition of greater career mobility. A number of hospital pharmacists had completed part-time MScs which qualified them to work in clinical pharmacy; others had studied for MBAs to enhance their opportunities to move into management; two—one a hospital and one a community pharmacist—had taken law degrees and the bar examination with a view to moving into the pharmaceutical industry; and three -only one of whom was an academic—had been awarded PhDs. In contrast, only one architect in the sample had acquired a doctorate, though one had MAs in both architecture and planning, and a number had taken MBAs. More than one in five of the sample of structural engineers held doctoral or masters' degrees, but there was a marked absence of interest in MBAs, stemming presumably from the more general view that engineers already know what they need to know about management.

The lawyers and accountants appeared to have a significantly lower interest in acquiring academic qualifications. The only direct references to a higher degree were made by a solicitor (L/30) who had taken a part-time Master of Law (LLM), "mainly out of interest rather than with an academic career in view," though he had subsequently taught in a university law school for a short period; and by a barrister (L/2) who had also acquired an LLM (and had practiced as an academic lawyer for several years before qualifying for the bar). The issue of the linkage between the universities and the professional worlds is the subject of more detailed discussion in the postscript. At this point, however, it is of interest to note Coulson-Thomas' (1991) prediction that "as academic qualifications become more practical and relevant...the differences between professional and academic qualifications may become blurred" (p. 12).

The Later Career Stages

For some years after they qualified, most respondents spent some time consolidating and extending their professional capabilities before deciding whether and in what direction to specialize. In the smaller firms, the amount of specialization was limited, and most practitioners continued to work as generalists. In the larger enterprises, a typical pattern was to become increasingly involved in management after a period working as a specialist. A distinctive management role was usually seen as out of the question in small practices, where "it isn't realistic to think of escaping into management, because it calls for very large overheads" (Arc/14). One respondent (E/30) saw the option between continuing professional involvement and a shift into managerial responsibilities in fairly stark terms: "As a senior engineer, you have to choose either to stay close to engineering in a small firm or to go into management in a large one." Along similar lines, another (E/18) commented that "as their careers develop, many engineers don't do engineering".

In large organizations—and particularly those involved in law and accountancy—management is accorded a higher status than practice, and an appointment as a manager is seen as promotion out of the professional rank-and-file. Accordingly, many of the most able practitioners are in due course drawn out of the work in which they are particularly skilled into activities with which they are generally unfamiliar.

As elsewhere, the later career patterns differ to some extent between and within different professions, as well as between large organizations and small. For hospital medics it remains possible largely to avoid administrative responsibilities, or to undertake them part-time, unless one wishes for a change in activity; for GPs, managerial tasks are usually shared, or in the larger firms devolved to a non-medical practice manager. Hospital and industrial pharmacists have the opportunity to go into management in their later careers, and many take it, as a form of promotion. As already noted, engineers, solicitors and chartered accountants in large firms are in a similar situation. However, barristers—as single practitioners—are not; neither, commonly, are management accountants, who operate in a service role. Architects, except in the largest enterprises, often succeed in combining part-time management with practice.

There is some evidence in my data to suggest that management is seen by a proportion of professionals as a welcome change from overfamiliar routines: but there is also another general consideration which relates to those who began their careers before about 1970. It emerged that computerization had affected different age-groups in different ways. As a rough approximation, it could be said that those under about 35 had grown up in a computer age, had encountered computers in the course of their education, and were generally comfortable with them. Those between about 35 and 45 found it less easy to adapt to the various forms of information technology with which they were having to deal, but were usually able to do so. A watershed seemed to mark off the senior professionals above the age of 45. Many of those in my sample admitted to a barrier of understanding and acceptance which they found it extremely difficult to overcome. Some found avoidance in a flight to management, where secretaries could cope on their behalf with the mysterious world of word processing, e-mail, and the like. Others feared that they were having to face "incipient redundancy" (Arc/14). As with many general claims, this one must admit of exceptions: but the same pattern cropped up time and again in the comments of interviewees across the range of professions, to an extent that suggested a quite basic and widespread phenomenon. Clearly, however, it is a passing one, disappearing after the retirement of the pre-computer generation is completed in the early twenty-first century, when the whole professional world can be expected to have adapted to the demands of information technology.

If managerial responsibilities have offered some senior professionals an escape route from the necessities of computing, they have posed a different problem in their turn. A surprising number of respondents seemed to have been quite unaware of, and taken aback by, the extent to which management activities brought organizational politics in their train. A hospital pharmacist (P/24) who had been given the responsibility for running the pharmaceutical services in a fair-sized provincial hospital trust commented that she had had no preparation for the politics she had encountered, especially with "doctors who use managers and other professionals as punch bags." A community pharmacist (P/14) appointed as superintendent in a major chain also noted, as a new experience in taking up the post, having to learn "how to influence key people and maneuver to your advantage in a large organization." An architect (Arc/27) employed by an oil company complained that he had been ill-prepared for the political aspects of the job, and particularly for the extent to which he had to fight his corner. A lawyer (L/27) working as head of the legal branch in a leading bank similarly acknowledged that his job "involves a lot of politics—I'm underdeveloped in it." A solicitor in mid-career (L/23) had identified some of the underlying mechanisms:

> Having clients means having power—clients tend to belong to individuals, even in a corporate firm. That's one reason why service departments don't have much power—because they don't have clients attached to them, their members can be hired and fired more easily...having clients gives you greater job mobility, and helps you to open your way into one of the big six firms.

The issue of how to cope with demands of this kind is not a new one. Even some two decades ago, Collins (1979) was able to claim:

> The overriding fact is that an organizational career is made in a political environment, and success goes to those individuals who recognize the fact and act on it most assiduously. The one who makes it to the top is the organizational politician, concerned above all with informalities, manoeuvring toward the crucial gate-keepers, avoiding the organizational contingencies that trap the less wary (p. 31).

It is only the rare professional in what Brown (1982) categorized as a bureaucratic setting who can afford in later career to claim, with one of the consultants interviewed (M/10), that "I don't interest myself in politics." It is perhaps the more surprising that so many senior people—including those who had had substantial management training—appeared so little prepared for the political connotations of managerial activities. Organizational politics are, it would seem, regarded as an example of tacit knowledge, as identified by Polanyi (1967): something that one is expected to pick up in practice, but which is not seen as an appropriate subject for airing in public.

Career Benefits and Disbenefits

Up to this point, the discussion has centered upon the externalities of a professional career. It remains to give some consideration also to the internalities—to the experiential aspects of engaging in a profession. Many of the respondents made, without prompting, some reference to what they found enjoyable and attractive in their work, and what were its negative aspects. On the whole, the advantages were held considerably to outweigh the disadvantages, serving to underline the notion of professionals as strongly committed to their calling.

The positive features of professional life mentioned by interviewees ranged widely. One of the most common was the perceived variety of the job. Even as a sole practitioner in a community pharmacy, where one might suppose that the work, involving long hours, would tend to fall into a routine pattern, "there is a great degree of varied activity" (P/11). A consulting engineer (E/3) also singled out the diverse nature of his work and the wide range of small to large assignments, while a partner in a medium-sized solicitor's firm (L/9) saw her job as interesting and attractive "because the pattern of the days is varied and you are largely in control of it." The notion of being in control, or of having ample scope for choice of activity, was picked up by a number of other respondents, including a barrister (L/17), who enjoyed the opportunity "to pick and choose what you want to do," and an architect (Arc/19), who saw his profession as "providing a choice and enriching your life." The sense of developing one's expertise and doing one's job better was singled out by a hospital pharmacist (P/2) and an architect (Arc/2), while for an accountant (Acc/25) "the most satisfactory aspect of my job is having a say in running the partnership"—a point echoed by an engineer (E/26), who found that becoming an equity partner in a large firm involved him in many issues which he found both interesting and challenging.

All these varied considerations seem to have been of relevance to practitioners in all or most of the six professions. A smaller number of topics were prominent among those mentioned only by one or two particular groups. The singularity may convey something to those with a psychometric turn of mind; otherwise, the particular linkages do not seem to reflect any obvious features of the professions concerned, and may indeed be no more than distortions inherent in a statistically small and unrepresentative sample. However, the coincidences may be noted for what they are worth, and what readers may choose to make of them. The attractions of involvement with other people were remarked upon only by pharmacists, among whom the industrial and hospital pharmacists also referred to the positive experience of working in a team. The excitement of having to meet a challenge or to solve a problem appeared to be specific to lawyers and engineers: a barrister (L/19), for example, referred to "the adrenalin of getting things right in court," while an engineer (E/4) maintained that "the challenges are what make the job fun." The satisfaction of a total involvement in one's work— though on other evidence quite widespread—was mentioned exclusively by barristers and architects: "The law is an all-consuming profession— we talk a lot about what we are doing" (L/6); "My life is enmeshed with my work—I see architecture as a way of life and I make no distinction between my job and the rest of what I do. It is in the nature of professions that they totally envelop you" (Arc/4).

One general source of satisfaction was touched on only by a small minority of respondents, and then only in a tangential way. The absence of comment on the point may reflect a delicacy, among those not yet comfortable about the idea of professions as businesses, about making an outspoken reference to money. Roslender (1992), in her study of accountants, refers to the perception of them—which she goes on to endorse—as being "very well rewarded for their efforts, being able to command high salaries and receive attractive perks in comparatively secure positions" (p. 40). The same is certainly true of solicitors in sizeable practices and of hospital consultants—although the latter will have had to work for excessively long hours for more than a decade at relatively low salaries before achieving consultant status. GPs are in a somewhat similar case, at a less substantial but nonetheless very comfortable income level. For single practitioners or those in small firms in most of the six professions, the situation is much more variable: a successful barrister may reap substantial rewards, while an unsuccessful architect may easily become insolvent. Generally, incomes in the construction industry have become depressed, while those of pharmacists are modest in comparison with their medical counterparts. But although money is not to be claimed as the main *raison d'être* of entering a professional career, the earnings are by and large one of its positive concomitants.

It is among the main contentions of this study that professionals are in general prepared to cope with changes and adapt to them in virtue of a strong sense of motivation and commitment. That some respondents expressed dissatisfactions with their working lives does not subvert that claim, especially as the negative comments were minor and limited in comparison with the positive ones. They centered particularly on the absence, in one particular field, of career mobility; on the concern about a possible blockage on progress; and on worries about the possibility of work becoming monotonous or boring.

Very few respondents indicated, either in their actual career patterns or in their potential career developments, a sense that they were necessarily confined to one particular role in one particular location. The clear exceptions were to be found among the hospital consultants. As one interviewee (M/29) put it, "A lot of doctors in senior positions are bored with their work because they have to stay in the same hospital and do the same job day in and day out—some of them since their early thirties." A cardiologist (M/10) remarked on the unchanging nature of his environment over the past 23 years: "I see the same old stream of patients with the same old problems"; a neurologist (M/13) confirmed the lack of mobility: "each appointment is seen as a 25-year stretch." Another respondent (M/24) explained that it was difficult to change jobs because of the structure of the National Health Service and the tendency of appointments committees to favor recently trained candidates. The situation appeared however to be changing in response to the Calman Report (1993). An optimistic picture was presented by a medical administrator (M/23), "There are some switches now at the consultancy level and could be more—but even if you don't change specialisms, you're unlikely to get bored with your job because it's very varied and because there are plenty of other activities on the side."

Some interviewees had reached a sticking-point in their current career stage, such as the industrial pharmacist (P/7) who saw her existing job as being "in dead-men's shoes," or the barrister in mid-career (L/13) who maintained that he, and others in his generation, were likely to be trapped by the absence of enough judicial openings. A structural engineer (E/16) referred to the incidence of mid-career crises in his profession: "people tend to find themselves in limbo in their thirties and forties." Adding to the litany, a solicitor (L/9) commented that "In one sense, when you become a partner, there is nowhere else to go—so you have to set yourself new goals to avoid being bored." The possibility of boredom was also touched upon by an architect (Arc/19) working for a large local authority who hoped to avoid "becoming stale" by taking on lecturing assignments and supervising student projects in conjunction with his existing work. A barrister (L/7) claimed that "the work is intensive and can get boring." He added that barristers rarely survive over the age of 55 and very few stay on over 60. The process of ending a career is a further issue raised by this comment, and an appropriate one with which to conclude the chapter.

Ending a Career

A professional career, in common with careers of other kinds, may wind up in a variety of different ways. The most conventional is retirement, usually—except in cases of self-employment—at a pre-specified age somewhere in one's sixties (judges are atypical in having a retirement age of 72, though High Court judges suffer no such constraint). This procedure is familiar enough to call for no special discussion. The very large majority of those I interviewed could be expected to follow the standard pattern, though a few indicated that they might deviate from it, or referred to others who had done so. The three categories other than normal retirement which emerged from the data, and which will now be briefly reviewed, were redundancy or dismissal; dropout or early retirement; and what has come to be referred to as burnout.

Reference was made earlier in this chapter to the tendency for large firms of solicitors and accountants to declare members of their staff redundant when the clients' demands for their specialist skills diminish; it was also noted in chapter 3 that one effect of the recession in the late 1990s was to generate massive unemployment among architects in particular. Structural engineers suffered less, but many individuals also lost their jobs. At the time that the interviews took place, in the mid-1990s, the two groups least affected in this way were the medics and the pharmacists. Nevertheless, one consultant (M/1) referred to senior colleagues who had in his view lost motivation, and commented that because they were "hard to get rid of," the possibility of compulsory redundancies was being considered. A hospital pharmacist (P/16) went further in arguing that serious breaches of professional conduct should lead to enforced resignation rather than to the "unnecessarily expensive options of redundancy and retirement."

For the most part, early retirement was seen a resulting from a voluntary or semi-voluntary decision, often because of a disenchantment on the part of the individual concerned with current work conditions. Watkins et al. (1992) quote one of the doctors they interviewed as remarking:

> In general practice you used to have GPs who carried on until they dropped. There is a mandatory retiring age now, but the big feeling among GPs is that you retire as soon as you can...I don't know anyone amongst my colleagues who want to go on a minute longer than they have to (p. 45).

Similar points were made among my respondents: a hospital doctor (M/19) referred to low morale leading to "more and more consultants over 50 getting out" and an academic (M/22) spoke of medical school colleagues "opting out in their early 50s" because of pressure of work and discontent about their salaries. A number of solicitors referred to the prospect of retiring at around 55, one of whom (L/1) added that "traditionally, they used to work on into their eighties." Even judges— whose job tends to be seen by other lawyers as a relatively soft option—were said to have begun retiring early, because the work was more demanding and less enjoyable than it had been in the past. The accountants, too, suggested likely premature retirement dates at various points between 50 and 55, particularly for those in "stressful top jobs" (Acc/12) and for older colleagues whose careers were adversely affected by the phasing out of audit. Among the disenchanted younger professionals, one recently appointed consultant (M/24) was contemplating an alternative medically-related career because of the disruption caused by his work to his family life; another, a senior hospital doctor, had chosen to resign as a result of being criticized in "a witch hunt on accountability," but had taken up a part-time research post at a medical school; a third, a former partner of a GP respondent (M/5), had dropped out with a depressive illness.

The phenomenon of burnout is related to this last incident. The study of the topic came into fashion in the early 1980s, when a spate of relevant publications appeared. It has been variously defined: for example, Freudenberger and Richardson (1980) describe it a "fatigue or frustration brought about by devotion to a cause, way of life or relationship that failed to produce the expected reward"; and Marlach and Schaufeli (1993), more briefly, as "prolonged job stress." Its causes, too, are said to cover a varied range: fears of incompetence, poor relations with clients, bureaucratic interference in work practice, and professional isolation (Cherniss, 1980); overload, and a sense of professional failure based on unrealistic demands (Wessells et al. , 1989); and among my respondents, incompetence and fatigue (M/10), long working hours and pressure from patients (P/5), and high levels of responsibility combined with uncertainties about the future (P/18). Commonly cited indicators of the likelihood of burnout occurring among a particular occupational group are alcoholism, drug dependency and depression (Cartwright, 1987), and suicide rate (Rosenthal, 1995). A medical respondent (M/8) added divorce rate as a further item. Attempts at amelioration cover different varieties of therapy (Wessells et al., 1989) including stress counselling (P/14). However, one respondent (M/8) commented that despite the need for it, "the ill doctor service is under-used."

It was striking that respondents in most of the six professions, while many of them remarked on the stressful nature of their work, were emphatic in denying burnout to be a problem. Only one lawyer (L/7) suggested that "It can be a phenomenon for barristers, unless they become judges," but his claim was flatly contradicted by others. Accountants saw their work a being "less stressful than GPs" (Acc/24): "people don't burn out" (Acc/25). Despite the recessionary problems they had had to face, the architects and engineers took a similar line. It was the doctors and pharmacists who most clearly acknowledged the incidence of the phenomenon within their ranks. However, though both community and hospital pharmacists raised it as an issue, a senior member of the profession (P/2) claimed that it was "not a major problem for pharmacists: though we're often stressed, it isn't a hands-on job." What seems apparent is that the burden of responsibility for getting things right, and the potentially drastic consequences of getting them wrong, puts greater pressure on those who deal with human lives than on those whose subject matter comprises documents or buildings. The level of stress is further compounded by the longer hours which doctors and pharmacists are expected to work—which is itself a consequence of providing a public service subject to constant Treasury restrictions. It is the self-employed professionals in single or small private practice who can most readily control their pace of work and the demands they put upon themselves: but even the larger firms have to treat their professional employees well enough to save them going to work for their rivals.

Given the costs of training a professional, it is as well that relatively few suffer from burnout: and despite the negative comments related to resignation, dropout and early retirement rehearsed in this section, it needs to be re-emphasized that the large majority of those interviewed showed a high degree of commitment to their work and, where relevant, looked forward to the continuing development of their careers.

Notes

1. Lord Chancellor's Advisory Committee (1997, p. 100).
2. This is not to suggest that redundancies and sackings never take place in modest-sized partnerships. Clearly, they did so on a significant scale even in small architects' firms during the major recession in the construction industry. But the sense of personal concern seemed higher, and recourse to devices such as part-time working greater, than in the intensely competitive world of City lawyers and accountants.
3. They sent a postal questionnaire to all medical qualifiers in 1993, receiving 2,621 replies.
4. Echoing this suggestion, a senior medical administrator (M/21) urged the need for joint training of junior nurses and medical staff, in that treating them separately made no organizational sense.
5. Some measure of the overall dissatisfaction with initial medical training is provided by Allen (1994), who reports that when surveyed in 1992, 58 percent of men who qualified in 1986, and 76 percent of women, claimed to have regretted their decision to study medicine.
6. "The drive to specialization must not be allowed to force intending lawyers into premature career choices. Specialization should be the function of continuing professional development after the point of initial qualification" (Lord Chancellor's Advisory Committee, 1996b, p. 17).
7. See also chapter 3, pp. 82–83.
8. This seemed to me a surprisingly high proportion, emphasizing once again that my sample of respondents was not necessarily typical.

5

Women Professionals

Structural Issues

Women have found common cause to fight for their rights in a male-dominated society at intervals over a long period of history. It was not however until the women's movement initiated in the 1960s that the arguments for gender equality began for the first time to catch the interest and sympathy of significant numbers of men as well as many women, and set in train a slow but apparently inexorable series of changes in social structures and collective attitudes. Those changes were still working their way through the professional community at the time at which the fieldwork for the present study was undertaken. Accordingly, in relation to women professionals, there tended to be a greater emphasis on the identification of problems than on success in resolving them: but there were also signs that some at least of those problems were being systematically addressed and were in the process of resolution.

The discussion of professionals' careers in chapter 4 was largely gender-neutral, in the sense that the considerations it addressed were as relevant to women as to men. There were nonetheless some highly significant differences, many of which emerged in the interview data, but even more of which became apparent in a review of the relevant literature. The writings on women in the professions in general, and in the six professions which comprise the subject matter of this study in particular, are extensive and wide-ranging. Most of them, as with the researches on other topics, are North American in authorship, but relate surprisingly closely to the corresponding scenarios on the opposite side of the Atlantic. I shall therefore draw on them as a substantial resource in the exploration which follows of the main issues affecting the lives and careers of women professionals.

One of the most striking phenomena has been the growth in the numbers of professionally qualified women in recent years. Allen (1994) records that, in the U.K., the proportion of women entering medical schools rose from 28 percent in 1970 to 52 percent in 1992. One of my respondents (L/1), in noting that the law was a male-dominated profession, acknowledged that the intake was now evenly balanced. The statistics more than vindicate his claim: by 1994, there were more women European Community students accepted for U.K. university first degree law courses than men (54.8 percent and 45.2 percent, respectively).[1] Elston (1993) similarly notes that the number of women general practitioners grew by 100 percent between 1977 and 1990, as against an increase of only 10 percent in men. A measure of the increase in accountancy is offered by Roslender (1992), citing the overall female membership of the four English professional bodies as 10–11 percent, but the female student membership as between 30 percent and 40 percent.[2] In a large accountancy firm, a respondent (Acc/5) noted that two-thirds of the current trainees were women. Even in 1983, the percentage of female first-year students in pharmacy degrees was reported as 62 percent, and in 1984 the percentage of women hospital pharmacists as 61 percent (Crompton and Sanderson, 1986). By 1994 it had risen to 69 percent.

No such claims were made for architecture, or for engineering, where the professional bodies seemed anxious to step up the number of women entrants (U.K. Inter-Professional Group, n.d.). The latter source gave the percentage of women engineering undergraduates as 12 percent in the mid-1990s[3], while the Annual Report of the Architects Registration Council for 1995–96 showed that even by the end of 1995 only 9.4 percent of registered architects were women (p. 32). An academic (E/1) maintained that it was essential for the future of the profession to attract more women into engineering, speculating that a dislike of mathematics was one of the crucial barriers. Other explanations, as mentioned in chapter 2, were less specific: that "women are too sensible to get involved in a rock bottom industry" (E/21); or that they are put off by "the image of the engineer" (E/15) or as a result of "early stereotyping" (E/29). But with these two exceptions among the six professions, it seems clear that when the present recruits become fully established in their careers, male superiority—in the matter of numbers at least—will be a thing of the past.[4]

Numbers, however, are by no means the only source of inequality. Atkinson and Delamont (1990), in their study of "women in elite professions," note that they "have not managed to achieve equality...in power and prestige" (p. 105). Referring more specifically to the legal profession, Thornton (1996) describes women as "fringe-dwellers of the jurisprudential community," faced with the problem of displacing entrenched thought structures (p. 291); Allen (1994), similarly, sees the careers of women in medicine as inhibited by uncongenial structure and organization. Roberts and Coutts (1992) offer two provocative explanations for the relative disadvantage of "women in a female niche on the margins of accountancy": first, that "occupations striving for professional status...will be particularly sensitive to any process [such as feminisation] which may threaten their status" (p. 392); second, that "allowing women access to the professional rewards of high pay, high status and autonomy, is in contradiction with women's subordinate status in society as a whole" (p. 393). Lorber (1984) is among those who point out that, in seeking the reasons for womens' career disadvantages, attention to underlying structural factors is more important than a focus on more superficial explanations: "Gender inequalities are pervasive and long-standing because they are built into social institutions and maintained by everyday assumptions about appropriate work for women and men in and out of the home" (p. 114).

The most deep-seated of these "everyday assumptions" relate to marriage and child-rearing. Married female professionals are still expected, except in the most liberal circles, to defer to their husbands' career demands and to take primary responsibility for the upbringing of their children: entrenched social values require their roles as wives and mothers to predominate over their roles as working women. Men's work commitments, on the other hand, are sanctioned to take precedence over their obligations as domestic partners. A useful analysis of typical career structures in contemporary society is offered by Céreq (1997):[5]

> Among singles or couples without children, men and women divide their time similarly.... What upsets this equitable distribution is the arrival of a child.... None of them [recent fathers] expresses the desire to reduce his working hours or reorganise his schedule...women [in contrast] fall into two groups: some recent mothers carry out their professional activity in areas (or ways) where their family least "disrupts" the job.... They sometimes opt for part-time work or a temporary interruption of their professional activity; others, like those who remain single, work full time—or maintain long working hours—and continue to demonstrate considerable availability for their career at the cost of a highly structured personal organization...women who exploit the margin of organizational autonomy available to them in order to respond to the imperatives of family life limit their possibilities of career advancement by abandoning the "promotional model"...those who adopt a structure in phase with that model preserve—eight years after their entry into the work force—the same career possibilities as men, on the condition

that their employer has gone beyond stereotyped representations of the female model of activity (p. 3).

This account ties in well with the interview data, but omits two important variants: first, that there are a limited number of cases in which the female partner has greater earning power than the male, and in which the male takes career time out as "househusband"; second, that there is a relatively higher dropout rate of women professionals as compared with men. Allen (1994) notes, for example, that less than 50 percent of female hospital doctors are still in the same specialty four years after registration. More generally, some women leave their current jobs because they consider themselves discriminated against, but stay in the profession; others, though, abandon their careers altogether, often through disappointment or conflicting loyalties (L/1, Arc/1, E/6). The sense of resulting waste was poignantly expressed by a woman medical consultant (M/2). "It's no better than cruelty to educate women to a high level and then give them nowhere to go."

There appears to be a trend towards the second pattern outlined in the above quotation from Céreq (1997), in which women professionals choose "a highly structured personal organization" of child care to enable them to return to work a very short time after their children are born. A solicitor in a medium-sized partnership (L/11) described the fail-safe arrangements she had set up in this context, and an architect (Arc/7) noted that she took breaks of no more than twelve weeks for the birth of each of her children. A senior member of the Pharmaceutical Society (P/20) noted a change from a typical ten-year break to one of a few months: indeed, the U.K. Inter-Professional Group (n.d.) records that "Over 80 percent of [women] pharmacists go back to some kind of professional work a few weeks after childbirth." The main motivation here may in some cases be economic, in terms of maintaining a previously high standard of family living, rather than being a direct consequence of career ambition. But whatever the grounds for making this choice, there are specific problems in resolving the competing priorities between personal and professional life, some of which will be discussed in the next section.

Forms of Gender Discrimination

The proclivity of young women to form heterosexual alliances and produce children creates an inevitable interruption, however brief, in their careers. Any such interruption is unwelcome to employers in large firms or to co-partners in small ones, in that maternity leave is costly and—in occupational as against domestic terms—gives rise to unproductive time.[6] Accordingly, given equally well qualified male and female applicants, the bias of recruitment choice may be in favor of the male. To make matters worse, some female employees may "play the system," returning to work only for long enough to qualify for the employer's maternity contribution before resigning. Even those who leave before their child is born represent a waste of the costs of training, while those who stay on may agitate for administratively inconvenient part-time working arrangements. It is not altogether surprising, therefore, that legislation is required to enforce gender equality that would not in many firms otherwise be available.

The existence of equal opportunities policies, while compulsory in principle, does not always result in appropriate practice. A solicitor respondent (L/5) commented that she had left her previous firm after an unsuccessful attempt to negotiate a four-day working week following the birth of her first child. But discrimination is more extensive than that associated only with early motherhood. A woman engineer (E/6), for example, was not appointed to a managerial job because it was considered that a man would be more suitable. Ten weeks later, after the firm had been unable to find anyone equally well qualified, she was invited back to fill the post. A male accountant in a local authority (Acc/12) acknowledged that the organization as a whole was "very sexist." More modestly, a recently appointed female member of a large accountancy firm (Acc/13) found its attitude to women employees "quite patronizing." However, the interviews also highlighted a number of positive examples, particularly in large enterprises. An international pharmaceutical company was rated by a senior woman employee (P/21) as having "a good track record in equal opportunities," showing no gender discrimination in promotion and an accommodating policy towards part-time work. A major firm of accountants was also said by a (male) senior partner (Acc/15) to be "keen to take on women returners and to offer part-time employment."

Even where the employing institution may have a supportive stance towards its women employees, the attitudes of individual male colleagues and contacts may be hostile. Shapland and Sorsby (1994), in an extensive survey of young barristers, came up with the surprisingly high figure of 26 percent of women who considered sex discrimination to be a major problem and 16 percent who claimed to have had direct experience of it. Around one woman in three reported having experienced minor and 5 percent major sexual harassment. In engineering, a U.S. study by McIlwee and Robinson (1992) noted that the sexual harassment of women engineers typically took the form of "sexual endearments, come-ons, suggestiveness and physical assault" (p. 99). Two of the engineers I interviewed (E/15 and E/21) referred respectively to women being "afraid of site experience" and to there being "still some discrimination on site," mainly involving building workers; an architect (Arc/14) added that young women professionals were reluctant to work on site "because of barracking." In accountancy, one of the woman respondents (Acc/13) commented that she had left her previous job with an industrial firm because of sexual harassment. In relation to the same profession, an American inquiry (Wescott and Seider, 1986) identified three typical client reactions to female accountants: (a) comments on their looks; (b) patronizing approval; (c) assumption of limited competence. One would have to be on the receiving end to know which is the less intolerable of overt hostility and underhand attempts to demean. It is clearly the latter that Brown and Klein (1982) represent in their account of "an insidious attack by primarily male subordinates and supervisors when they neuter her [a senior physician] by such pseudo-compliments as 'I don't think of you as a woman, you're too good!' which suggests that being competent is inconsistent with being a woman" (p. 162).

A less evident but in real terms much more damaging form of discrimination has come to be referred to as "the glass ceiling"—a barrier to women's careers which, though not readily observable, effectively operates to cut off the higher reaches of promotion and preserve them for men. There is very substantial evidence for the existence of this phenomenon, both in the interview data and in the relevant research literature.

In medicine, to take a U.S. example, Brown and Klein (1982) observe that

> Women must be loyal, must make themselves invaluable to male superiors, must be non-threatening to them as well, and ultimately must function best in a secondary position, moderating the internal boundaries so that men reap the rewards and advance...women in medicine may also find that if advancement is not blocked altogether, it may only proceed to the point when a woman reaches a second-in-command, woman-behind-the-throne position (p. 163).

If this is seen as a somewhat dated portrayal from a different cultural setting (albeit one in which feminism would appear to hold a powerful sway), it may be added that by the mid-1990s in the U.K., only 15 percent of consultants and 23 percent of GP principals were women (U.K. Inter-Professional Group, n.d.). Even in hospital pharmacy, despite the atypically large majority of women practitioners by the mid-nineties, the proportion of them in senior positions was very considerably smaller (P/20).

In many solicitors' firms, one respondent commented, it is only "the least troublesome women who are promoted—women's careers are a universal problem" (L/5). Spurr (1990) calculated that, despite an increase in the proportion of women entering law firms in the U.S. from 3 percent in 1968 to 33 percent in 1983, a representative sample of the cohort during this period were approximately half as likely as men to be promoted to partnership, despite a lack of any significant difference in academic credits. A later study by Wood et al. (1993) of women law school graduates from the University of Michigan found that, with virtually identical qualifications to men, they started their careers earning only slightly less. Fifteen years later, however, they were earning only 60 percent of male incomes. An econometric factor analysis suggested that 41 percent of the difference could be attributed to child care responsibility, 11 percent to a larger number of job switches and 3 percent to a shorter period in practice. However, a quarter to a third of the earnings gap was "unexplained by objective factors."

McKeen and Bujaki (1994) noted that in the six largest Canadian accountancy firms the proportion of women partners ranged from 0 percent to 22 percent out of a partnership pool comprising some 33 percent of women. The comparable figure quoted by a woman respondent in my sample (Acc/6) was 3 partners out of 140, of which she was one. In local authority employment, too, "there are very few women treasurers" (Acc/12). Roslender (1992) comments wryly that

> men have gifted some of the least rewarding jobs in the profession to their female colleagues...while 26% of male ICAEW [Institute of Chartered Accountants in England and Wales] members were partners in public practice only 12% of women fell into this category...while three-fifths of female ICAEW members are presently consigned to lower status jobs only one-fifth of the men are there with them...it is the men who succeed in making their careers away from the less prestigious, more routine functions of the accountancy profession (p. 41).

The picture is no different in architecture ("a male-dominated profession—Arc/1) or structural engineering. In the former, a respondent (Arc/13) noted that in his relatively small firm the staff was equally divided between men and women and that "the women are very good indeed": but none of them were partners. Berkeley (1989) confirms that the same discrimination is to be found among U.S. architects. In the case of engineering, a respondent acknowledged that "the firm has many female engineers, but it has not had much success in promoting them to senior posts" (E/14). A number of senior male interviewees in the same field expressed a wish to take on, and subsequently to promote, more women, but claimed to be frustrated in this by a shortage of successful candidates. The leading U.K. firm, Ove Arup, provides a case in point. In an interview with *The Guardian* newspaper (*Guardian*, 1996), the chairman is quoted as remarking that the firm recruits and retains a relatively high proportion of women engineers, but that "we are failing to pull them through on promotion." He was unable to say why, but a female member of staff attributed it to "the ingrained attitude, particularly among the older staff."

It is anyone's guess whether the overall position will improve as steadily increasing numbers enter the professions and a critical mass develops of senior and highly qualified women. Roslender (1992) adopts a pessimistic view in relation to accountancy, speculating that it may be "more a case of 'room at the bottom' rather than at the top," with women "leaving the best jobs, careers and control of the accountancy profession in the hands of their male colleagues" (p. 41). In contrast, a senior male solicitor (L/1) saw "the balance at the top end of the firm...as gradually changing in favor of women."

The Demands of Domesticity

It is not a matter for much controversy or debate that "women become and remain marginal when...the emphasis on commitment places professional ahead of personal life, creating conflict for [those] who desire both career and family" (Martin, 1989, p. 233); or that serious problems can result from career interruptions of marriage and childbirth (Wescott and Seiler, 1986, p. 154). Such problems take a variety of forms. In some cases, women professionals opt to cut down on the more avoidable commitments. Among my female respondents, a pharmacist (P/8) did not, as a matter of policy, go to professional training sessions scheduled for weekends; an architect (Arc/11) had placed an embargo on all courses and conferences, however relevant they might seem. A solicitor (L/11) had ceased to take any work home with her after her first child was born. At the same time, such professionals "must also convince potential superiors that their commitment to their work will not be put in jeopardy because of personal demands...a challenge not made of men in the same position" (Brown and Klein, 1982, p. 163). A woman consultant (M/16) had succeeded in meeting this requirement by cutting down drastically on family and leisure commitments. She explained that she started her working day at 5:30 a.m. and got home usually at 10 p.m. She did not watch television, read the papers, take exercise or read novels. She hardly saw her children at all between Sunday evening and Saturday morning.

A distinct set of issues arises in relation to mobility. When a husband's career involves a major change of location, his professional partner often feels constrained to interrupt her own career to move with him, as in the case of a hospital doctor in the sample (M/2); conversely, when a woman's own career development involves a move, she is liable to feel constrained to give up the opportunity and stay, as with a woman GP, "tied to a particular place" (M/3). A woman engineer (E/6) made a related point, remarking that her family commitments had significantly reduced her commuting range. In accountancy in particular, Wescott and Seiler (1986) pinpoint the problem of geographical mobility in multi-office firms: an issue which can also arise in large legal practices.

Part-time working presents another range of difficulties. A number of employers are reluctant to enter into part-time arrangements. Particular cases among my respondents were in a solicitor's firm, where a woman partner (L/5) carried a full workload, although working a four-day week, and in an architectural partnership in which "taking time out is awkward because the firm's arrangements aren't flexible enough" (Arc/13). General practice would seem to be an exception. Elston (1993) records that over 40 percent of women GPs were working less than full-time in 1990. However, she modifies the impact of this statistic by noting that "working 'part-time' in British medicine often involves what passes for a normal working week in most professions" (p. 40). The Céreq (1997) study was quoted earlier in this chapter as suggesting that women who "respond to the imperatives of family life limit their possibilities of career advancement" (p. 32). The problem is exacerbated if the professional in question takes a significant career break as well as subsequently returning to work part-time. What one must hope to be an extreme example was offered by the hospital pharmacist (P/26) who held a senior managerial job for five years before she had her first child. At this point she stayed at home for six months and then returned to a part-time post in a different hospital. It took her thirteen years to regain her previous level of seniority. A hospital doctor in a regional hospital trust (M/2) fared considerably better, moving steadily from part-time jobs as a Registrar and later a Senior Registrar to her present consultant post, at the top end of the medical hierarchy.

The same respondent (M/2) commented that "as a woman professional you need a certain degree of flexibility." Two community pharmacists had achieved this, keeping their hands in, one (P/1) by taking up occasional locum jobs and the other (P/8) by continuing to work for one day a week, before gradually increasing their part-time commitments. While there can be rigidities in both large firms and small partnerships, sole practice offers the most flexible context of all, in that the individual concerned can make a free choice of how to allocate time between work and family. General medical practice and community pharmacy, as already remarked, can offer some sort of approximation to such flexibility. A comparable situation was presented by an architect (Arc/11) in a small joint practice with her husband, who was able to experiment with doing some of her professional work at home. To her regret, this strategy was not noticeably successful: "Friends pop in, and it's hard to establish a routine. Also, people ring up outside working hours. There is a hard line to draw between work and home life—you could say that the whole thing is psychologically embarrassing."

The Channeling of Careers

The incidence—or even the potentiality—of domestic demands can have a further, and highly significant, effect on the development of women's careers. The phenomenon is particularly well-documented in medicine where, as Brown and Klein (1982) observe,

> the "professional socialization" that women in medicine undergo...invisibly channels these women into certain specific areas (pediatrics and psychiatry), and only when typical male/female family roles change can these covert but powerful features of medical structure and organization begin to be addressed (p. 156).

Specific examples of career channeling can be seen among hospital doctors where, as Elston (1993) points out, women "were overrepresented in certain fields of medicine, including... 'service' specialties... such as anesthetics and radiology and in primary care. In contrast, women were underrepresented in the major fields of acute adult medicine, especially surgical ones" (p. 10). It is of course the service fields that are time-circumscribed, as against the major ones where doctors are liable to be on call. According to one informant (M/8), "There are fifteen women general surgeons in Britain, as against about a thousand men.[7] There are relatively few women consultants in obstetrics and gynecology. More of them become pathologists, anesthetists and the like."

Previous researches suggest that there may be other factors operating to constrain career choice, not all of them related to the anticipated demands of marriage and a family, though some would appear to be so. Allen (1994) suggests that surgery, for instance, has become a "white male preserve" (p. 253) because of strong competition and a "macho" image as well as a long demanding training and very limited provision for part-time work; and Cartwright (1987) suggests that women remain concentrated in lower-status and "caring" career options because of the organizational structure of specialties and informal social pressures as well as of sex role compatibilities and the wish to avoid acute time demands.

Domestic factors are generally agreed to play a large part in the decision to opt for a career in general medical practice, as against hospital medicine. Elston (1993) records that more young women than men "are shying away from a hospital career," and that the attraction of women to general practice shows "no decrease over time" (p. 45). A woman GP (M/5) explained that although she would have liked to specialize in obstetrics and gynecology, the field was very competitive, and would have entailed "dashing around the country and working long hours," features which she considered to account for the low proportion of women consultants. As far as she was concerned, "general practice is good for motherhood."

Similar considerations help to explain the preference of female pharmacists for jobs in community pharmacy. One respondent (P/24) recommended it as "a good subject for picking up and putting down," while another (P/29) saw it as a largely self-employed profession which suffered less from discrimination than many other professional jobs. However, this last assertion, made by a training consultant, needs to be modified. Muzzin et al. (1994) point out that, in Canada, only some 10 percent of small community pharmacies are owned by women because of the problem of working a 70-plus hour week. The figure for the U.K. is unlikely to be significantly different, which implies that most women in this, the largest, branch of the profession are in a supportive rather than a leading role.

Law and accountancy follow a similar pattern. In the former, "There's an implicit assumption that women will take time out to have children, and this tends to limit their career choices and prospects" (L/4). In the latter, Wescott and Seiler (1986) refer to the notion of "suitable" assignments for women, often not mainstream in career terms. One relevant specialism was highlighted by a woman engaged in corporate finance (Acc/17), who referred to one of the rare female partners in her section as having "a girlie job as a tax specialist."

The labelling of particular specialisms as preferred areas for women is less evident in architecture and engineering, but one might infer that this is not only because women are not attracted to either profession in very large numbers, but also because there is no strong pattern of specialization requiring a choice by those who are. For the rest, the irony is that as long as some career options can be seen to make relatively fewer demands incompatible with family requirements, those options will continue to attract women. Insofar as they tend to lie outside the mainstream, they will also be less likely to lead to high status appointments; and insofar as they are seen as offering "girlie jobs," their standing within the profession will be yet further diminished. One is thrown back to the pessimistic contention of Brown and Klein (1982), quoted above, that an effective resolution of the problem can only be contemplated "when typical male/female family roles change."

Social Deprivations

In the teeth of legislative attempts to promote equal career opportunities for women, a flourishing culture of underground discrimination survives. One of the more covert practices is exclusion by deliberate or inadvertent ostracism. Several writers, along with a number of my respondents, have pointed to the importance in career advancement of belonging to key social networks. In general, these tend to perpetuate themselves as male preserves, so effectively cutting women off from the opportunity to develop strategically useful links with influential and knowledgeable colleagues. In medicine, for example, Brown and Klein (1982) maintain that

> all too often, networking remains restricted to 'old boys' and to all-male social clubbing: inside knowledge is transmitted only to those who fit the typical picture of 'promising young physician' (primarily upper-middle-class white male) and aspiring young women physicians are left out in the cold (p. 157).

Elston (1993) suggests that this exclusion may in part be the result of "the demands of young children [which] limit women's participation in the informal aspects of hospital medical life." Clearly, part-time appointments or sizeable career breaks limit access to such forms of interaction in any occupational group, but the evidence suggests that this is also often the case with full-time women professionals. Brown (1989) argues that exclusion from the colleague system ("a men's club"—p. 242) is one of the reasons for the denial of advancement among women architects, and McIllwee and Robinson (1992) make a similar point about exclusion from "grapevines and social interactions" among women engineers.

A partial resolution of the difficulty, it is sometimes proposed, is to adopt the retaliatory measure of setting up rival women's networks. Lorber (1984) advances the case for doing so in the medical profession, independently supporting the claim by Brown and Klein (1982) that "Until more senior women develop 'old girl' networks, identification and entry issues will remain problematic for young women physicians" (p. 161). Carter and Kirkup (1990) also emphasize the importance of networking among women engineers within professional societies, especially in the identification of senior job vacancies. This possibility has been institutionalized in the U.K. in two of the six professions most adversely affected by gender discrimination, through the establishment of a Women Architects Group (which one of my respondents, Arc/9, had joined) and a Women's Engineering Society. A solicitor (L/5) and an insolvency practitioner (Acc/6) each described the activities of the informal network of senior women professionals to which they belonged, most of the members being in client organizations, including insurance and banking. However, this group seemed to function more in terms of offering moral support than in enhancing career progress, and its activities, as described, were predominantly social (going to the theater, to the races, and so on). In any event, the establishment of a separate network structure for women is unlikely to achieve the required equalization of career opportunities, since it would almost certainly be accorded the status of a fringe organization and would therefore be denied the chance effectively to match any long-established male counterpart group in terms of political effectiveness. The best hope here must be for a change in climate sufficiently fundamental to allow women into previously male-dominated groups on an equal footing: a change which is already happening in relation to learning networks (see chapter 7).

A closely related issue, also a commonly noted cause for concern, is the absence among women professionals of suitable role models and mentors. Allen (1994), in her study of medical careers, notes that—in a profession which relies quite heavily on the support of patrons—female consultants are rarely identified as being in that category, and suggests that their lack of availability presents a disincentive to younger women doctors. Brown and Klein (1982) in their turn described "mentor-protégé relationships" as "often crucially important" for young upwardly mobile physicians (p. 157) and note that, in lacking them, women's careers are handicapped. Vytlačil (1989) similarly identifies the scarcity of women role models in architecture as an obstacle to career progress. All this should not be taken to imply that men seldom provide mentorship to women: but the recognition that few women are available to do so may nevertheless be taken to convey a strongly discouraging message.

One effect of being denied access to male networks and female patrons is to create a sense of marginality: as Martin (1989) puts it, "women become and remain marginal when the hierarchical and elitist nature of the [architectural] profession (relying on 'old boy' connections) serves to exclude them from opportunities for achievement and advancement" (p. 283). In the same vein, Spencer and Podmore (1987) subtitle their discussion of women lawyers "marginal members of a male-dominated profession." To be marginalized is by the same token to lack credibility: as a senior woman in a medium-sized accounting firm (Acc/6) pointed out, "when you're in the company of men, it's always assumed that a man is in charge." A comparable remark was attributed to a woman engineer in an article on the large engineering firm Ove Arup, who claimed that a senior colleague had automatically "assumed I must be a secretary" (*Guardian*, 1996).

If women are excluded by the structure of informal networks as predominantly male preserves, it is more a case of self-exclusion when it comes to their joining formal organizations whose membership shares with such networks a career-related political aspect. "There are not enough women" commented a highly active woman GP (M/5) "ready to get involved in committee and policy forums."[8] A medical consultant (M/16) demonstrated clearly how the mould could be broken, given the will to do so: she regularly participated in the major conferences relevant to her specialism, belonged to the main specialist groups, and was a member of the editorial boards of four academic journals. Understandably, quite a few of the other women professionals interviewed saw such activities as being in competition with their domestic commitments, and opted against participating in them. Some at least seemed to be unaware that such involvement could create connections and promote causes which might help to enhance their professional visibility. This apparent obliviousness to the political aspects of their working lives provides some justification to the claim by Wescott and Seiler (1986) that women are "less likely to create the conditions which lead to career advancement."

Attitudes and Feelings

Up to this point, discussion of the problems affecting women professionals' careers has focused on those which are in some sense externally imposed, through the way in which social attitudes are structured, gender discrimination operates, marital and family pressures intervene, or access to support mechanisms appears to be lacking. There is however a further set of issues which relate to predominantly psychological considerations—that is to say, those which stem from feelings of inadequacy or a perceived lack of the personal qualities considered necessary for a successful professional career.

One such issue concerns a suggested difference between men's and women's main incentives and ambitions. A woman solicitor (L/4) claimed that, in general "women are assumed to be—and often are—less ambitious than men." As acknowledged earlier in this chapter, many women professionals experience divided loyalties between their marital and family commitments and their careers. A sizeable proportion of the women respondents in my study were frank in their assertion that in a conflict of priorities their prime commitment would have to be to the former. As one general practitioner (M/3) explained, "having a family can affect your ambition, change your sense of priorities and make it harder to 'get back up'." This, she suggested, could explain why there were "quite a few single or childless women GPs."[9] Brown and Klein (1982) echo this latter point in their reference to an "option open to women in medicine to become entirely married to career." For the most part, however, such single-mindedness seems as rare among women as it is said to be common among men. A different contrast between men and women is identified in Maupin's (1993) study of recent U.S. graduates in accountancy.[10] He suggests that while the acquisition of money is the main job incentive for men in the profession, the quest for "independence and self-fulfillment" provides the strongest driving force for women.

Another consideration has to do with the experience among many female professionals (which they may be held to share with women in general) of a deep-seated lack of confidence, linked with related concerns about deficiencies in assertiveness and competitive aggression. A revealing set of comments stemmed from a respondent who was a partner in a medium-sized accountancy firm (Acc/6): "women in accountancy certainly have a different outlook from men, and I don't think they're as tough"; it took her about a year to come to terms with being a partner, and she started off by being "aggressive and unsure." For some time she found it extremely difficult to go into the otherwise all-male partners' dining room. Wescott and Seiler (1986) confirm that women accountants at a senior level "need to be assertive" (p. 112), while Berkeley (1989) comments that for women architects "the ability to express confidence.... is critical."

The right balance between assertiveness and aggression can however be difficult to strike. Brown and Klein (1982) refer in this connection to a "double-bind" in which "women in the medical profession are expected to exhibit assertive, stereotypically 'masculine' qualities, but then are castigated for not exhibiting more unabrasive, stereotypically 'feminine' qualities" (p. 158). It is not easy to win either way: a woman engineer (E/6) observed that women who "adopt a hostile attitude" tend to be eased out of the profession, while McIlwee and Robinson (1992), also concerned with female engineers, suggest that the power structure in the workplace causes them to lack an appropriate degree of aggression. They further postulate that women's absence of confidence is related to their earlier lives. A long experience, from early childhood, of being regarded as in some respects second-class citizens, with males taking a consistently dominant role, would indeed appear to account for some of the problems experienced by women in this regard. It remains to be seen how far such problems may be ameliorated by an apparent reduction in the general level of gender discrimination during the later 1990s.

One by-product of women's uncertainty about their own worth is well documented in the research literature and the interview data. It concerns the widely held notion that female professionals are expected, and expect themselves, to outshine their male counterparts. The point is made in general terms by Pugh and Wahrman (1983): "Our data[11] indicate that there may be some truth in the folk wisdom that being as good as a man is not enough to enable a woman to succeed" (p. 760). More specifically, a woman GP (M/3) was frank in owning to the feeling that she "had to do better than men—to be super-qualified," in line with the observations by Brown and Klein (1982) that women in medicine "tend to underrate their professional contributions. They feel that they should be superwomen and they feel pressured to perform fully in all areas of life" (p. 156), and that "A number of women felt that women had to be better, brighter, more talented, more resourceful than men to be placed in comparable positions in the medical hierarchy" (p. 163).

The same theme is taken up in relation to accountancy by Wescott and Seiler (1986), who refer to the need for a female aspiring partner to "prove herself far more than a male would have to do" (p. 130), adding that "women need to be much better qualified and work much harder to equal the progress made by men" (p. 178). In architecture, according to Berkeley (1989), "men are expected to be competent while women are expected to be outstanding" (p. xvii). A woman respondent among the engineers in my sample (E/6) argued that "women can't afford to be mediocre and have to give more than the men," while Carter and Kirkup (1990) similarly comment on the feeling among their informants (comprising 21 U.K. and 16 U.S. women engineers) that they had not only to prove their competency, but also to demonstrate that they were even more competent than their male colleagues. Whether or not the need to establish such superiority is an objective, if generally unstated, requirement, it seems undeniably to be an assumption made by many women professionals.

Because of this "greater pressure to prove their ability and serious purpose," Vytlačil (1989, p. 26) suggests, women fear failure more deeply than men. Brown (1989) takes up a similar theme, maintaining that when male colleagues' careers advance more rapidly than theirs, "women lacking feminist awareness feel that the failure to achieve is their own fault" (p. 242). Both are writing about professional architects, but the tendency towards self-blame and a sense of failure seems unlikely to be confined to them, any more than a heightened sense of stress is necessarily peculiar to women doctors. Nonetheless, it is understandable that women in a highly pressurized calling should be more prone to stressful experiences than their female counterparts in other professions and their male counterparts in their own. Both Schreiber (1987) and Cartwright (1987) quote the same statistic, claiming that suicides among female physicians in the US are three times as high as the norm for all women (the corresponding ratio for men is 1.5:1); as a further indicator, Schreiber (1987) cites the divorce rate as one-and-a-half times higher for women physicians than for men.

The Picture in Perspective

Any attempt to review a particular category of problems in a reasonably extensive way is bound to end up running the risk of giving an unduly doleful impression: of falsely portraying what may not in actuality be an irremediable situation. Even though there is ample evidence to suggest that some professional women suffer some of the problems adumbrated in this chapter in the course of some of the phases in their careers, not all women are necessarily alike in sharing all the same negative experiences. As has been noted, one common difficulty affecting those women with marital or cohabiting partners relates to their often unequal potentialities for geographical mobility; another, even more apparently intractable, is the competition between work and home engendered by their young children. Even here however, it is possible to discern, in the course of the 1990s in particular, a continuing if gradual change in what Lorber (1984) was quoted in the introductory section to this chapter as designating "everyday assumptions about appropriate work for women and men in and out of the home" (p. 114) This shift, taken together with an increased reliability of and reliance on family planning, and with changing patterns of child care (the readier acceptability among the professional classes of child-minding arrangements and the greater availability of kindergarten and pre-school provision) must help to ease women's career choices from the pre-set channels identified and discussed above.

According, too, to those who make it their business to forecast the prevailing patterns of future society, the rise of information technology, foremost among other factors, will introduce profound changes in the structure of most occupations, promoting the "outsourcing" of workers. Insofar as this proves to be the case, the resulting flexibility in the demands of space and time, enabling both women and men to work from home at hours partly of their own choosing, is likely to have significant implications for some professions—such as law, accountancy, architecture, and structural engineering—if less evidently for others requiring face-to-face client contact, such as medicine and to a lesser extent pharmacy.

Another factor likely to ameliorate the largely negative picture of occupational disadvantage among women professionals relates to men's heightened awareness and acknowledgment of discriminatory situations and practices—a phenomenon which became apparent in interviews with male respondents across the whole range of professions covered. This, coupled with an increasing readiness to give recognition to the highly competent level of women's professional performance (occasioned, it was suggested earlier, by a belief in the requirement for them to be better than men) promises to tilt the balance towards a greater level of gender equality, or at least to reduce the grosser inequalities which still persist.

It is important also, in recognition of the positive aspects of women's position within the professions, to recall the point made at the outset of this discussion about demographic changes. Unless the rate of increase of women entering the professions reaches a sudden and dramatic halt, the time will come—as it has already in pharmacy—when the women in practice in medicine, law, and accountancy (though not foreseeably in architecture and structural engineering) will outnumber the men. The situation in which men command all the senior posts will not easily persist, particularly in a rising generation in which women are increasingly prepared to recognize their rights and to exercise a tactful assertiveness in attaining them. There are, it can confidently be claimed, cracks beginning to appear in the glass ceiling and in the other invisible barriers created by male exclusory tactics. In particular, there are already fewer discernable differences than in the past between men and women in their access to formal and informal learning opportunities (see chapters 6 and 7).

Looking collectively at the women interviewed in this study, the overall impression which they gave was certainly neither despairing nor rancorous. Some were understandably resentful of what they saw as inequitable treatment or unreasonable behavior by senior male colleagues: others were content at the balance they had achieved between their personal and their professional lives. Many had managed, despite the familiar handicaps of gender, to achieve highly successful and rewarding positions. Two in particular commented on the advantages of being a woman. The first, an engineer (E/6), considered that it had been a factor in gaining her membership of the council of her professional association at a relatively young age, and hence in opening up a wide range of influential contacts and job opportunities; the second, an industrial pharmacist (P/21), had found special political and career advantages as a woman "in dealing with aggressive men."

Finally, in considering some of the crucial and often debilitating differences between women and men in the professions, it seems appropriate to conclude with a reminder of the significant similarities. If one considers the three elements in the subtitle of this book—change, commitment, and capability—it has been argued of the second that some women may currently differ from men in the division of their loyalties between profession and motherhood, but that to balance this they manifest the third—capability—in a higher degree. When it comes to change, while women may have to face more career disruptions, and often to overcome significant problems after a break for child-rearing, they also share the same occupational cultures, and therefore encounter the same set of pressures—delineated in chapter 3—as men. They also experience comparable career patterns, as reviewed in chapter 4, with the exception, here noted, that they do not in the main enjoy the same access to the more senior posts. They have similar needs for continuing professional learning, as will be seen in chapters 6 and 7, and face the same general demands relating to quality assurance, as set out in chapter 8. These commonalities make it possible to discuss most issues in a largely gender-free way, using interview testimony without the need for marking constant distinctions between men and women respondents. Even so, when considering the varied aspects and activities of professional life, it remains important to recognize and acknowledge the special issues which affect women professionals.

Notes

1. Lord Chancellor's Advisory Committee (1996a) Appendix F, p. 153; see also Hughes (1994) p. 65.
2. The process of feminization has gone further in the US: by the late 1980s, the female:male ratio was almost 50:50 (Reid et al., 1987).
3. The Latham Report (1994), reviewing "procurement and contractual arrangements in the construction industry," observed that "women are seriously underrepresented in the industry. There is no obvious reason why this should be so at a professional consultant level...a survey of the number of women professionals amongst the membership of 14 of the professional institutions in the construction industry...showed that in 1992/3, there were 12,406 women out of a total collective membership of 239,700 across the 14 disciplines, equal to 5.2% of the total" (§7.24).
4. The phenomenon is not confined to Britain and the U.S.: in France, "between 1986 and 1996, the proportion of women among the 'managers and higher intellectual occupations' went from 27 to 34 percent...In 1991, five out of every ten women went on to higher education, as opposed to four out of every ten men" (Céreq, 1997. p 2).
5. The account of 'The Necessary Trade-Offs of Young Women Managers' in France was based mainly on in-depth interviews with 20 women and 20 men eight years after they obtained their diplomas, and a matching group who were still at the outset of their working lives.
6. A prime example of a backwoods employer's attitude is given by Scotland (1998), quoting from one of her interviews with general practitioners:

    No, I would never employ a female GP. She would be here five minutes, then she'd be off. Off having babies, she'd have one then another, and I would be paying the bill. It would be me who would have to pay for the maternity leave, and have to pay someone to replace her (p.76).

7. The U.K. Inter-Professional Group (n.d.) puts the proportion at "less than 1% of consultants."
8. Although the respondent was herself the senior partner in a busy five-partner practice, and married with two young children, she had managed to find time to act as a member of her district health authority and the local medical committee, as well as taking part in the activities of the British Medical Association and three other professional bodies.
9. Schreiber (1987) puts the figure for single female physicians as high as 31% of the total, as against only 8 % of males in the same category.
10. The research findings are based on a survey of 141 female and 120 male graduating students in accountancy, supplemented by 30 in-depth interviews.
11. The enquiry took the form of two fairly elaborate psychosociological tests carried out on 87 male-female pairs.

Part 4

Capability

6

Continuing Professional Development

Definitions, Origins, and Purposes

It is sometimes said that a definition reveals more about the person doing the defining than about the subject being defined. While that may be to underline a point by large exaggeration, it is nevertheless the case that the different ways of representing the concept of continuing professional development throw some light on those who advance them.

For example, Vaughan (1991), writing from a stance as an academic researcher, offers a brief and uncontentious, if mildly inelegant, formulation:

> "Continuing Professional Development" is the term which is increasingly being used to describe the on-going learning that professionals need to undertake throughout their career in order to maintain their professional competence (p. 5).

Later in the same text, he quotes, approvingly, the "clearest and most comprehensive definition of the purpose of CPD," put forward by the CPD in Construction Group (a consortium of professional bodies related to the construction industry):

> The systematic maintenance, improvement and broadening of knowledge and skill and the development of personal qualities necessary for the execution of professional and technical duties throughout the practitioner's working life (p. 29).

Apart from the muted bureaucratic and legalistic overtones, this statement is interesting in its reference to personal qualities alongside "knowledge and skill."

The Lord Chancellor's Advisory Committee (1997), perhaps with more of an eye on its political masters than on its practitioner constituents, points in a somewhat different direction:

> In this report, continuing professional development ("CPD") means regular, structured educational activity designed to supplement the practitioner's experience by

enhancing any aspect of his professional competence at all the different stages of his career. CPD in this sense is closely related to practice because it is important that CPD should add, by means of suitably structured activity, an element of reflection designed to clarify and enhance the effect of practical experience (§1.13, p. 15).

The exclusive use of the male gender is remarkable in a profession in which there is now a high proportion of female practitioners;[1] but it is perhaps even more remarkable that, with a couple of metaphorical strokes of the pen, all informal and unstructured professional learning is discounted, alongside any advanced qualifications which, in their nature, are unlikely to be "closely related to practice." The effect of this formulation can only be to divert the legal profession's continuing education into a more narrowly mechanistic channel than it currently occupies.[2]

Most contemporary perceptions of CPD are less illiberal, allowing at least some scope for informal, self-directed learning and including contextual as well as strictly technical topics. Curiously, the proceedings of the "Consultative Conference" leading to the 1997 report (Lord Chancellor's Advisory Committee 1996c) contained an account by a leading American legal executive, V.J. Rubico, of how the matter was viewed by the U.S. legal profession. This made it plain that CPD covered many other topics beside continuing legal education, strictly conceived, including management, communication, interpersonal skills, computer literacy and marketing.

The broadening of the earlier boundaries to include themes which are not directly related to the technical knowledge base of the profession is as noticeable in British medicine as it is in American law. Nicholls and Hind (1996) suggest that this is a general trend throughout the European Union; some support for the contention is also found among my respondents. A senior medical administrator, for example, argued that CPD has a much broader connotation than CME (Continuing Medical Education):

CME is, in the view of most doctors—and Royal Colleges indeed—training or insuring that doctors do what they were trained to do rather better, although they've kept up to date. I see it, in the way it's coming together, as essentially a principally backward looking process. Whereas I see CPD, with a judicious use of CME within it, as something driven by the individual as a response to the question: Where do I want to be in a given period of time and how can I best get there? It's a forward looking process and it's a process that the individual really needs to grasp their own destiny…one of the problems is that medical training prepares people to pass obstacles; it doesn't really prepare them to think of their own personal development (M/30).

There is, then, no single and agreed conception of CPD, even though—or perhaps indeed because—it is not a new coinage. Its etymology is doubtless as subject to contest as its definition, but it may be relevant to note that the notion of lifelong learning appeared on the scene, as a relatively novel idea, in the 1960s, giving a boost to the then somewhat marginal activity of adult education. The new doctrine was that the pace of growth of knowledge and the rate of change of society were such that no vocational qualification could be expected to survive for more than a few years, and would therefore require periodic renewal.

Some professions picked up the cue more rapidly than others. Thus, as early as 1971, the Ormrod Report referred to the value of continuing legal education after qualification in enabling lawyers to become fully equipped members of the profession. By 1974, Acheson had already undertaken a survey of opinions about the organization of continuing education from a random sample of GPs in England and Wales. It was not until four years later, in 1978, that the Institute of Chartered Accountants established a requirement for continuing professional development—a forerunner by several years of most professional bodies' schemes, although the Royal Institute of British Architects published a discussion document on the subject in 1979.

However, it may be of less significance to delve into the historical record than to ask the sociologist's favorite and familiar question: who stands to benefit, and in what ways, by promoting the systematization of CPD? Here, the answers are evident. First, the professional bodies must be major stakeholders, in that it is they who will be expected to administer the necessary arrangements. This will extend their administrative staff, bringing more status to their senior managers, and enhance their power over their members. To some extent, the government departments in the background, together with their responsible ministers, will benefit by being at least partially absolved from having to answer for or take action on the perceived inadequacies of the profession in question, and from the costs of implementing quality assurance procedures to safeguard the public interest. The public, as potential clients—insofar as they are made aware of the pressures on professionals to keep up-to-date—will also see some advantage. And finally, amidst the drawbacks of having to meet extra demands (and in many cases to be out-of-pocket for doing so), the professionals themselves may gain by having a clear framework within which to meet their needs to respond to change, maintain their capability, and the like.

It is at any rate incontestable that CPD activities in general have grown in both number and scope in recent years. Vaughan's (1991) study records a significant increase between 1987 and 1991 in the number of professional bodies with formal policy statements, in those requiring members to record their CPD activities, and in those claiming regularly to monitor such records. Among the six professions which form the subject of this study, three at least of the medical Royal Colleges—the General Practitioners, the Obstetricians and Gynecologists, and the Physicians—introduced formal schemes between 1990 and 1995; so did the Royal Pharmaceutical Society, the Law Society, the Chartered Association of Certified Accountants, and the Chartered Institute of Management Accountants, the Royal Institute of British Architects, and the Institution of Structural Engineers.

Various suggestions have been put forward about the purposes which CPD programs might serve, in addition to the general one of keeping up professional standards of competence and capability. For example, Vaughan (1991) advances "three common reasons for professionals to engage in CPD:...to update themselves in new developments...to train themselves for additional roles...to help provide wider job-satisfaction and personal effectiveness" (p. 5). Madden and Mitchell (1993) offer a nearly identical trilogy: "updating of knowledge and skills...; preparation for a changing role...and increasing competence in a wider context."

At the Lord Chancellor's Advisory Committee's Consultative Conference (1996c), the main purposes put forward in discussion were somewhat comparable: updating knowledge, including new topics such as European Union Law; consolidating experience; specializing; and changing career or direction. For the purposes of my subsequent analysis, I shall adopt a simpler threefold categorization based on my interview data, namely keeping up-to-date, enhancing professional capabilities, and solving specific problems.

Formal Requirements and the Related Debate

There is not a great deal of purpose in listing the various sets of conditions which professional bodies have elected to impose on their members in the way of continuing professional development: these are so frequently subject to modification that any detailed tabulation would soon be misleadingly out-of-date. However, some general observations can be made to indicate the wide variety of practice, even across the limited sample of six professions under review.

The specifications themselves vary in terms of whether they involve the whole professional population or only sectors of it (e.g., those recently qualified or those aspiring to a Fellowship); whether they refer to hours or working days spent or whether they base themselves on points earned. However, as an approximation, the points awarded can be translated into equivalent full-time hours. On this basis, the Institute of Chartered Accountants ranks highly, with an annual equivalent of 50 hours of structured learning: it is exceeded only by the norm for some hospital doctors. In the case of the latter, the Royal Colleges differ in their stipulated time allocations, but the Royal College of Physicians calls for 100 hours a year, or 10 days, half at least of which should involve external activities. The annual norm for the other four professions appears to be around 30–35 hours, though both the Institution of Structural Engineers and the Law Society required 20 hours or less in the late 1990s. The Bar Council at that time made no demands on its members. The extent of CPD commitments, as can be seen from these figures, bears little or no relation to the perceived status of the professions concerned (see chapter 2).

My discussions with officials in the relevant professional bodies brought to light a certain ambivalence about the extent to which CPD requirements were binding on practitioners, and—assuming that they were—in what ways conformity to such requirements had to be certified. The first of these questions yielded, in one case, the assertion that CPD was "mandatory but not obligatory"; in another, I was assured that it was "obligatory but not mandatory."

A clue to the source of such otherwise puzzling equivocation was provided by two respondents in particular. The first, an academic accountant (Acc/21), found it difficult to see how a statutory demand for CPD could be enforceable, remarking that the professional bodies would be cutting their own throats if they alienated the large numbers of their members in small practices as a result of such insistence. An architect, although an active member of the RIBA, was critical of its stance on CPD which, he claimed,

> could definitely be called pathetic—in the sense that it's not mandatory anyway and effectively very few people do it...I'm not saying they haven't done CPD but they haven't filled in those forms...in the end, the RIBA is frightened of losing membership and they're backing off from any exercise, because of course a large body of the membership who work some of the time perhaps just don't have the money and the time to do this (Arc/18).

He went on, however, to observe that

> On the other hand I think as a profession it's absolutely ludicrous—we can hardly

hold ourselves ineligible for CPD unless we think it acceptable to qualify by the age of 25 and then stay the same for the next 25 or 30 years. In actuality, CPD is a natural part of architecture—it would be professionally very evident if you didn't do it (Arc/18).

That observation reflects the tendency, already noted as a salient characteristic of professionalism, to aim to achieve capability in order to maintain a professional reputation. But it also points up one of the key dilemmas related to CPD. To avoid any definitive minimum requirement could serve to raise questions about the continuing claim to professional status; to insist on one could alternatively—since membership of a professional association is not invariably a *sine qua non* of continuing practice—cause dissenters to vote with their feet. But the considerations for and against mandation are more extensive than this argument suggests.

Vaughan's (1991) study, to which reference has already been made, sets out several points which its proponents have advanced in favor of mandatory CPD. Prominent amongst them is the demon-round-the-corner warning: if we don't put our own house in order, somebody else (most likely the government of the day) will do it for us, in a much more painful and damaging way. Other arguments include the need for a given profession to protect its patch and maintain its image and—a consideration advanced particularly in the 1990s—to be in a strong position to outdo competitors from other European Union countries. The considerations against compulsion include the importance of retaining a sense of autonomy and responsibility among professionals; the need to recognize the significance of informal, not easily measurable, learning activities; and, more pragmatically, the costs of setting up and running formal CPD schemes.

Further objections to mandation, interestingly, are voiced more frequently in relation to law and medicine than to the other four professions.[3] Crandall (1990), for instance, in a study of continuing medical learning, makes a point which seems more widely applicable:

learning occurs when content is relevant, applicable to practice, and of some perceived benefit to patients...When change is primarily extrinsically provoked... usually it is viewed negatively and the commitment to change or learn may be superficial (p. 346).

Bashook (1993), writing for a similar audience, contends that

CME [Continuing Medical Education] participation becomes converted from a learning opportunity to a measure of competence through designating credit hours for participation and offering recognition awards for attendance at accredited CME programmes. The hours and the awards have little to do with learning and are questionable measures of competence (p. 33).

And in his turn, Armytage (1996), in a well-informed and authoritative work on the education of judges, refers to

a deeply held view that professions generally, and judges in particular, see themselves as the best arbiter of their learning needs and how to meet them and, within this self-image see any notion of external prescription as anathema....There is no compelling evidence from any source that mandatory education promotes effective learning (pp. 172–3).

He adds that "mandatory education is best explained from the perspective of the profession as an elaborate and costly, but apparently compelling, public relations exercise" (p. 175). In his turn, Hughes (1995), from his vantage point as head of a training and consultancy organization for law and accountancy, observes that "The usual type of CPD system operated by professional bodies, based on a quota of points and hours, is not effective in ensuring that members obtain CPD which is relevant to the needs of the clients they serve" (p. 75).

As a variant on what can be labelled as predominantly pedagogic objections of this kind, another set of criticisms relates to the bureaucratic limitations of mandatory systems. In this genre, Evans (1985) claims that his in-depth review of the literature relating to CPD supports his respondents' objections to the lack of quality control of provision and the absence of adequate monitoring of conformity. He concludes that

there is no evidence that practical performance has been affected by MCPE [Mandatory Continuing Professional Education—in this case for lawyers]. What has emerged is a system which appears to place more emphasis on participation than on sound educational principles. New bureaucracies have developed, bureaucracies which are costly and increasingly intrude on the autonomy of the individual professional. For all these reasons MCPE, as it exists today, cannot be justified (p. 42).

Jewell (1991) complains more specifically of the "fatuous insistence" of the Department of Health that GPs' study time should be equally divided "among the wholly arbitrary categories of practice management, prevention and disease management" (p. 54) and further chastises the Department for the bureaucracy of its course approval and evaluation procedures. Woodward (1990) shows a related concern about the Law Society's CPD program, observing that in a single year (1989) the paperwork dealing with accredited courses in a large solicitors' firm filled eighteen lever-arch files, and speculating on how much space the Society must need to house the paperwork arising from its nationwide accreditation of training events.

A more extensive critique is to be found in the Lord Chancellor's Advisory Committee's First Report on Legal Education and Training (1996a) in the section on "Continuing professional development":

> our solicitor respondents consistently identified two main defects in the current system of CPD. First, it was said that CPD is often seen simply as a "numbers game" in which a number of points or hours have to be collected. CPD places a cost burden on firms, and often a financial strain on smaller firms, resulting in courses being selected for their cheapness rather than for their value to the individual trainee or law firm. Secondly, CPD courses are widely considered to be of variable quality or at inappropriate levels, and to be overpriced. There is a lack of specialist courses outside London. The system of accreditation and monitoring of standards is said to be inadequate (§6.29, p. 96).[4]

A brief diversion to review the developing scenario in North America may be of interest here. Abernethy (1994) offers a starting point in his claim that continuing medical education in the US is a statutory requirement, involving attendance at 50 hours of lectures a year, "very much bums on seats" (p. 644). Yet a decade before this comment, Phillips (1983) referred to a recent resolution of the American Medical Association calling for a moratorium on mandatory continuing education and on any mandatory reexamination or recertification programs, pending further study of their value in assuring competence. In 1987, the same author noted that, in a context in which individual states were entitled to demand mandatory continuing education, 47 had done so for accountants, 36 for pharmacists, 21 for physicians, 20 for lawyers, 3 for engineers, and 1 for architects (Phillips, 1987): not, one might say, at that stage a clear justification for the reference by Cross (1981) to the "rising concern about blanket legislation that would require continuing education in the professions" (p. 42).[5]

More recently, McKee (1997), referring to the impending introduction of a compulsory CPD program by the North American Institute of Architects, noted that it called for 18 hours a year, as against the existing requirements for lawyers of 12–15 hours and for doctors of 25–50 (the latter figures at the upper end being not too far removed from those for their U.K. counterparts): any member of the Institute failing to comply would be "deemed inactive." McKee records a catalogue of doubts, familiar to British practitioners, relating to the erratic coverage of subject matter, the narrow range of provision, and the lack of quality control in reliance on an "honor system." He also notes a concern on the part of the Institute to stem defections. If one detects in all this a stronger transatlantic emphasis on compulsion, it is more a nuance than a clear-cut case: there is the same sense of disputed validity and the same apparently random variation in requirement as between one profession and another. However, it seems clear that professionals in both Britain and the U.S. share what Nicholls and Hind (1996) identify as a general antipathy to compulsion.

Providing and Implementing CPD

Whatever the particular policy adopted by the professional body concerned, there remains the issue of how the policy in question can be put into effect: how an appropriate training program can be made available and how conformity to it can be monitored.

In relation to formal learning requirements, there is commonly a variety of course providers in any given field. For the most part, the professional body concerned sees it as its responsibility to organize at least a basic range of courses; many activities are generated within the profession itself; others are provided by commercial agencies set up for the purpose; and there may also be a marginal involvement by related university departments. Most of these providers, inevitably, draw on the limited pool of people who are knowledgeable and experienced enough to count as experts in their subject.

The professional bodies are in a difficult position, in that the courses they put on are seen by participants as in some sense officially approved. They therefore tend to be judged critically and often to be found wanting. A number of my respondents commented that CPD activities generated from this source, among others, were either run by people with specialist knowledge but no teaching skills or those with teaching skills and no specialist knowledge. Maintaining a uniformly high level of quality is particularly difficult when an effort is made to avoid an excessive concentration on the geographical area in which the professional body is located—London, in the case of the six professions, and most others in the U.K. A more widely distributed regional program usually relies, for both practical and political reasons, on the initiative of local branches, so attenuating the degree of control that can be exercised by central headquarters.

My interviews brought to light a surprisingly large proportion of self-help provision, especially in law and accountancy—both proce-durally-based professions in the terminology put forward in chapter 1, whose practitioners would hence be particularly responsive to general surveys and specialist updates of a broadly codified field of knowl-edge. These two professions, as noted in chapter 2, have given rise to very large firms, whose combined resources enable them to run their own training departments and to provide many of the CPD programs needed by their staff from their own resources:[6] one respondent (L/21) compared his firm's in-house scheme to "a free university for trainees."

Small and medium partnerships in law and accountancy who lack the funds and the personnel needed to maintain a facility of this kind are able to take one of two choices. They may either buy in to the pro-grams put on by larger firms (the latter are often ready, in terms of public relations as much as anything else, to open most of their courses to practitioner colleagues from smaller organizations) or join in con-sortium arrangements with comparable partnerships. The latter choice is generally adopted by provincial practices—often spanning a wide geographical area—in view of the scarcity of large firms outside met-ropolitan centers. Training consortia of this kind can also serve other useful functions, such as negotiating lower insurance costs to mem-bers, generating inter-firm specialist groups, and opening up wider so-cial and professional contacts.

Commercial firms occupy another niche in the training market. In order to survive, they have to be competitive with the provision made by professional bodies and the professional firms themselves. They tend to achieve this by energetic and carefully designed marketing, the choice of attractive venues, the identification of topical themes, and the cooption of well-established and reputable members of the relevant profession as presenters. Not all commercially run programs achieve every one of these desiderata, and are the more fiercely criticized when they fail to do so, particularly as their costs tend to be high in relation to those of other providers.

University departments do not feature prominently in CPD provi-sion. Their main contribution is through the offering of advanced quali-fications (see chapter 4) and through occasional short courses on spe-cialist developments and techniques. In medicine, it is the Royal Colleges that take the lead in the specifically technical courses charac-teristic of continuing medical education (CME); there are a handful of references in my data to university-based CPD courses in law, accoun-tancy, and engineering; and virtually none in architecture. Pharmacy offers a contrasting case in point. Aside from a number of updating programs for community pharmacists run by university schools of pharmacy in their regional areas, there is in England a major, officially funded Centre for Postgraduate Pharmacy Education based on the University of Manchester which provides a nation-wide pattern of course offerings. Another source of provision, in both pharmacy and medicine, is the pharmaceutical industry. Drug companies clearly see a commercial advantage, as well as some benefit in terms of public relations, in putting on informative presentations related to their products.

Across the range of providers and topics in each profession, there is an extensive choice for those wishing to embark on formal development activities: Cervero (1988) provides a useful tabulation of providers' strengths and weaknesses (p. 88). Those who attend them, because already by definition highly educated, tend to be severe in their judgments of merit. A fairly frequent complaint, among professionals in private more than public practice, and among those in small firms rather than large, concerns the time and cost involved in course attendance. A rough norm of £300 to £500 a day (at mid-1990s prices) was quoted for commercial course fees—which, taken in conjunction with earnings foregone, could amount to a substantial sum. Perhaps because of this, few courses are designed to occupy more than two and a half days at most, and some are packed into a half day or an evening after work. Some are run as a series, often weekly, of short sessions on the same broad topic.

When it comes to courses put on by professional bodies, the costs may to some extent be subsidized by the income from members' subscriptions. This, together with the fact that large firms provide and pay for their own staff training, led to the comment by one respondent that the smaller firms are subsidized by the larger, both because they are the main beneficiaries of low-cost CPD from the professional body and because, in addition, many of them are given access at favorable rates to the larger firms' provision. Even so, the cost to small firms, and even more to sole practices, operates as something of a disincentive. For some practitioners in the public sector, it must be said, there is an easing of the burden. In medicine, GPs are in effect fully subsidized through a postgraduate education allowance payable on completion of a year's CPD requirements; this is a source of some irritation to hospital consultants, who may or may not—depending on the financial situation of their employing hospitals—have basic travel and attendance costs paid for. Community pharmacists also compare their absence of compensation for earnings foregone unfavorably with GP provision.

Drumming up enthusiasm for formal training activities in general can be an uphill task, especially where the imposition of a compulsory scheme gives rise to widespread resentment. Neither of the proverbial alternatives of offering the carrot or wielding the stick seems to have proved fully effective. Positive incentives include the establishment by the Royal Pharmaceutical Society of a College of Pharmacy Practice, intended to be seen as an elite group of practitioners whose membership requires a certified minimum of twenty hours a year of continuing education: but as one of my respondents pointed out, it had only attracted a small number of pharmacists and was not generally recognized as an important body to join. Another approach, adopted by the Institution of Structural Engineers, is to make the award of a Fellowship conditional on active involvement in CPD over the previous five years: but this stipulation no longer obtains after the Fellowship has been awarded. As noted above, GPs have to fulfill their CME obligations in order to qualify for their postgraduate education allowance, which seems the most powerful incentive of all. The take-up rate is correspondingly high (Kelly and Murray, 1996).

At the other end of the scale, examples of sanctions to ensure conformity are provided by the Royal College of Obstetricians and Gynecologists, who have established a publicly available register, updated annually, of Fellows and Members who have met the stipulated requirement of 200 credit points over a five-yearly cycle, and by the Royal College of Physicians, who maintain a similar register, available to prospective employing bodies, and provide those who meet the specifications over a five-year period with certificates of participation. The Lord Chancellor's Advisory Committee (1997) refers to the possibility of both the solicitors' and the barristers' professional bodies calling on "the major sanction of withdrawal of right to practice," but ameliorates this by allowing that "It may also be possible to devise lesser sanctions" (§2.25, 2.26, p. 26).[7] The concluding paragraph of the Committee's 1997 report refers to the need for "active and sustained intervention by the professional body to ensure the profession's progress towards adequate CPD" (§4.32, p. 43). This injunction is addressed specifically to the Bar Council, given that "The Law Society's compulsory scheme has already brought real advantages to the solicitor's branch of the profession. The Law Society appears very much committed to further progress" (§4.30, p. 42).

Individual practitioners are however quite capable of brushing aside the efforts of their professional bodies to define their best interests and determine their needs in relation to continuing education. One modest but indicative example was offered by a community pharmacist (P/8), whose testimony made it clear that she was quite active in keeping in touch with new developments. To inspire its members to higher achievements, the Pharmaceutical Society had issued a free year-planner for CPD. The respondent, in mentioning this in passing, remarked that she had found it useful as a bookmark. A solicitor commented that "it's hard to take CPD seriously, because you don't get marks for relevance: nor does the Law Society police the standards of lectures" (L/5).

This last comment points to one of two particular problems occasioned by a compulsory CPD policy. If professionals consider themselves to be under duress to complete training requirements, they generally see it as reasonable for the professional body responsible for enforcing that policy to ensure that the courses provided or recommended are of a satisfactory standard. That expectation may place a heavy demand on the training department concerned in calling for course specifications from other providers far enough in advance to allow for the completion of approval procedures and the distribution of details to the members of the profession or sub-profession at large. Life is simpler under a laissez-faire system in which it is necessary only to "wander through the supermarket" (L/22) to make one's own choices and to take personal responsibility for them.

The second difficulty that arises in the context of mandatory program is to ensure practitioners' compliance with their requirements. In the case of any but the smallest membership groups, demanding and examining documentary proof from every individual every year that the necessary numbers of hours have been clocked up or points accumulated would demand an impossibly large workload. Some professional bodies have compromised by requiring the necessary evidence but only sampling the returns. Others have gone for the weaker solution of self-certification, under which practitioners merely have to confirm in writing that they have fulfilled the stipulated requirements.[8]

Practitioners' Attitudes and Motivation

There have already been a number of indications in this chapter of the views of professionals in relation to CPD. As in any articulate and thoughtful group of people, attitudes can differ sharply, though sometimes the differences relate less to divergences in underlying values than to dissimilarities in working context.

The data from my sample confirm the comment by Hughes (1994), that "European architects...tend to work in small practices and they have been severely affected by the crisis in the building sector and the resulting unemployment. Both these features contribute to their low average take-up of CPD" (p. 29). She adds that "The attitude of architects towards CPD is a serious problem. The main cause of non-participation is the view that CPD is not necessary" (p. 44).

A clear instance was given by a woman practitioner working in a two-partner practice:

> In fact we do have, as they probably told you, a continuing professional development requirement now from our body...It was voluntary. I think it is about to be, or perhaps this year supposed to be, more than that. But they would only know if you hadn't if they came and inspected, basically. And one would then perhaps fill in bits of paper which say "well we did do this, and we did do that"...I'm afraid I'm not terribly up to date with it. I've got it all here. I've looked at the stuff that they send out but it's not always what I'm interested in (Arc/10).

Another informant (Arc/29) considered it "appalling that it [CPD] is necessary", and found the demand for it "a demoralizing sign of the times." He did not dispute the contention that continuing learning must be at the heart of a professional's responsibility, but considered it entirely inappropriate to formalize it. A third (Arc/16) echoed the same sentiment, claiming to be "slightly cynical" about the RIBA's policy, "because in a good practice you ought to develop professionally anyway": being of the old school, he had gained his own professional skills from building buildings. He added, with a touch of superciliousness, that engineers, being very qualification-conscious, were much more amenable to CPD requirements.

An engineer's response, made quite independently, belied the accusation:

> Well, I think we're all aware that you're supposed to be doing some formal CPD but, apart from the fact that I've got the booklets somewhere in my drawer, that's about as far as I've ever actually got to reading it, because to me CPD is something set up really by people who envisage a situation where an engineer is actually working one discipline in a big company, county council, civil servant—he never gets exposed to anything other than what he sees day in, day out, coming across his desk, whereas in reality in a company like [this]—which is why I'm here—every day is a new element of career and professional development. To have actually gone on to my five day's worth of CPD in a year...yes I could have done it, but it wouldn't have really meant very much. It would have just been ticking the box and saying you've been on a few courses. Getting involved with it first hand is far more rewarding (E/17).

This view is by no means unanimous in either architecture or engineering. A number of respondents, even if critical of the existing arrangements, supported the concept of CPD. For example, one architect (Arc/20) contended that people should keep up and maintain their skills—provision should not be too structured, but the current RIBA scheme was not structured enough. Similarly arguing in favor of formal requirements, an engineer (E/3) claimed that "if you're a professional it's your duty to keep up-to-date." Compulsion would prevent one from getting in a rut: "in the present climate, you have to change or die." A second engineering respondent (E/15) thought that CPD was important, but that it would be of more value to him, as head of a medium-sized firm, if it allowed scope for courses on marketing and accounting.

Nevertheless, a sizeable majority of interviewees in these two professions were at best lukewarm about and at worst overtly hostile towards the formalization of professional development—noticeably more so than those in the other four. It would seem, from their explanatory comments, that they considered their professional work to have a strongly practical bias, largely unsuited to enhancement by conventional lectures or other mainly verbal forms of provision. This would accord with their designation in chapter 1 as processually based professions. One might conjecture that the reasons why respondents in the third profession in this category did not reflect a similar view were that medicine, being the most heavily academicized profession, is more amenable to formal training, and that, apart from surgery, most medical specialisms have a high, rapidly developing factual as well as theoretical content calling for systematic CME.

But again, the pattern is not a homogeneous one, in that medics have their own criticisms to offer. Al-Shehri et al. (1993), in their review of provision for GPs, make the telling comment that "the uptake of continuing medical education may not be a valid measure of competence-oriented learning by general practitioners" (p. 253). That is a useful reminder of a point which advocates of formal training are prone to overlook, or to sweep under the carpet: that learning and teaching are not opposite sides of the same coin, since teaching can occur without learning and learning without teaching. The same sentiment was voiced by one of my GP respondents (M/11): "when it comes to professional skills, you can't organize that sort of teaching; and the other thing is that the person has to be receptive. If you're not in a receptive frame of mind, you're not going to learn anything." Another GP turned academic (M/22) saw "brownie point collecting" as one of the drawbacks of CME:

keen members of the profession take it seriously, but the less keen go for easy options and are liable to sleep through lectures.

The question of the relevance of programs to practitioners' needs was raised by a number of respondents: "No one I've ever spoken to goes on them" said one (Arc/11) dismissively. As Dowlatshaki (1996) notes in relation to engineers, "the importance placed on continuing education programs is moderate...the continuing education needs of the respondents are either marginally or poorly met."[9] Davis and Fox (1994) observe that doctors have "the perception that 'CME' consists primarily of didactic activities or programs unrelated to clinical settings or outcomes (p. xi)."

If one looks for reasons why people do or do not pursue CPD, the available literature offers some clues. Pitts and Vincent (1994), enquiring into why a group of GPs registered for a course but failed to turn up, concluded that the decision not to attend resulted from work pressures rather than antagonistic attitudes towards continuing professional education. The Royal College of General Practitioners (1990), never neglectful of public relations, identified "two main incentives for participation in continuing medical education, one fostered by the nature of the doctor/patient relationship and the personal satisfaction of performing well as a doctor, and the other from the intellectual stimulus of discussing one's work with one's colleagues" (p. 35). Armytage (1996) supports more directly my contention that professionals are strongly motivated to go on learning by considerations of collegial esteem and the maintenance of a good reputation, remarking that "judges possess unusually high levels of pre-existing professional competence, they are rigorously autonomous, they have an intensely short-term problem-orientation, and they are motivated to pursue competence for its own sake rather than for profit or material gain." In extension of the point, Partington (1994) refers to "a remarkable change" in the attitude of the judiciary towards more systematic training, citing it as "another example of the stealthy evolution of the English legal system" (p. 335).

In response to all the doubts and caveats, a chartered accountant in a very large firm advanced a staunch defense of the concept of CPD. He began by pointing out that all the larger accountancy practices have well-developed training schemes, and all of them work to a higher standard than that specified by their professional institute. That institute's policy, therefore, has little application or relevance to such organizations. However,

It seems to me that the [continuing education] requirements, taken in the context of the small practitioner, where there would be no in-house training provision, where there is much greater risk of the guys not being kept up-to-date...have a very different application.... There are a lot of changes coming through and therefore if we are going to get those changes bedded down over a very short time scale, you've actually got to do some fairly intensive training to get that consistent message.... I would be horrified if we abandoned our technical training programmes, because I think our quality would suffer (Acc/11).

A second respondent had a comparable concern with maintaining the quality of professional work, and a far-reaching suggestion about how that quality might be ensured:

I think what we probably need to come into this country is a system similar to the one that they have in the States, whereby you all have to show that you have attended a certain amount of postgraduate ongoing education. At the moment it's done informally: [consultants] have up to 2 weeks' study leave a year, but nobody monitors whether you take it or not....here am I using potentially life threatening drugs—ought I not once a year to be grilled on whether I know what I'm doing? And that is quite a terrifying thought (M/2).

Aspects of Course Provision

A similar range of conflicting views emerges when the focus of attention is shifted from continuing professional development as a whole to its constituent elements, of which courses of one kind or another are the most prominent. Training courses were perceived in a drearily depressing light by some interviewees, including one (L/5) who admitted frankly that "I hate courses." She detailed her nightmarish, recurring vision of a day lecture program put on by a high-pressure commercial organization in an airless, overheated room, unconsciously echoing Nowlen's (1988) portrayal:

In what is typically an intensive 2- or 3-day short course...fairly large groups...sit for hours in an audiovisual twilight, making never-to-be-read notes at rows of narrow tables covered with green baize and appointed with fat binders and sweating pitchers of ice water (p. 245).

However, even if this stereotype holds for a significant proportion of courses, others are able to project a more attractive image. One of the salient characteristics of my data on course provision is their huge variety and range: not only across professional and sub-professional groups, but in terms of duration, functions and purposes, styles of presentation and types of locale. At one end of the scale, one may come across short, one-off lectures on new aspects of the law or new regulations in accounting, or after-work evening programs on professional topics for community pharmacists. At the other, one may find extensive weekly or monthly sessions for GPs on topics such as family therapy, or intensive annual weekend programs for judges on sentencing policy and related issues, and for tribunal chairs on strategies for handling difficult cases. Three- and four-day courses, though less common, exist for putting across complex techniques in surgery, learning how to use new materials in architecture and structural engineering and the like.

The purposes served by such courses are usefully summarized by Sparkes (1984). Although he refers specifically to continuing education in engineering, his taxonomy seems to apply quite aptly to the other five professions: promoting awareness of new developments; updating, particularly in specialist areas; upgrading (i.e., leading to more advanced qualifications, including academic awards); and practitioners' courses focusing on skills and know-how. Unless the last of these items is interpreted very broadly, it is necessary—given the lapse of time since the list was compiled—to add contextual courses dealing with wider non-technical issues, such as the development of management capabilities and the enhancement of relationships with clients. These and related topics will be reconsidered at a later point in the chapter. The theme of upgrading, touched on earlier (in chapter 4) falls into a rather different category from the rest, since it usually calls for sustained involvement in an award-bearing—and therefore assessed—program over a sustained period.

Within this range of purposes, CPD provision is by no means confined to traditional lectures. Respondents mentioned a variety of other forms of learning activity, including more participative methods such as role play and the use of case studies. Multimedia presentations comprise another attempt to enliven the content of conventional teaching. Distance learning plays a particularly significant part in community pharmacy, where the sole practitioners who form the majority of the sub-profession find it difficult to combine their long working hours with attendance at updating courses. Audiotapes and videotapes may be used either as components in correspondence courses or as forms of communication in their own right. A heart surgeon (M/10), for example, mentioned a widely subscribed series of tapes, produced by the American Council of Cardiology, containing useful up-to-date information about his specialism which he played in his car on the way to work; and an accountant (Acc/7) in a small four-partner firm commended the regular video training presentations, bought on subscription, which were viewed by all the professional members of the firm fortnightly over lunch. Compact discs are a more recent addition to the armory of alternative modes of structured presentation of course materials.

Partly in response to these developments in presentational technique, the locations in which courses are presented have also become more diverse. In large firms, in-house courses, often in designated training centers, predominate; professionals in small firms rely mainly on external provision. Distance learning and the use of discs, videos, and audiotape may bring the classroom into the home, the office, or the car; even in more conventional programs, informally appointed seminar rooms may replace the "rows of narrow tables covered in green baize" portrayed by Nowlen in the quotation above. At times when the exchange rate is favorable, one medic (M/22) remarked, quite a few courses are organized in attractive locations overseas: "it's cheaper to go on a package to Cyprus than it is to stay in a hotel in Bournemouth."

Some respondents took a highly positive view of courses, seeing in them major professional benefits. Among the sample represented in my research, the accountants emerged as particularly enthusiastic proponents. One remarked that going on a course

> builds up that body of knowledge [so that if] at some point you are faced with a new challenge, instead of having to ask and going to scrounge around and look for information you can just say 'I've got the notes from that course tucked away, I'll go dig those out.' So it widens that body of knowledge that you've got and hopefully it covers you for more situations of change that you inevitably face (Acc/3).

An engineer (E/3) also adopted a generally positive attitude, but qualified it by stipulating that course attendance "has to be need-driven: you need to know in advance what the course is actually about, and the content has to be specific to be useful."

A GP was less concerned with assimilating knowledge as such, and was in fact critical of a didactic approach, but welcomed the opportunity to interact with colleagues and to stand back from the daily routine:

> I love it [going on courses].... There are two aspects to it...not only what you are learning from the course but meeting other GPs as well and preparing notes, and talking about practices and moaning about the government or something; forging contact and perhaps making new friends or whatever it is, so it's a double pleasure if you like. People sitting in front of me talking at me like lecturers used to do, filling me with biochemistry or pharmacology or something—I just switch off completely, but when you're involved yourself...you can actually think about what you are doing. Whereas when you are doing it, sitting there day to day seeing the patients, you don't actually have time to do that. It's actually very refreshing. Extremely tiring I may say. At the end of a week's course I'm probably more tired than I would be at the end of a week's work (M/5).

One problem, identified by a number of fellow-GPs, was that some courses seemed to be geared to those who were neither interested nor motivated. Compulsory course attendance did not, as a result, have the required effect on the "bad apples," who took the opportunity to use their postgraduate education allowance for "Glaxo lunches" (a coinage in the profession for lavishly provided but undemanding sessions sponsored by drug companies). An officer of a professional association (M/0), acknowledging that formal courses did not necessarily meet the needs of lively and conscientious members of the profession, nevertheless claimed that they could help to ensure minimum standards: "What else can you do with the people at the bottom end who don't want to take account of change?"

Respondents from diverse professions put forward somewhat negative views. A community pharmacist in a small multiple firm (P/10) found the courses he had attended, put on by the Centre for Postgraduate Pharmacy Education, to be "very time-consuming and not always helpful." A solicitor in a small urban practice (L/10) complained that the courses she had attended involved "nearly all talk and hardly any workshop or practical activity." An engineer argued that in a highly specialized field the leading proponents can gain little from formal courses, in that they already know what there is to be known:

> it's the people we know, the people we talk to, the people we work with, handing out information that they've already given us, that we've used on jobs in the past. Once you get into a specialised field, there is very little available…to keep people up-to-date with what's going on, because the level at which we need it is generally above that level at which it's commercially viable—it's at the front of research almost (E/7).

The element of cost in CPD activity has already been mentioned as a potential drawback. It was objected by some senior partners in some of the smaller professional firms that course attendance, even where it might be of benefit to the individual concerned, was of little collective benefit to the other non-participating members of the organization, and was not therefore evidently cost-effective. A number of partnerships had however developed a strategy to ameliorate the problem, at least to some degree, by requiring any colleague returning from a course to make a detailed presentation of what he or she had learned to those who had not had the chance to attend it.

The evanescent character of courses was cited as another problematic issue. An industrial pharmacist (P/7) noted that, even after a useful course, "you get sucked back into your job, and although you may be fired up you are soon put back in your place. If you don't put what you learn into practice, it soon goes away." A management accountant (Acc/4) observed that those of her colleagues who went on a time management course "soon reverted to type when they came back." And along the same lines, a consultant surgeon, recollecting the courses which had made an impact on her, commented:

> I think one of the most memorable was the week I spent at the King's Fund [a major non-profit organization concerned with medical education]...you thought 'This is great, I shall come back and it'll all be wonderful'. Within a week or two you thought 'Oh dear, I really can't understand any more than I could before' (M/8).

She added that a course was only useful if one could apply its results shortly afterwards.

A similar comment was made by one of the lawyers interviewed by Gear et al. (1994) in their study of professional learning:

> I have been on courses which dealt with aspects of immediate concern to me, but quite often it's a question of going on a course and thinking, oh yes, that would have been extremely useful to me about six months ago. I wish I'd known that then (p. 68).

A structural engineer, working in his own practice (E/11), also referring to the question of putting new learning outcomes into practice, invoked a familiar saying: "If you don't use a skill you lose it." Following on the same idea, a senior architect in the planning department of a large local authority (Arc/19) had adopted the principle that "you should never learn anything until it's clearly a disadvantage not to know it." These various considerations lie behind the advocacy of "just-in-time learning," explained by an accountant (Acc/15) as the development of new skills at precisely the point at which they need to be applied. Unfortunately, course provision—as noted above—rarely dovetails so neatly with need.

Contextual Courses

In the case of some professional bodies, the only recognized form of continuing education comprises technical courses, dealing explicitly with the subject matter of the profession in question: any activity which relates to wider contextual questions is, accordingly, sidelined and discounted. In actuality, however, it would seem that contextually oriented courses are rated by practitioners as being more important than technical ones. Besides the extensive evidence supporting this claim from my interview data, Sherr's (1993) pilot study of eight solicitors from varied backgrounds, carried out for the Law Society, is of particular interest. Among the skills noted by them as calling for further learning, the related topics of staff supervision, personnel management and general management were accorded six out of a total of sixteen responses. In contrast, among a scatter of specifically legal issues, advocacy was mentioned twice and European Union Law only once.

Management, in one aspect or another, is a significant element in the training needs of most professions, especially—as might be expected— at the more senior levels. Anderson (1989), anticipating Sherr's findings, emphasizes the importance of training in effective personnel and practice management for solicitors. He singles out personnel-related skills such as interviewing clients, effective delegation, communication, and teamwork as being the more important for having at least until recently been neglected at the prequalification stage. At the practice level, he identifies marketing and staff appraisal as key aspects in the professional development of partners. A professional body related to architecture, the Royal Town Planning Institute, draws an even wider net to encompass business and financial planning, managing uncertainty and stress, staff management, and information technology.

As a consequence of the frequent politically inspired changes in the structure of the National Health Service, both hospital doctors and general practitioners have found themselves drawn inexorably into taking on managerial responsibilities. Many of them, conscious of their lack of previous experience, saw the need for more systematic training. A GP in a medium-sized local Health Center emphasized the point that he and his colleagues needed:

> more structured training in certainly financial and managerial aspects…if our colleagues in industry knew the budgets that GPs are dealing with and having to spend, and the amount of money we're spending with absolutely no training, they would be absolutely horrified (M/7).

The consultants' point of view was expressed more tentatively by another respondent:

> most of my management training has been by osmosis rather than by taught course…that probably is regrettable because I think there are aspects, particularly if you are managing a fairly large group of people with a fairly large expenditure.… To be involved in the direct management of that, I think one would be better to have some concept of how people do things in other organizations (M/18).

The training deficiency here would seem to be the consequence more of lack of time, money, or motivation than of absence of opportunity. The consultant just quoted prefaced his comments by remarking that he had twice been offered a place on one of the relevant King's Fund courses, but had been unable to take up either offer because of pressure of work. Similar assertions were made by other medical interviewees. The available provision in this field seems generous by comparison with that of the other professions. Besides a wide range of well-regarded short courses organized by the King's Fund, respondents referred to a diversity of other training programs provided by Imperial College, the Industrial Society, the Regional Health Authorities, and the Royal College of General Practitioners. There are also two more extensive and ambitious programs offering MBAs geared specifically to the needs of medical managers, both organized on a modular basis to allow for different levels of commitment: one is sponsored by the British Medical Association and the other by a more recently established organization, the British Association for Management in Medicine.

In pharmacy, a certain amount of in-house management training is available for senior staff in large firms in the pharmaceutical industry; similar provision in community pharmacy is mainly confined to headquarters staff in the bigger multiples. Hospital pharmacists, who—like their medical counterparts—have begun to take a larger share in management activities, are relatively well provided, though largely reliant on distance learning techniques. One interviewee in a large teaching hospital (P/30), for example, had been given the opportunity to take an MBA through the Open University which had had the effect, in his daily work as a senior manager, of "making things seem very easy."

It will be evident by this stage in the discussion that my interviewees were in general possessed of a healthy scepticism. Few issues were taken for granted: on most of them, at least some respondents had a critical point to make. Management training was no exception. A solicitor (L/4) had four different reservations: that the quality of courses was difficult to judge; that they were often very expensive; that she was wary of management jargon; and that it was not in any case obvious that training was necessary in order to be a manager. An engineer (E/29) picked up the last point in remarking that "basic commercial awareness is a talent and not a skill."

Management as a general concept is broad to the point of amorphousness: that may in part lie behind the reluctance of some respondents to involve themselves in training programs. But even when it came to discussing more specific aspects of the subject, some hesitations remained. Only two people in the sample mentioned attending courses on team building. In this instance, both were favorable. The first (Arc/6) was sent on a weekend residential course, as one of a group of six colleagues, involving several mini-lectures, videos, and question-and-answer-tests: "We learnt about ourselves and our partners, found our strengths and weaknesses—it wasn't technical training." The second (Acc/14) recalled a very different experience, involving a three-day management development activity in the Lake District, run by ex-policemen, which he reported to have been enthusiastically received by both the senior managers and the partners in his firm. Time management courses were also mentioned by a few respondents, one of whom, a management accountant (Acc/4), was quoted in the previous section. Her comment about the short-term effectiveness of the learning experience was corroborated by an architect (Arc/12) who remarked that a recent in-house course in his firm had seemed effective for a couple of months, adding that "things haven't relaxed entirely, but there's been a good deal of slippage."

Developing effective presentation skills is seen as particularly important, understandably enough, in professions which have in some sense to sell themselves to their clients: particularly architecture and engineering, and perhaps to a lesser extent law and accountancy. A solicitor (L/4) had found a short course on public speaking useful, but would have liked it to be at least twice as long: she felt the need for further guidance on self-presentation, if only to help her "in these days of beauty parades and touting for jobs, to know what is the state of the art." The barristers in my sample were also concerned with improving their self-presentation, though not by going on courses—"everyone is aware now of the need to be more user-friendly" (L/7).

A senior official in the Institute of Chartered Accountants, reporting on the current situation in his profession (Swinson, 1991), portrays an ambivalent response among its members:

> One of our recent efforts has been to change the basis of education and training in our Institute to move from the all knowledge based scheme, to a scheme that takes account of...[i]nterpersonal skills, communication skills, and so on.... We can get these through the large commercial firms, there is no problem, but the tail end of our small members, which is pretty enormous, is very difficult to move on this point. They do not believe that we should move away from the traditional knowledge base which they claim is at the core of accounting (p. 18).

A substantial proportion of the respondents in engineering—most of them from large or medium-sized firms—mentioned that they, along with a number of their colleagues, had experienced various types of training in self-presentation, confidence building, public speaking, client relations, and the like. There were some passing suggestions that it was more important to know and have good rapport with one's clients than to be able to charm them with deliberately cultivated techniques, but on the whole the reactions were favorable. A typical comment, from a senior member of a sizeable firm (E/14), was that engineers had to be good at communicating, but that many members of staff, though highly intelligent, had given little thought to self-presentation. Accordingly, the firm had sent groups of ten people at a time on two-day training courses on the topic. Another more junior respondent (E/18) had had the support of his employers in attending an extensive program involving attendance for four hours a week over a twelve-week period and covering a wide span of topics, including stress reduction and memory improvement.

Architects were in general comparably positive about this form of training. One of the largest U.K. practices had, in the calendar year before my interview with its senior partner (Arc/30), sent between 40 and 50 staff through a complete course in presentation and report writing. Another interviewee (Arc/6) had recently been to a one-day course of novel design run by two American actresses. All twelve participants had had to give a speech on a specified topic and were videotaped doing so. Each performance was reviewed critically by the other participants and the actresses then mimicked it. "At the end of the day," he added "we were all fairly pleased." A third (reflecting a point made in the previous section about cost-cutting strategies) added to the series of enthusiastic responses:

> I went with two of my partners and one other senior person on a two-day presentation skills course which was very, very interesting because however good one thought one was, when you have been all through that and seen the video...it sharpened up our presentation and I found that extremely valuable...as a result of that I have given two or three in-house talks on that to other groups in the office. If one was feeling rich, one would have sent these people on the course as well [laughter].... Intellectual property and that sort of thing (Arc/1).

There were voices of dissent nonetheless. A founding partner of a medium-sized firm priding itself on the quality of its work (Arc/13) contrasted his own colleagues, all of whom he saw as "committed and at the forefront of the profession," with "people in firms which are commercial with a big or a small 'c'." While the latter, being more concerned with public relations than with professional work, might need to be trained to attract commissions, clients came to his partnership by recommendation and needed no blandishments to do so. For a quite different reason, another architect reacted strongly against an RIBA course he had attended several years ago on self-presentation:

> It was for me, personally, a deeply disturbing experience…it was actually a terrible mistake. I think I formed a wrong view of what it was I wanted to learn, but it took me some time to realise that…. Now I'm better [at presenting myself] than I used to be—but it was nothing to do with the course (Arc/3).

He commented that he had never been on another course since.

It is scarcely surprising that the contextual courses remarked on by the professionals in my sample echo the main pressures for change discussed in chapter 3. The advent of managerialism has provided the main impetus for the various management courses to which reference was made earlier in this section, much as the change in client attitudes has spurred the growing concern with training in presentational and marketing skills. Another factor identified in chapter 3, the rising tide of computerization and information technology, has also triggered off an interesting series of perceptions of training needs and possibilities.

The nature of the response to the challenges and opportunities opened up by information technology depends on various factors. The character of the profession in question is obviously one; the range of its activities another. The size of partnership can make a significant difference, as can the ages of the professionals concerned. Some issues are common to all six professions under review, while others are specific to particular fields or specialisms. It will be easiest, for the purpose of exposition, to look at the common features first.

The most evident, and perhaps the most surprising, feature revealed by the fairly extensive interview data on the subject is how little is called for in the way of formal computer training. The limited demand was attributed by many respondents to the user-friendly, straightforward, and comparatively unsophisticated character of most of the commonly used facilities and their associated programs. Introductory courses were widely available, but many of them were of quite short duration: in some cases they lasted only a couple of hours, while at a maximum they might run for one or two days. The larger firms often provided in-house training, while the smaller ones tended to rely on bought-in or external training expertise. A strong thread could also be discerned of "handed-on knowledge" (M/24): as one GP (M/7) explained, "one of my partners showed me the right buttons to press." Colleagues who were already knowledgeable, or who had gained the necessary knowledge on a course, seemed willing without hesitation to share their particular skills with other members of their firms.

There was also, however, a staunch tradition of self-help. Reference was often made to the possibility of picking up new techniques by playing around, learning by trial and error, or working things out on the job. This process of independent learning might on occasion be reinforced by access to suppliers' helplines, built-in training programs or accompanying manuals. But however the necessary knowledge might be acquired, "you can only," as one architect (Arc/24) pointed out, "become competent in information systems by both learning a lot and doing a lot." Regular involvement is called for to keep in touch and stay up-to-date.

The departures from and exceptions to this shared pattern of experience are relatively few. As might be expected from the discussion in chapter 3, the volume of the training need is greater in medicine than elsewhere, because the profession was slow to latch on to the possibilities of information technology. But even here, although the number of professionals striving for greater familiarity with the subject is large, the amount of initial training required by most individuals seems generally modest. In industrial pharmacy, fairly extensive training may be necessary for specialist applications. One respondent (P/9) had recently followed training courses in computer graphics, quality control procedures, purchasing and stock control, and the firm's raw materials safety system. Another, who had enjoyed a highly versatile career, was required to take a three-week course and a subsequent examination when she left her industrial pharmacy employers to work in an international computer company as a liaison consultant with pharmaceutical responsibilities. Advanced courses in computing are also available for hospital pharmacists under the auspices of the National Health Service, though a beneficiary of three of them (P/18) claimed to have remained technophobic.

The lawyers among my respondents presented no significant aberrations from the norm, but accountants would seem more amenable than their counterparts in other professions to formal training courses lasting for one or two days. The limited evidence from my interviews suggests that this may be related to the complexities of computer-based auditing systems. Architects and engineers—see chapter 3 again—have access to special facilities for computer-assisted drafting and computer-assisted design (commonly referred to as CAD). While learning how to exploit the former is relatively easy, needing only two or three days to pick up the essentials, the latter presents many more complexities. An architect (Arc/16) commented that the CAD system installed in his medium-sized firm was far from user-friendly and needed about three months to master. Two structural engineers (E/13 and E/17) independently estimated the timespan as six months. They were however apparently referring to a state of full expertise in the techniques, as against a lower-level working competence.

Management training, client-oriented courses, and the achievement of familiarity with information technology were the main examples of contextual programs to emerge from my interviews. There was however one theme of minority interest worth singling out from the rest, in that it may come to seem more generally relevant as the unification of Britain with the rest of Europe begins to have an impact on professions other than architecture and engineering, where nearly all existing instances of it are to be found: namely the learning of another language.

As noted in chapter 3, it is the architects and the engineers who have shown the greatest interest in developing connections and entering into commitments outside the U.K. This has been almost entirely the result of the catastrophic recession in the construction industry in the late 1980s and the early 1990s, which led many enterprising firms to avoid extinction by actively canvassing work opportunities abroad. Europe usually proved the easiest option, both in cultural and geographical terms, provided that the inevitable language barriers could be overcome. For understandable reasons, it was in nearly all cases the larger partnerships who felt able to invest in the necessary resources to tackle the problem.

The two strategies most commonly adopted were predictable enough: namely, to build on and improve the existing language skills of key practitioners, and to buy in the necessary language expertise. Some firms played safe by doing both. As noted in chapter 3, a partner in one of the top ten U.K. architectural practices in terms of size (Arc/25) remarked that, in the twelve months before my interview with him, twenty percent of its income had been from overseas: however, because it had existing in-house language skills it had not on the whole sent people on language courses. In an even larger multidisciplinary firm, the job leader in a recent linkup in Germany was encouraged to go on an appropriate language course, but the firm had also recruited German architects into the team. The interviewee, one of the senior managers of the partnership (Arc/17), remarked that he would have liked to develop his own language skills but had been unable to find the time to do so. His counterpart in another large firm had gone further than merely to express an aspiration:

> I've learnt German. I have somebody who comes here twice a week for 4 hours in total and I try to fit my homework in with everything else. And yes, I listen to tapes as well. Extremely difficult it is, you can't just go in there…, there are subtle points and you have got to be lucid in the language. Having a sort of working knowledge of it is nonetheless helpful but you've got to recruit proper German speakers (Arc/1).

In structural engineering, a similar picture emerged. According to the founding partner of a medium-sized firm (E/8), twenty percent of the staff were currently working on a major project in Berlin, and the firm had accordingly organized in-house language lessons in German. In anticipation of similar developments it was also providing tuition in French. The respondent himself, however, was not involved in either activity. A larger firm which incorporated several other professions alongside structural engineering gave its staff "strong encouragement to learn a second language" (E/26) but did not provide them with the time and money to do so. An earlier program of lunch-time courses with bought-in tutors had been discontinued for financial reasons. The current policy was to encourage staff interchanges with joint venture firms in the country concerned as a directly practical form of accelerated language learning.

If there seems something slightly half-hearted in many of these ventures—as compared, say, with the warmer enthusiasm shown by members of the medical profession for management training and by architects and engineers themselves for self-presentation courses—there was at the time of my interviews virtually no interest at all in language learning evinced by members of the other four professions. In fact, among the total of 128 respondents in medicine, pharmacy, law, and accountancy, only one—an accountant in a three-partner firm (Acc/1)—volunteered that another partner had been taking a course in French, even though "the links with Europe are not too relevant at the moment." None of the other interviewees made any mention of languages in their discussions of contextual learning. If surprising, this is perhaps understandable in the light of the comments on internationalization in chapter 3.

The Margins of Formality

The discussion up to this point has focused on different kinds of formal provision of CPD, including both technically and contextually oriented activities. It is evident that if a points system, or its equivalent in hours spent, has been adopted for calculating the minimum requirement for any given group of professionals, structured programs of this kind can be readily fitted in to the specified bureaucratic pattern. The number of hours occupied by a particular public event, whether a longish course or a shortish lecture, can be straightforwardly recorded and checked, and the attendance of the professional concerned can be certified (though, as mentioned earlier, this procedure can say nothing about what learning if any has taken place). It is, however, much less easy to account for less formal or private engagements in continuing education, of the kind to be discussed in chapter 7: a state of affairs which seems particularly unfortunate since, as will there be argued, such engagements occupy a prominent part in all professional learning.

Be that as it may, one concession is made by all professional bodies, however constrained their designation of acceptable forms of CPD, in relation to what are at best semi-formal and loosely structured activities. These, usually designated as conferences and seminars, have a superficial similarity to formal courses and lectures, but internally reflect a quite different constitution. The terms are not consistently used, but what are meant in this context are activities run by members of the profession itself—as against commercial or other external providers—in which the input is also professionally contributed. Would-be participants in some conferences are allowed to compete for a slot in the program by submitting their proposals for papers to a panel of selectors. The theme may in some cases be quite general, but in others highly specialized. The content usually comprises a single set, or a number of parallel sets, of papers on more or less related topics, but the structure, because it is not as deliberately planned as a course would be, lacks close articulation. The duration tends to be longer than that of a typical course, running usually from two-and-a-half to four days, or more rarely five. Seminars are much shorter, covering a day or half-day, and with fewer participants. It is however the expectation, as in conferences, that those attending will take an active part, offering their own input to the discussion rather than remaining passive listeners, as in typical lectures or lecture courses.

These characteristic features of conferences carry certain implications. In particular, they tend untidily to open up rather than neatly to pin down professional issues. The point was succinctly made by one of the interviewees in the study by Gear et al. (1994):

   ...you can actually get quite narrow-minded by picking the brains of your consultant colleagues, because that's only four or five people, and then you'll go to a

College meeting and you'll be meeting consultants from all round the country who will express widely different views and expect people to have a debate on it (p. 66).

Because, too, the contents are not bound together in a tight sequence, it is not difficult to skip a particular session which seems unpromising: the intellectual fare is provided on an *à la carte* rather than a *table d'hôte* basis. This gives rise to a much easier possibility than on an orthodox course to "sit back and skive" (M/8). It also seems evident from the interview data that reasonably regular involvement in professional conferences serves to mark off, in terms of the useful distinction by Gouldner (1957), the cosmopolitans from the locals—that is, those who enjoy a wide reference group as against those confined to a narrow circle. In common with attendance at courses, it can help to reinforce existing professional contacts and to initiate new ones. Participation in international conferences is, moreover, a symbolic marker of status, and at the same time offers a valuable opportunity to enhance one's reputation in the field.

As in so many cases in professional practice as a whole, there are interesting variations between the professions in respect of attitudes towards conference-going. The hospital doctors are unquestionably the most energetic participants in the genre. One informant (M/22) described a five-day conference in the U.S. from which he had recently returned as comprising some hundred different 15-minute contributions, sledge-hammered across at the rate of twenty a day. One important attraction is clearly the sense, in a carefully chosen event, of finding oneself, as a consultant, "at the rolling edge of the subject" (M/10), and being able to keep abreast of the latest research findings. A less serious-minded general surgeon (M/8) explained that international conferences were normally arranged in attractive locations, "just to cheer things up." The roll call of venues mentioned in my interviews with medics bears out the point: it included (in alphabetical order) Antwerp, Montreal, Munich, Paris, Prague, Rome and Sydney. For general practitioners, there seem to be few such opportunities, in part because they lack the research funding which could help to pay their conference fares and fees. Even in hospital medicine, the conference pickings go to the consultants rather than to their junior colleagues, though in a couple of cases mention was made of taking along one or two promising research fellows to help launch them on their careers.

Among the other professions, none stood out particularly strongly as supporters of professional conferences, perhaps because, as one senior engineer (E/0) explained, they "don't contain as broad a range of roles as medicine": the degree of specialization is not unconnected with the incidence of conference-going. In pharmacy, even the hospital pharmacists showed little evidence of shadowing their medical counterparts, while community pharmacists were evidently more interested in attending short courses and lectures than in participating in the annual British Pharmaceutical Conference organized by the Royal Pharmaceutical Society. Some brief mention was made, however, of conferences catering for particular interest groups such as the Young Pharmacists and the pharmacy advisers employed by the National Health Service to keep an overview of drug provision in each region. It was only the industrial pharmacists who offered much evidence of involvement in conferences, with one respondent (P/21) recording that her employers supported her attendance at two or three meetings of international professional bodies each year.

Lawyers pleaded the constraints of time and cost in extenuation of their limited involvement: as one (L/11) explained, "solicitors don't go in for long programs." Seminars were allowable, but the same respondent dismissed conferences as "really just little jollies." Nonetheless, a senior solicitor in a large urban authority (L/26) commended the Local Government Group of the Law Society for its useful three-day annual conferences, and a solicitor in a medium-sized provincial firm (L/28) remarked that he had recently been to a conference in New York on anti-trust laws and to another in Brussels on mergers. None of the barristers I interviewed made any reference to conferences. This seems to be squarely in the tradition of one of the few remaining professions composed of one-man or one-woman bands, to which collective activity is largely foreign, and in which to suspend fee-earning professional activity is necessarily to forego income. The accountants in my sample, like the lawyers, preferred to involve themselves in shorter and cheaper seminars, though one regularly attended the annual conference of his professional body, the Institute of Chartered Accountants, while another planned to take part in a conference on international taxation, to be run in San Francisco, organized partly as a public relations venture by a large international accountancy firm. The two professions in the construction industry showed a similar profile. Apart from an architect who had participated in a one-day conference at the RIBA on sheltered housing and an engineer who had been to an international conference in Deauville on aspects of bridge design, there was a general silence about collective professional activities of this kind.

Conferences, though lacking the formality and close structure of courses, share with them the potential benefits of helping practitioners to catch up with new developments and—though to a lesser extent—to acquire or reinforce professional skills and develop contextual capabilities. How far such potentialities of formal and semi-formal CPD are realized is another question. Evaluating them is not a straightforward matter, since neither courses nor conferences are sharply isolated from everyday professional life, and such learning as takes place may not be solely attributable to them.

Where evaluation is attempted, the verdict is not unequivocally favorable. Thus Wergin et al. (1988), in a telephone follow-up survey of 102 participants in CME programs organized by the American College of Cardiology, found that the changes they brought about were ones which "reflect refinements of clinical practice rather than radical alterations in patient care" (p. 155). They went on to comment that the process of change is typically continuous and incremental, and that CME is most effective when it occurs in conjunction with other sources of influence such as local colleagues. A similar finding emerges from another study, by Davis et al. (1995)[10]: "Widely used CME delivery methods such as conferences have little direct impact on improving professional practice. More effective methods such as systematic practice-based interventions and outreach visits are seldom used by CME providers" (p. 700).

The suggestion that stand-alone activities in formal CPD are less effective than those undertaken in conjunction with informal approaches was borne out by a number of my respondents, but in particular an architect who had successfully completed both an MBA and a PhD:

> The way of working which incorporated learning—action learning is what I call it—had become basically second nature and I've actually refined that a great deal, particularly through the MBA where—you know—the cycle of actually doing and learning...computing is quite a good example of that. Where necessary I took courses way back in the early 80s when actually part of that was my PhD research. I had to do all my number crunching on a PC and PCs had only just come about then. But I learnt a lot from going to formal courses, a lot of self taught work, I often had little projects going which were not mainstream work projects but which were, you know, developing my own learning in particular areas (Arc/24).

The motivation to learn, shown to a high degree by this respondent, is one of the key issues in considering the effectiveness of both formal and informal CPD. As Tough (1971) points out, "Most adult learning begins because of a problem or responsibility or at least a question or a puzzle, not because of a grand desire for a liberal education" (p. 72). The evidence in support of that assertion deriving from my literature search and interview data is set out in the next chapter. Its general theme is the one—all too characteristically—"not touched on" in a series of detailed case studies of continuing education in architecture by Harris and Rymer (1983), namely "the independent learning going on outside formal CPD provision."

Notes

1. The statistical tables in the same publication show that, in 1996, nearly one-third of the solicitors on roll (28,822 out of 87,081) and a comparable proportion of the barristers on record (5,288 out of 17,279) were women (Lord Chancellor's Advisory Committee, 1997, pp. 99 and 101).
2. Something of the same attitude emerges in Griffith's (1983) account of education and training in engineering, where he contrasts continuing engineering education unfavorably with "training, [which] has as a goal the development of task-specific competencies for immediate professional practice...training is job- and task-oriented , with strong emphasis on 'how-to' procedures and techniques" (pp. 70 and 71).
3. It would be no more than speculation to suggest that, in enjoying the highest status (see chapter 2), practitioners in these fields may consider themselves to have more personal authority to lose and a stronger existing base to defend than their counterparts.
4. It seems curious, to say the least, that the same Committee's Second Report, issued just over a year later, should apparently have ignored this evidence—and should further have overlooked the relevant and easily available findings of recent research—in its unequivocal demand for a compulsory CPD program for lawyers.
5. However, a more recent survey (Lord Chancellor's Advisory Committee, 1997) records that 38 of the U.S. mainland states had by 1996 adopted some form of mandatory requirement for continuing legal education (CLE), and only 11 had by that time failed to do so.
6. Some exceptions mentioned were management courses and those dealing with highly specialized topics: though even in these cases some firms bought in the trainers rather than farming out the staff concerned.
7. It is possible to interpret this uncompromising stance as evidence of the Committee's irritation with the supine response of the Bar Council to the consultation paper on CPD circulated in 1996.
8. It should also be remarked that professional bodies have no formal jurisdiction over those holding professional qualifications but working in other roles than that of standard private practice. Such individuals are free of the obligation to undertake any CPD except that required by their employers. The proportions in this category can be quite substantial: for example, in 1996, they were around twenty percent for solicitors and slightly higher for barristers (Lord Chancellor's Advisory Committee, 1997).
9. His study was based on responses from engineers in 378 firms in Midwestern US.
10. Their findings derived from a review of 99 studies of continuing education in the health professions published between 1975 and 1994.

7

Informal Learning

Some Basic Considerations

In contrast to the deliberately structured types of provision discussed in chapter 6, informal learning manifests itself as a natural by-product of professional activity. In the context of medicine, Jennett et al. (1994) usefully characterize it as including "journal reading, *ad hoc* conversations with colleagues or recognized experts...interaction with pharmaceutical or equipment representatives, attendance at regular CME [Continuing Medical Education] events (such as grand rounds), preparation for lecturing or writing..." (p. 52).[1] These and other cognate activities will be reviewed later in this chapter. First, however, it may be useful to consider how significant a role informal learning can play in professional life, how it relates to the familiar (but none too precise) distinction between theory and practice, how far it is susceptible to planning, and how far it takes an explicit as against a tacit form.

Many of the respondents in my study seemed inclined to play down the value of formal course provision in comparison with the learning undertaken on their own initiative as part of the natural ebb and flow of their professional lives. They were not invited to quantify the relative importance of each, and made no attempt to do so. The research literature, however, contains a number of examples of quantitative enquiries into the issue. Most of them were conducted during the 1980s, when such studies were more fashionable than they have subsequently become: as noted in chapter 2, investigations into medical education are prominent among them. In the event, they indicated with some consistency that practitioners relied more heavily on informal sources than on organized continuing professional development.[2]

But given that this evidence points to the significance of informal, self-directed learning and serves to cast some doubt on the contribution of formal courses in maintaining professional competence, it is easy to

FIGURE 7.1
The Informal Learning Tree

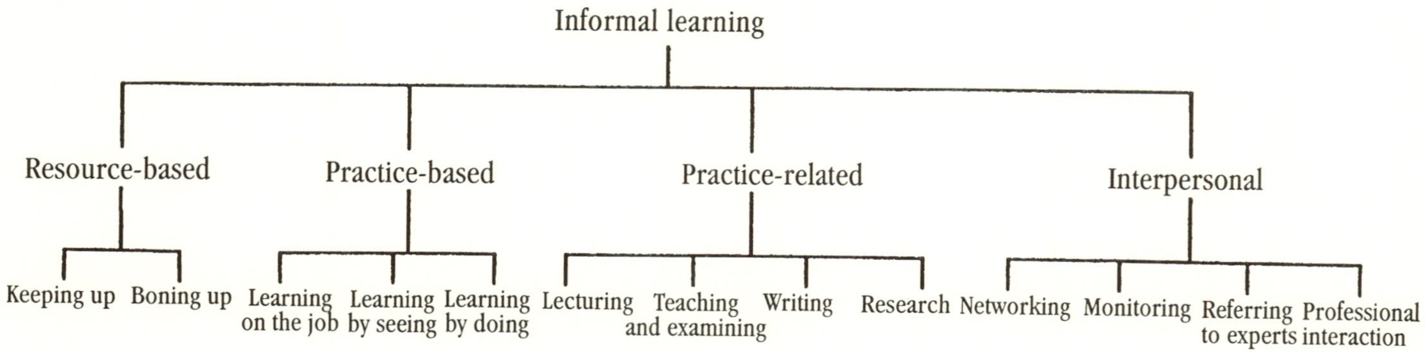

predict the responses of those concerned to promote more structured CPD provision. In the first place, the findings might be dismissed as out-of-date: the context of professional work has changed a great deal in the intervening years, and conditions in the late 1990s bear only a distant relationship to those in the early to mid-eighties. Secondly, a large preponderance of such enquiries are based on a North American constituency, whose traditions and legislative frameworks are different from those of the U.K.: that consideration may be held to cast doubt on comparison between the two settings. Thirdly, some questions may be raised about the research methods employed in such enquiries, and scepticism voiced about the spurious precision of the results (with percentages even in some cases embellished with decimal points). And finally, it might be said, the actual behavior of professionals is no reliable guide to their needs for continuing education and development. A proper assessment of such needs has to be made from a more independent and impartial standpoint.

Be that as it may, the way professionals think and act in relation to maintaining their capabilities and their reputations constitutes an important starting-point for would-be reformers. There is a substantial body of research, to be noted only in passing, which suggests that reforms cannot effectively be implemented in a top-down manner, but instead demand a bottom-up approach, starting where the potential beneficiaries are, and patiently enlisting their acquiescence.[3] One might expect this to be especially the case where those involved are generally well-educated, self-confident, and independent-minded people. It is therefore worth giving some attention to the actual response of professionals to the new demands which face them and the new problems they encounter, as a counterpoint to what may from an external perspective be deemed as necessary aspects of professional development.

The well-worn distinction between theory and practice, though relevant, does not quite catch the difference between formal and informal approaches, in that not all formal learning is theoretical, while informal learning, though predominantly practical, can also give rise in some of its manifestations to theoretical understanding. To complicate things further, while the theory-practice contrast seems familiar enough at first glance, on closer scrutiny—as with so many aspects of cognition—it emerges as having a variety of possible interpretations. Among the classic formulations are Ryle's (1949) dichotomy between "knowing how" and "knowing that" and Aristotle's more complex set of distinctions between *theoria, praxis,* and *poiesis* (the theoretical, the practical, and the productive), well explained in Squires (in press).[4]

Cervero (1992) is in no doubt, as far as the professions are concerned, that "the primary goal of continuing education should be to improve professionals' ability to engage in wise action," adding dolefully that "we have witnessed the delegitimisation of practical knowledge in favor of abstract knowledge" (p. 98). Addis (1990) conducts a wide-ranging discussion of the theory-practice divide in the education and training of structural engineers, and similarly laments the dominance of engineering science and the consequent neglect of design as a central element. In his turn, Griffith (1983) comments that "most continuing education…is an abstraction of general principles speculatively applied in practice. There is too little simulation of practice or curricular development drawn from observation" (p. 70).

These commentators seem more concerned to give formal training a strongly practical slant than to take into account the role of informal learning in the development of professional expertise. A somewhat different range of considerations emerges from my interview data. A senior accountant (Acc/30) noted "a very interesting balance…the difference between awareness and skills," going on to observe that "I must have been on three or four kinds of courses on computer awareness, and played around, but it wasn't until I rolled my sleeves up and decided that I was going to do something with this wretched machine that it became much more comfortable." So from his point of view, the informal, hands-on involvement was a crucial element in the process of coping: as an academic pharmacist (P/23) put it, "competence to practice and breadth of knowledge are two separate things."

Other respondents noted the distinction between their initial training, which they saw as largely theoretical, and their subsequent experience in the world of practice. Speaking of the step "from being a student who had been through the educational mill into becoming a consultant" in structural engineering, one interviewee (E/26) referred to "using your educational training rather than engineering training. So one was still quite young, still questioning and I did a learning process, there's no question about it. During that stage, one is very receptive to being involved in a learning process rather than an application process." The context makes it clear that he was contrasting the informal acquisition of the know-how needed to become a consultant—"a learning process"—with the application of the formal knowledge acquired in going through the educational mill—"an application process."

Along the same lines, a recently qualified accountant (Acc/10) referred to her experience in acquiring an additional qualification as an insolvency practitioner:

> I think when it came to the final exam and going on the crash course, it was very much: this is the exam technique you need to get through this exam, regardless of whether it's going to make you a good insolvency practitioner. I'm quite happy to accept that, and I realised to get the qualification I wanted I needed to pass an exam...passing an exam and being good at your job are very often two different things. So I was quite happy to sit down and do it exactly the way they wanted me to, whether I thought it was practical or not.

Here again, the implication is that theoretical knowledge, conveyed and tested by formal procedures, needs to be differentiated from the practical skills demanded in "being good at your job."

For some respondents, theory is to be consciously avoided. One accountant (Acc/29) declined to go to courses on the management of working capital, on the grounds that they were put on by theorists. A less drastic position was adopted by another accountant (Acc/11), who had earlier in his career been responsible for his firm's training activities. Referring to a formal induction scheme for recruits from universities, he noted that a number of the associated training materials were "akin to learning by doing," and that their emphasis was always on the link with practice. Similarly, he reported that management development training had moved away from formal programs to group work, with the instructors becoming more like consultants. Here, then, was a case in which the ideal strategy was taken to be informal, practical learning, to which more formal provision was required to approximate.

But even if it is conceded that informal learning activities constitute an important element in maintaining professional standards, there is a line of argument that the informality needs to be contained within some kind of formal structure: that is to say, that learning needs to be systematically planned. Jewell (1991), for example, while critical about the then current policy governing continuing education for general practitioners, and stressing the need for them to take responsibility for their own provision, nevertheless calls for each of them to plan a coherent program rather than attending "a random selection of courses" (p. 512). A more limited measure of systematization was advocated by one of my respondents, in talking of the desirability of working out long-term solutions to the problems he encountered:

> The textbook in the manager's office...goes into some areas which you wouldn't exactly call bedtime reading, but nevertheless for an accountant it's written in highly

readable language. It introduces the element of debate about the subject and the theory as well as saying this is what is good practice. I found that quite enlightening...just to take some time and go back to basics, to use that awful phrase, read it, work it out, plan it, take into account the practical problems and come up with an organised plan of how to do it. (Acc/3)

Most professionals, however, do not seem to operate in such a tidy way. Gear et al. (1994), in their interviews with members of six professions (having a considerable degree of overlap with those covered in the present study) concentrated on various aspects of informal learning. The report of their research notes that "Less than a fifth [of the learning projects recorded] were described unequivocally as having followed through a pre-determined plan. The learning process proved not to be the kind of linear, step-by-step process conventionally associated with formal education and training.... Serendipity was clearly a significant factor" (p. 27). Their illustrative quotations elaborate the point:

> I don't get time to sit back and think what do I want to learn about next. You're driven by whatever problem, or whatever situation arises, and if something comes up and you think 'I'm vulnerable in that area', I'll try and develop the skills to answer it. (p. 32)

> Yes, well you start and then you see what you get and then you follow it where it takes you. You certainly don't plan, because you are not sure what you are going to find. (p. 36)

An example from my data advances the further argument that

> specific jobs require specific skills and so when they do come up I will gen up on them then...But I couldn't sit down and say, now I really need to understand this or that...there are so many things that I didn't know about: it would be an endless task. (E/9)

Informal learning, it would therefore seem, tends to relate quite strongly to the practical as opposed to theoretical aspects of professional knowledge, arising largely in response to circumstances rather than as a result of deliberate planning: when it comes to formal learning the opposite characteristics seem dominant. Another difference between the formal and the informal lies in the observation that the first is by definition explicitly articulated, while the latter is not necessarily so. What Polanyi (1967) referred to as tacit knowledge is not, with a few important exceptions, afforded much attention in discussions of "learning in the workplace," as Marsick and Watkins (1990) term it: as they contend, "an overriding interest in how best to organize learning through training has taken attention away from the natural opportunities for learning that occur every day in a person's working life" (p. 4).

A clear account of tacit knowledge is offered by Gerholm (1990) in relation to the induction of postgraduates into academic research:

> Any person entering a new group with the ambition of becoming a full-fledged, competent member has to learn to comply with its fundamental cultural rules. This applies also to academic departments. To function smoothly within the group of teachers, fellow students and secretaries, the student needs a considerable amount of know-how. Most of it will be acquired slowly through the interaction with others and without anyone ever making a deliberate effort to teach the newcomer the rules of the game. Nonetheless, failure to comply with these implicit rules will undoubtedly affect the student's standing within the group (p. 265).

In contexts other than the academic, Hanlon (1994) gives considerable prominence to the notion, remarking that "An accountant's training is not really about developing technical expertise, although this obviously is a factor, it has much more to do with becoming acceptable, trustworthy, commercially aware or whatever other term one cares to use" (p. 215). One of my respondents (E/9), taking up the notion of the implicit rules of the game, remarked that learning professional behavior and parlance "comes with experience, not on a course." Another (M/27) commented that, in picking up how to conduct oneself, it was important to notice what key people didn't do, as well as what they did.

Having now considered a number of the salient general characteristics of informal learning, we may usefully turn to examine some of its more specific features. For convenience, these can be grouped under four broad headings: resource-based, practice-based, practice-related and interpersonal activities.

Resource-Based Activities

The great Samuel Johnson gave it as his opinion that "Knowledge is of two kinds. We know a subject ourselves, or we know where we can find information on it." Both kinds of knowledge are relevant to professional practice: here we shall be concerned with the second. The finding of information is dependent not only on the availability of sources but also on the facility to exploit them. An important set of skills consists in the competence to learn how to learn, the capacity to teach oneself, and the capability to know where to look.

Powell and Banks (1989), in their study of a group of research scientists, quoted a respondent as remarking that "What I brought from university is mostly an ability to learn rather than a set of facts in my head...factual information is lost so quickly anyhow. The only thing worth learning is where to look it up" (p. 36). A number of my respondents reinforced the notion that an academic training fosters this particular talent. An architect (Arc/15) observed that, for the most part, he kept up to date by self-learning (which was how, in any case, his university time was spent). A consultant physician (M/15) developed the point:

> if you depend on being spoon-fed and you don't train yourself, then as medicine changes over the years you haven't learnt how to adapt and learn for yourself...it's throughout the whole of general medicine, the whole of my working life, that as things change, techniques develop, I'm happy to take them on because I've taught myself all the way. So I can continue to teach myself.

Besides enabling them to learn how to learn, two interviewees in particular saw an academic training as enhancing their analytic skills. The first, an accountant (Acc/29), held that "your degree teaches you to look in a structured way at problems." The second, a hospital consultant who had recently completed a higher degree in medical law and ethics, advanced the view that

> It made me much more able to think and articulate and construct logical arguments. In my professional work I've become more effective as an analyst—not necessarily as a communicator, but I'm much less sort of passionate and trying to beat people down in arguments. I dismantle the logic of people's arguments now because I've had a bit of a legal training and I find that actually I've become more effective at talking to people (M/14).

Both these abilities—to learn for oneself, and to approach issues in an analytic way—are essential to the business of exploiting sources of information. But what have been grouped together here under the label of resource-based activities clearly depend, as noted earlier, both on the skills of the enquirer and on the availability and accessibility of relevant data. It soon became evident in the course of my investigation that such data existed in abundance: indeed, that in some instances its voluminousness constituted a serious problem. Because the nature and extent of the key data sources varies from profession to profession, it seems appropriate to review each of them in turn.

Medical practitioners are largely dependent on journal publication. The staple diet of most doctors is the *British Medical Journal*, but there is in addition a substantial number of other general and specialized publications: one consultant (M/15) commented that to do justice even to the publications in his own field would call for a whole day each week. There were also occasional references to textbooks; and a number of hospital and community doctors acknowledged publications by drug companies as another relevant source.

In comparison, pharmacists have access to a much wider range of information. Although the number of journals is relatively limited, there are standard textbooks covering a variety of topics, and several regularly updated reference sources, including the *British National Formulary*, which is issued every six months. As in medicine, drug company publications provide an additional body of information. There are also various microfiche and computerized databases. The library of the Pharmaceutical Society provides a further back-up system, as do networks of information centers on drugs, poisons, and other topics.

There is a comparably heavy reliance on textbooks in law, supplementing the traditional dependence on journals. A number of respondents read the *Times Law Reports* as an effective way of keeping in touch with current developments. More basic, long-term references include compilations of statutes and cases, and sourcebooks on rules, procedures, and legislation. There are various databases on CDROM, along with a number of computerized databases (the general view was that these were more expensive than useful). The Law Society Library is an important reference source: and many chambers and large solicitors' firms have extensive library collections. Some of these firms issue their own periodic newsletters and information digests.

Accountants, with predictable economy, make extensive use of "tasters and summaries" of current developments in their professional journals, in newsletters, bulletins, and weekly updating circulars. But they also have recourse to textbooks, databases on disc and CDROM, research publications from professional bodies ("not big sellers"—Acc/0), and reference books. The latter include a handbook setting out accountancy and auditing standards which is revised every two years. Two respondents had made use of updating videotapes marketed commercially. Professional bodies were cited as a useful source of information. Those working in large firms had access to in-house libraries and technical departments.

Architects display a very different pattern of information-seeking. Their main source of ideas and inspiration lies in looking at relevant existing buildings, rather than in having recourse to the written word. However, many respondents commented on the excellence of the Royal Institute of British Architects' library, not only for its large book collection but also for its half-a-million drawings, its million or so photographs, and its comprehensive CDROM digest of architectural journals. Other reference materials include magazines and journals, trade literature, and videos. Only a very limited use appears to be made of textbooks and standard reference sources.

Finally, structural engineers, like their architectural counterparts, claim relatively little reliance on written sources: looking at buildings, maps, and drawings constitutes an important part of information-gathering. Some passing reference was also made to journals, trade publications, directories, and official documents, including codes of practice. One heavily research-oriented firm had established an on-line data link with a nearby university. Another claimed to make extensive use of the RIBA's comprehensive information system, on CDROM, about building materials.

Two comments in particular are called for on this very brief conspectus. First, in support of the taxonomy elaborated in chapter 1, pharmacy, law, and accountancy emerge as more strongly dependent on an extensive information base than do medicine, engineering, and architecture. This is in keeping with their designation as procedurally based professions: one might expect those engaged in activities strongly conditioned by procedural formulae, precedents, and rule-bound constraints to draw more heavily than their processually oriented counterparts on manuals, reference texts and compilations of relevant data. Second, although the overall profile of source materials differs from one profession to another, it has to be emphasized that there is an additional dimension of diversity, in that individual practitioners manifest their own distinctive patterns of use of such materials. The observation by Bucher and Strauss (1961) that "the journals a man reads, in any branch of medicine, tend to reflect his methodological as well as his substantive interests"[5] (p. 328), applies not only to medicine and not only to journals.

The ability, then, to teach oneself, or learn by oneself (often, as it seems, promoted by an academic training) is one key element in resource-based activities, and the ready availability of adequate resources is another. The next questions to be addressed relate to the purposes which are best served by such activities and the attitudes and concerns of those who carry them out.

Harking back for a moment to the discussion in chapter 6 about the main functions of continuing education in the professions, the evidence suggests that resource-based activities can—though apparently only to a limited extent—help in the development or enhancement of existing skills and capabilities; they may also play an important part in helping to solve particular problems, through a process of focused enquiry or background research; above all, however, they form an essential element in staying up to date.

This concern—to remain in touch with current developments in their profession—was voiced by many of my respondents. A predictable difference between generalists and specialists could be seen to lie in the range of coverage involved in keeping abreast of the literature. The former, understandably, tend to concentrate on publications offering regular summaries of what has been happening across a wide spectrum; the latter look to in depth accounts of significant findings in a more sharply focused range of journals and sourcebooks.

A tribunal chairman (L/10), reflecting on his responsibilities, regarded his lack of detailed expertise as one of the perils of being a generalist and so of having to keep up with many different branches of the law at once. An engineer saw no case for regret or apology in his role as a non-specialist in his company:

> if you're any good you should have an awareness—not a competence level but an awareness—of most of the potential disciplines into which you could have gone should you have chosen to go one way or the other at college. Going through your chartered process does actually theoretically set you up quite well for a diverse range of interests and, on the basis that you should continue to read and be interested in what's going on, then you should be able to walk into any discipline which is basically civil or structural engineering and be able to talk in a general sense to clients so that they realise that you don't know everything about it: but we work on the basis that we know a man who does (E/17).

In contrast, a specialist medical consultant commented on the difficulty, in a financially straitened Health Service, of getting hold of all the journals to which he needed to refer as he became more highly specialized. Many individual consultants, he considered, find it hard to keep up-to-date; and as a result, the more senior among them remain with the medicine of their day and tend to become steadily out of touch. A more positive view of the possibilities of remaining *au fait* was advanced by a barrister specializing in commercial law. Speaking for her peers as well as herself, she remarked that:

> Most of us do get the relevant journals, the relevant reports. We always have up-to-date textbooks. More and more the textbooks are the loose-leaf kind which are updated every month or quarter. It's not that difficult to keep up to date—to some extent, obviously, we don't know it all like that. But as soon as we get a problem, it's pretty damn easy to find what one needs (L/6).

There were those who showed some hesitation in spending the time needed to fit in the requisite amount of background reading: some of them admitted that they did so only as a result of strong peer pressure. There were predictable complaints at the excessive number of journals and the amount of rubbish published in them. Various strategies were described for coping with the load of reading to be done. The most obvious—and hence the most common—was to resort to skimming materials rather than reading them in depth. Others included drastically narrowing down the focus; introducing a regular routine of reading at least one article each day; or using impending retirement as a way of avoiding the obligation. Some respondents had worked out ingenious devices for incorporating a review of current literature into their mainstream professional tasks. For example, a consultant (M/14) had undertaken to provide periodic summaries of journal articles for a drug company, while a solicitor (L/11) had created "a strong incentive for keeping up" by agreeing to serve as librarian to her practice. In conformity with these general findings, but as a useful supplement to them, Huberman (1983) conjectures, on the basis of a study of classroom teachers, that information-seeking among professionals is directed towards readily available knowledge which pays off rapidly and which is guaranteed by other professionals.

Across all six fields, it has become evident that the pace of development and the accompanying volume of documentary information together exercise a kind of tyranny on those attempting to come to terms with them. A sole practitioner accountant (Acc/7) poignantly remarked, "it's a nightmare keeping up"; a medical researcher (M/0) commented on "the real danger of information overload." One of the scientific researchers studied by Powell and Banks (1989) put the position succinctly:

> I find the information explosion exceptionally difficult to keep up with.... I don't get much further than the abstracts in most things. It is very difficult to keep up with the discipline: there is too much else going on, too many demands on time (p. 38).

A lawyer working as a senior consultant in a large accountancy firm pointed out that it is impossible to read everything you might need to read and important to avoid becoming over-specific. It needs a lot of self-control to avoid getting submerged in the flood of available data. She had recently adopted an alternative approach to the problem:

> I had a briefcase full of stuff that I ought to look at and I took an executive decision...that this is crazy—that we have an increasingly efficient database on screen

if we need it. I also have 40 people out there, you know, one of whom is going to
know something about it. We have a technical backup and I've now got to the stage
that I've realised I've got to let go—I cannot expect to be able to know everything.
What I need to know is what is going on and where I can find the detailed information (L/24).

In other words, an encyclopedic database becomes an essential replacement for an encyclopedic mind: being able to access information becomes a substitute for being able to assimilate it.

This notion of selective culling of professional subject matter finds
an echo in many of my interviews. It seems especially prevalent in law
and architecture, but examples also occur in other fields. In conversation, it tends to be labelled in terms of "boning up" on an issue, or as
"doing research." The usage of the latter phrase needs to be distinguished from the sense in which "research" designates an academic or .
quasi-academic enquiry which is in some sense self-contained, designed
to explore an issue in depth and often leading to some form of publication. It is, in contradistinction, short-term, small-scale, and localized,
arising from or feeding into an identifiable professional demand.

As an architect (Arc/2) explained, when it comes to a new challenge—
such as the design of a research laboratory—you "bone up on the subject." In this way, you can acquire a new expertise for each job, hiring
specialists in where necessary to give added support. As another (Arc/
18) confirmed, every new job entails research, even though design is
an iterative process: you have to read up the appropriate regulations
and study the relevant background information. How the building operates will vary from one case to another, and needs to be understood.
You look at other buildings, engage in library research, scan magazines
and journals, and key into the latest thinking. You may also have to do
background legal research.

Many firms of architects are reluctant to be type-cast as specialists
in school buildings, offices, sheltered housing, or whatever. A partner
in one such, highly successful, firm put the point as follows:

Researching buildings is the essence of good architecture, and creating an innovative building is the most exciting area in which to work.... There's no necessary
virtue in looking at precedents in what other architects have done. And often, if
you start by drawing up a schedule of areas you miss the underlying philosophy.
You need to explore the total intention of the building. The components may need
researching too. Here you might have to bring in specialist planners—for instance,
theatre consultants if you're designing a theatre (Arc/7).

As one might expect from a profession which is quite distinctive in content, structure, and organization, the concept of research has a different embodiment in legal practice. The contrast can readily be brought out by citing a lawyer's account of marshalling a wide variety of arguments in a very short space of time:

> Doing litigation, I've had to be an expert in the baking of pies, the making of sausage skins, the whole question of how you can defeat pain by transcutanial electro-neural stimulation. I'm actually going to be arguing about whether a PCTV is actually a PC or a TV, whether iced tea should be zero rated...this wonderful collection of different things where I have to get a grasp for the facts, so it's fascinating...within a space of two days, you can become a really in-depth expert on something—and having absolutely lived it, three weeks later you might have sort of forgotten (L/24).

One can discern again here a significant difference between a generalist of the kind typified by the last informant and one who specializes in a particular area. A barrister whose work dealt exclusively with tax law put forward an alternative notion of research:

> The sort of questions which come to us, which are research type questions, are usually ones where there is a dispute...Your level of knowledge about the subject is likely to be such that you have a view as to what the answer is before you start your research...and probably what you'll do there is simply go and re-read the relevant cases.... You're almost certainly, in a specialist field, you're going to know the relevant authorities by and large. Also in our field the authorities only go back to 1875 (L/32).

A concluding comment from a solicitor provides a helpful resumé of how both initial training and subsequent experience can support the research process:

> One would hope that through having done a degree or worked for a while that you have at least, even if the field is unfamiliar, you have got certain skills as to research, or how you would set about finding things you don't know...Indeed, the longer you've done the job the more you can filter as to 'this is an important point and I must go and do my research about it'; 'This is not an important point' or 'I know from a case I've done before that this is how this should have gone' (L/9).

In summary, it has been argued that resource-based activities play an important part in helping to keep professionally up-to-date (though with the caveat that too great an abundance of information can prove overwhelming) and in contributing to the solution of problems through purposeful and closely defined research. The second group of activities now to be considered offers a clear contrast to the theoretically oriented, documentary-based concerns that have been the subject of this section.

Practice-Based Activities

A surprisingly large number of my informants commented on the extent to which they learnt new skills and developed new understandings in the ordinary course of their work. In each of the six professions, a similar message came through—though with interestingly different overtones, depending on the particular characteristics of the sub-profession or specialism concerned.

For example, two pharmacists referred to the move they had made from industrial to community pharmacy—one (P/7) temporarily, as part-time locum to earn extra money, and the other (P/11) permanently, in embarking on a new career path. Both were already well-equipped with the necessary technical background, and neither felt the need to go on a course: but applying their knowledge in a very different context involved, in their terms, "learning on the job." That particular phrase cropped up in interview after interview. As a barrister, "advocacy is a skill which has to be learnt on the job" (L/7); in accountancy, one respondent (Acc/6) learnt to specialize in insolvency in the same way, up to the point at which "it suddenly clicked." while another (Acc/20) reported adopting a similar approach to the intricacies of corporate finance. A traditionally inclined architect (Arc/4) complained that current professional training was over-theoretical, and hence that "the products of architecture schools don't know what a brick is—they're a complete liability and their technical expertise is non-existent—they have to learn mainly on the job." A consultant engineer (E/4) referred to a similar phenomenon: "You develop on the job through a gradual incremental process, learning from other people's mistakes, trial and error, literature, and seeing other colleagues at work." You sometimes notice the existence of new learning only in retrospect: but in any event, "part of the fun is pushing the boundaries out."

Other near-synonyms for this prevalent mode of informal learning include "learning on the hoof"; "learning by osmosis"; "learning by trial and error"; "learning by experience"; "learning as you go along"; and "flying by the seat of your pants." The notion of learning on the hoof is neatly exemplified by a fragment of dialogue with a chartered accountant who had recently carried out a major exercise in management consultancy:

[What you've described sounds more like a piece of organizational research than a piece of accountancy.]

Oh, it was. It was organizational behavior, it was management development, it was a change process.

[Where did you learn about that?]

On the hoof—plain and simple (Acc/11).

One of the researchers interviewed by Powell and Banks (1989) is similarly quoted as saying "I learned by osmosis.... It was a gradual process but very people-dependent" (p. 37). Lawyers seem especially prone to this approach. As a solicitor (L/1) explained, much of the subject matter develops gradually, so learning it is a matter of gradual absorption: confirming this, an academic lawyer (L/0) characterized the profession as "learning through accretion and absorption rather than radical shift." Referring with all the impartiality of a high court judge to current pressures for formalizing barristers' continuing education, one interviewee (L/3) noted that the profession had in the past relied heavily on on-the-job learning, with a strong tradition of informal support, but that this was now beginning to change. At a less exalted level, a member of the county court judiciary (L/8) observed that, in spite of the now quite extensive provision of training for judges, "ninety percent of my work involves flying by the seat of my pants." He went on to point out that, in addition to knowing the legal background, one has to develop "a general feel for the case—an instinct rather like that of a doctor for diagnoses."

Indeed, a major part of professional work goes beyond the straightforward application of standard routines. There are certain things (the same judge commented) that "can't be trained and don't need training." Among these are the personal qualities which often lead people into a particular line of work—advocacy, say, in law; insolvency practice in accountancy; restoration in architecture. For the most part, however, the necessary know-how may most effectively be acquired through what has here been termed practice-based activities. There is, said a solicitor (L/10) in a small firm, "nothing like having to learn as you go along." A sole practitioner in a community pharmacy (P/17) concurred that "you accumulate a lot of knowledge just through working."

A fairly strong thread of pragmatism can be seen to weave through professional practitioners' attitudes. It is well-exemplified in this interview with a senior partner in one of the larger architectural firms, taking up the subject of management training:

I've picked it up, basically. I did go on a marketing course and was doing PR and marketing. I actually have a theory that management is a lot of basically commonsense and…I'm astonished every day at the amount of literature I get at the moment for courses—personnel courses, human resources. I mean it's people as far as I'm concerned. Inter-personal skills—I think that means getting on with people, doesn't it? The jargon sends me absolutely round the bend (Arc/21).

Among professional pedagogues, there is an often-quoted Chinese saying: "I hear, and I forget; I see, and I remember; I do, and I understand." The implied condemnation of formal learning is, as chapter 6 has pointed out, not in reality justified: but the importance accorded to practice-based activities is amply confirmed in the interview data.[6] Among such activities, learning by seeing is a variant which is more noticeable in medicine and architecture than in other fields.

It was remarked earlier in this chapter, when referring to data sources in different professions, that architects depend heavily on looking at existing buildings in the process of coping with unfamiliar challenges and maintaining their expertise. One senior practitioner (Arc/2) claimed to spend his holidays looking at the work of great architects: "it gives you a particular vision of the world—you can see buildings…as answers to a problem determined by the site." "Architects," said another, "don't tell the truth about how much they look at other peoples' work…you look at buildings all the time. In London one is part of a huge conversation at the technical and professional level, forever looking at so-and-so's new building and discussing and critiquing it" (Arc/3).

The reason for the particular emphasis on visual learning was explained briefly by a senior partner in a large firm: "architecture is by nature an active, problem-solving discipline where you have to go out and see how the problem can be tackled" (Arc/30). The point is developed more fully in Cuff's (1991) portrait of the profession:

The architect's constant litany—that every problem is unique—is an appropriate response to an ambiguous situation. Knowing that problems and outcomes cannot be predicted, the architect emphasises "experience." As with the seasoned lawyer or the country doctor, direct experience with a range of problems is considered the best foundation for professional practice. Thus, although design problems may be unique and complicated, professional knowledge generalises from one problem to the next (p. 85);

and again, "Only with years of experience do architects become experts in, say, hospital design, or development projects. Experience will always play a significant role…." (p. 258).[7] For many of my respondents, both the generalization from one problem to the next and the progressive acquisition of experience were enhanced by examining the solutions adopted by other members of the profession. In the related field of structural engineering, too, "it's very important to look at what other people have done: there are very few new inventions, and most things derive from other ideas" (E/9).

The apparently similar emphasis on learning by seeing in medicine stems from a different source: as so often, the distinction lies in the contrasting characteristics of the professions concerned. All medics have a common initial training which entails some basic operational techniques on patients: giving injections, taking blood samples, and the like. Such techniques are clearly best acquired by imitation and practice, rather than by verbal instruction. So, traditionally, medical education has taken the form of "apprenticeship and the process of osmosis" (M/19); "Competent medicine comes from seeing, not from books—I didn't read any books when I trained" (M/25); "Everyone has to learn by watching somebody else" (M/0).[8]

Moreover, even practitioners who are newly trained in a particular technique may be called upon to pass it on to others. Parodying the speed with which assimilation and subsequent demonstration are expected to take place, a catch-phrase has emerged which played a prominent part in my medical interviews. It is "an old saying in medicine" (M/2) but one hardly calculated to reassure patients, so it is not in currency in the public domain: "see one, do one, teach one." Here is one of the contexts in which the slogan appeared:

> It has always been the case in medical training in this country that most of what you learn, you learn by picking it up as you go along…you're chucked in at the deep end as a medical student, you're chucked in and you have to check patients and you have to put up drips and things and you are just expected to know what to do. See one, do one, teach one—that's always been the philosophy (M/7).

Surgery is a branch of medicine in which seeing and doing play a prominent part. You pick up specialized techniques, a consultant urologist (M/9) explained, both by being told how they work and by watching them in action (nowadays there are even sophisticated camera systems that enable junior doctors to watch an operation involving fibre-optic-based surgery). At the next stage you practice part of the technique under supervision, and gradually build up to a complete performance. Another surgeon, specializing in the treatment of breast cancer, gave an essentially similar account:

> [In] almost any operation I would have done as a new one, I would have watched somebody else…I would have seen other consultants do them…. That's really the way one learns, and when the junior doctors are learning that's roughly [what they

do]:....they assist me with operations and then I get them to do a bit of an operation and one day they do all of it. Then they do all of it with me sitting outside—and so there's a gentle progression (M/4).

A more general variant of practice-based learning, which permeates other professions besides architecture and medicine, is commonly referred to as "learning by doing"—leading, in the optimistic terms of the Chinese proverb quoted earlier, to ultimate understanding. To quote one of Powell and Banks' (1989) informants once again: "I learn something new everyday. It may not be momentous but it makes me feel more and more able to do the job effectively. You can't learn that in a book—you have got to actually do it" (p. 39). A senior accountant in my study reflected that

the way you learn is by doing...there isn't that much in the way of directing of how to do things. You tend to learn by watching others. If you're not very observant, then you suffer (Acc/30).

The phrase "learning by doing" seems to imply a more directed or focused approach than that denoted by "learning on the job": the former suggests that the concern is with practicing some specific skill to the point of mastery, while the latter signifies a general stance towards professional practice as a whole. However, the distinction is not sharply drawn in the references to practice-based learning by my informants.

This general review of practice-based activities will, it is hoped, make it evident how pervasive a part they play in professional life, as well as suggesting how they can contribute to the different purposes which continuing professional development activities may serve. Their role in developing and extending practical skills is perhaps preeminent, in that resource-based activities would appear to make a stronger claim on the ability to keep up with current developments, and—as will be seen later in this chapter—interpersonal activities are particularly effective in the task of solving short-term problems.

Practice-Related Activities

There is another set of activities which can be quite clearly distinguished from those that have been considered so far. The distinction lies at least in part in the fact that they are not so much practice-based as practice-related: that is to say, they are carried out, not as a part of everyday professional work, but rather as a review of or commentary on such work. The family of engagements in question comprises giving lectures to colleagues, teaching new entrants to the profession, acting as examiner to such students, writing about the subject, and carrying out fairly substantial pieces of research.

When someone becomes eminent in a general field, or is recognized to be authoritative in a particular specialism, he or she is liable to be invited to talk to groups of fellow-practitioners. This happens quite commonly in architecture—a profession in which the quality of performance is highly visible—but also, albeit to a lesser extent, in law and accountancy. One of my respondents (L/24) took a frankly instrumental view of the matter, considering the preparation for such talks to be time-consuming and their presentation not a particularly effective marketing device. She did, however, participate in a commercial seminar and give one or two talks each year for her professional association in order to keep her name in the "list of luminaries." Other informants focused on the benefits to their professional skills: "giving talks produces useful feedback" (Arc/5); "very often it is the questions people ask that make you think hardest and develop new ideas" (Arc/2).

Quite a sizeable proportion of those I interviewed had direct experience of the related activity of teaching students. Here, medicine provided the prime examples, though there were also instances in each of the other professions under review. Gear et al. (1994) quote a clear exposition by a general practitioner of the benefits of working with trainees:

> They are the ones that keep me on my toes more than anything else, because they're constantly asking awkward questions, which I've got to go and find out about in order to answer. Which is why I went into training in the first place, to have a fresh person in the practice every six months so they're going to make me think and make me look things up and question what I'm doing. Because they're the ones that are coming in with the new ideas so it really is a challenge to me to re-evaluate the things I'm doing day-to-day (p. 60).[9]

In becoming a GP trainer, incidentally, one has to overcome various hurdles: "I had to do a one-year course which was taught in the evenings and in two residential weekends. Then my practice was inspected by 'three wise men' who looked at the records and at how the practice was being run" (M/12). As a training manager, the GP in question has to attend a workshop on one or two evenings a month. No such provision is made for those in hospital medicine who are called upon to pass on their knowledge. A consultant in a non-teaching hospital (M/2) remarked that "a lot of teaching goes on in medicine," but added that although she was responsible for giving courses to GPs and pharmacists, there was no training at all available in teaching methods or communication skills.

As well as situations in which aspiring professionals on university courses are taken on to learn in a practice setting, there are cases of a traffic in the reverse direction, in that experienced practitioners may be invited to participate in academic programs. Teaching, a senior architect (Arc/7) pointed out, is important in the sense of meeting the challenges posed by students. For that reason, not only was there in his practice a trainee in the office, but a number of partners taught in universities or became external examiners. A handful of well-established architects and engineers went beyond establishing an *ad hoc* connection by taking on appointments as visiting or part-time professors.

Examining, as an offshoot or by-product of teaching, was also acknowledged to make a direct contribution to professional understanding. One GP examiner for her Royal College explained that she and her colleagues were required themselves to sit the examinations in order to work out the marking schedules:

> You go through a lot of hoops and hurdles to do it, but it's the best course I go on...my biggest learning curve is there, because I constantly have to keep up-to-date. I have to be on my toes...whatever the exam questions are, I will probably then read up.... I find it very stressful, but it's very good learning (M/3).

Writing books and articles provides another variant of the kind of learning that both depends on and promotes professional knowledge. This form of activity seems to be more common in the processual than the procedural professions (see chapter 2)—those whose conduct depends mainly on knowing how to do things in a practical, hands-on sense—namely medicine, architecture, and engineering. At first glance this seems a paradox: writing about processes would appear to be less straightforward than writing about procedures. The latter, however, tend to be fixed and subject more to categorization than discussion; the former would seem to offer more scope for writing about in an analytic or reflective way.

Too much should not be made of the distinction. There are certainly one or two instances in the data of lawyers as authors: one barrister (L/32) reported contributing to a basic textbook on tax, and another (L/24) was shortly to publish a book based on the fellowship thesis submitted to her specialist professional body. A solicitor in a small, three-partner firm (L/19), speaking of the journal articles he had written, remarked that publication was encouraged by the senior partner because it helped the firm's as well as the author's name to be better known. No similar examples emerged in either pharmacy or accountancy, though that could well be consequent on the particular sample of respondents.

Architects would appear to have particularly ready pens. One (Arc/4) saw himself as having developed a second career as a writer; he had produced a textbook on his specialism as well as contributing to professional architectural magazines and to some more popular national journals. Another (Arc/5), who had been invited to contribute to a book on housing for the elderly, remarked that "I've always enjoyed writing because it clarifies the mind." A senior partner, running one of the largest practices (Arc/17), had nevertheless found time to write two books as well as a number of magazine articles on building procurement and professional practice. There are, observed a non-equity partner in a small firm (Arc/12), "many more opportunities nowadays to get work published as a form of career reward."

A consultant in a London teaching hospital (M/24) saw the publication of papers as his biggest source of job satisfaction. For those who claimed to have written best-selling textbooks (M/22, M/28), the rewards were presumably financial as well as professional. A consultant in pathology (M/1), commenting on the issue of continuing education, argued that the books he had written and the annual series which he edited were especially helpful in enabling him to keep up with his specialism. There is competitive pressure on young doctors, especially at Registrar level, to publish, another consultant (M/2) explained: but added that the quality of such publication is highly variable.

Although structural engineers may also engage in conventional publication—the senior staff members in one small firm had between them produced "at least six refereed papers and a book on deep excavations" (E/28)—the writing activity in this field would seem to concentrate mainly on the production of codes of practice. These firm guidelines to aspects of engineering practice are commonly drawn up by combined task forces of academics and practitioners, the latter's main function being to "make the document usable" (E/3). Various aspects of masonry formed the main topics of the codes in whose compilation some of my respondents had been involved. Two—the first a university teacher (E/1) and the second an academically inclined partner in a firm of consulting engineers (E/24)—had been working on procedures to be applied throughout the European Union, "retained", as the latter said, "by the Department of the Environment to represent U.K. interests." Preparing successful codes is clearly a complex business: the practicing engineers in the group, besides coping with political considerations and "controlling the boffins and acting as a bridge between academics and practitioners" (E/24), must necessarily have a sophisticated technical knowledge of the theme under consideration.

Those involved in writing codes of practice, along with some others in my sample, had had research experience at a more substantial level than that—referred to in the previous section—akin to a short-term "boning up" on a topic. Some had made a career move from an academic setting or a research organization into a job with a research aspect; others had retained an interest in the study of professional issues after taking a higher degree early in their careers. "Doing research," said one of these, "is not synonymous with being academic" (E/3).

Many of the medical practitioners I interviewed, particularly in hospital medicine, were also currently engaged, or recently had been, in significant research activities. As remarked in chapter 2, medicine is a profession in which the academic and the practical aspects are intertwined to an exceptional extent. Their close relationship is illustrated by the phenomenon of teaching hospitals, in which leading academics commonly engage in aspects of medical practice and specialist consultants often participate in research enquiries, so that the line between them is sometimes quite difficult to draw. Among various illustrations of the point, a consultant (M/15), particularly hard-pressed because of staff shortages, was waiting for an opportunity to do research: "even if it's in a relatively narrow area, it will keep my interests going." He added that research, besides being enjoyable, could help to give juniors career opportunities, and that it was in any case important in teaching hospitals to advance the knowledge base of the subject.

As noted in chapter 4, there has been a common expectation (not however amounting to a compulsion) that doctors, in the course of their training subsequent to their first degree, should enlist for an MD or MChir, or more ambitiously an MSc or PhD, involving a substantial element of scientific enquiry. Quite a number of the more senior medics I interviewed, looking back on the experience, were dubious about its value, beyond offering "paper kudos" (M/17). One remarked, acidly, that while the contribution of MDs to professional competence was open to doubt, one might say charitably that they were character-building (M/2). Another commented that the work she had to do on her thesis was "not a complete loss": it was useful to have learnt to do statistics, to judge the validity of other people's statistically based publications, to be able to undertake a systematic literature review, and to use a word processor (M/8). A third, who had found the activity "interesting and enjoyable—and a useful career break"—claimed that he would nevertheless have been no worse off it he had not taken the degree, except in his ability to interpret scientific papers more critically (M/15).

The experience, in spite of its detractors, has apparently succeeded in encouraging a generally research-minded attitude in members of the profession. To take a case in point, a breast cancer surgeon, working in a non-teaching hospital, explained an approach which was enabling him to cope better with his current concerns:

> When we started screening, we started getting a lot of these patients with one or two centimetres of this very early change, and we really didn't know what to do with it. So we've got various trials going for that and we need to discuss the pathology—the actual pathology becomes complicated, which is why we have a meeting every Monday lunch to go through this (M/4).

Even those not themselves engaged in research have to remain *au courant* with it. Apart from the substantive content, the language impinges on how practitioners manage disorders. "Research has an overall effect on how we think about diagnosis and management. If you don't keep up you don't understand others and you don't really know what is happening in the field" (M/2)—a comment which brings one back to resource-based learning.

Interpersonal Activities

As with the strategies for informal learning already considered, those which can appropriately be labelled as interpersonal activities have a number of cognate but analytically distinguishable components. All of them, however, involve some form of personal contact with fellow-professionals, leading to the acquisition of new information or the establishment of a potential means of doing so.

As a substantial body of research confirms, the most widespread—and hence the most familiar—form of contact is through what is commonly designated as networking.[10] Gear et al. (1994), for example, report that "Whether learning was described as planned or evolved, there was no doubt that people were the most important resource for it...nearly all of the interviewees (92 percent) drew on the help of other people at some stage" (p. 29). They go on to quote a specialist in obstetrics and gynecology:

> The nice thing about going to ask somebody, you can ask a specific question and get a specific answer. You go to a book and you have to wade through a chapter and a half and you may get an idea of the answer to the question that you asked. You can go and listen to a lecture for a day and they may sort of pass over the topic for half an hour, a quarter of an hour or just a sentence. So if you've got a specific question, go and ask somebody for a specific answer (p. 40).

Again in relation to medicine, Putnam and Campbell (1989) report that, in their study, "interaction with other physicians" came high in practitioners' ratings of learning resources (pp. 85, 86, 90), and add, in summary, that "the most important resource…was one's colleagues or peers" (p. 96). Hanson and DeMuth (1991) report in their turn that the most common form of learning in pharmacy is "communicating with one's peers" (p. 29); and Twining (1994a) records that

> One survey suggested that partners in solicitors' firms in a major Scottish city spent less than 15 minutes per week referring to books and that a remarkable amount of information about law is acquired by telephone (pp. 92–93).

My interviewees offered numerous examples of the same phenomenon. Among them an anatomy teacher in a leading university medical school, who was also a part-time GP, claimed to place a heavy reliance on networking:

> I never look anything up in a book. If I want to know something about a specific disease in any depth…I ring up personal contacts…. If I have a disease that I haven't seen for 10 years and I'm not sure what is going on, I pick up a phone and I'll speak to someone who I know is an expert in that disease and say, look, I've got a finkleback syndrome, what's the next stage? Because there's no way in medicine you can learn about everything in great detail all the time (M/22).

Along similar lines, a barrister explained that, when confronted with a difficult problem, she went for advice to the most influential person she knew:

> What I tend to do…is not to read a book, as that's too much like hard work; and it's not to take a course, because frankly I don't have a great deal of faith in courses. At the bar, experience has a great deal to do with things…Who you know and the way in which you approach a problem is very important…. The bar is a very cooperative profession, so if I have a problem I will invariably talk to one or two or three people in chambers whose opinions I trust (L/6).

Accountants have, it would appear, a more utilitarian than altruistic attitude towards information exchange. One, currently working as the financial controller of a small enterprise, had made numerous contacts when employed by one of the largest accountancy firms. They had proved professionally useful in floating the company on the stock market at no cost, and in providing free advice on tax questions. In return, he had offered guidance on issues such as the management of import quotas and foreign exchange (Acc/29). Another accountant, working in corporate recovery in another large organization, was one of the few respondents to express a preference for referring to books rather than people (Acc/5).

Architects emerge as somewhat ambivalent about networking. While one (Arc/29) claimed to do "a lot of picking of brains" and to be "a great believer in people as a key resource," and another (Arc/26) commented that as a member of the management group of a large-ish firm he could not survive without an extensive set of contacts, there were a number who claimed or implied that there was not a strong tradition of networking within the profession. One inhibiting factor was said to be the increasing competitiveness of architectual work (as referred to in chapters 2 and 3): professional discussion becomes guarded because people see themselves as businessmen in competition with one another rather than as professionals (Arc/4).

The hesitancy in consulting fellow-practitioners in rival firms also manifests itself in other commercially competitive fields, and notably law and accountancy. Most of those remarking on this ambivalence suggested that a careful line needed to be drawn between candor and confidentiality. The resulting tension was well expressed by a respondent straddling both fields, as a lawyer working in a large accounting practice:

> There are areas where we are all, you know, in very much cut-throat competition and there are other areas where I can pick up the 'phone to any of my competitors and say look, what do you think about this? So we share knowledge to a certain extent, but not completely. It's a very, very interesting tension but on the whole it works (L/24).

There is a clear distinction to be drawn between a process of consulting a variety of colleagues on an *ad hoc* basis, usually referred to as networking, and one involving frequent references by young professionals to one or two more experienced practitioners, to which the term mentoring is often applied. Again, examples of this interpersonal activity can be identified across a number of professions. A woman engineer (E/6) remarked that several aspects of her career had been furthered by the head of the first firm she worked for: "he had faith in me and prompted me to do a lot of things I would not otherwise have tried," including writing a technical paper for a prize competition, which she subsequently won, and going to social events and specialist meetings. An experienced accountant, reviewing his career in retrospect, observed that

> You need some grounding, whether through training or through a mentor or somebody else along the years.... There've been various people down the path. Everybody, I think, in this sort of an environment would have somebody who has been a good source of advice, either when sought or when not asked for (Acc/30).

In medicine, a recently appointed consultant in a London teaching hospital gave a closer view of the process:

> A formal training requires that somebody teaches you and I've not been trained in that way...I read the books, I say how do I do this and you ask people like Nigel B...: and he'll say "Have a look at this paper, have a look at this other paper, this is what I do, this is what they do down the road. I'm not sure what's right, you'll have to make your own mind up: here's the evidence." Now that's a different kind of training, it's a very different kind of training. At the end of the day you're training yourself.... But there's a safety net. When you are not sure it's right, you go and say "I really think this is wrong and I don't know why it's wrong"—and as long as you're reasonably intelligent and don't think you're infallible, you always have that fallback (M/24).

Another variant form of reference to one's professional colleagues is found in consulting an acknowledged expert for advice. This extension of the concept of mentoring may seem preferable in some situations to a networking process, in order to avoid losing face (as suggested by a barrister informant) or—as implied earlier—for fear of giving away trade secrets or of losing a client. The process is conveniently built in to the legal and medical professions, in that barristers are recognized reference points for solicitors, as are hospital consultants for GPs. A management accountant might similarly find it appropriate to draw on the wider experience of an auditor; an architect will very frequently collaborate closely with a structural engineer, but may also have a need for other forms of expertise—quantity surveyors, servicing firms and the like. Charging for such services will depend on circumstance: how far the query is a substantial one, whether the expert is also a personal friend, and so on. In a number of cases—it would seem particularly in technically oriented professions such as medicine, pharmacy, and engineering—the relevant professional schools in universities provide an additional source of help in tackling unfamiliar problems.

There are of course different levels of expertise. Thus, a consultant in cardiology (M/10) spoke of the need for a few very difficult cases to be dealt with by highly specialized cardiologists on a nation-wide system of tertiary referral. Similarly, a consultant dermatologist (M/2) referred to the opportunities for advice on esoteric problems afforded by the periodic professional meetings involving a number of leading experts. Rather than "having to write about a query," she enjoyed the chance to take advantage of "actual personal contact" with the relevant specialist.

At a more day-to-day level, a chartered accountant in a four-partner practice provided a further example:

> We've slowly built up a team, or a network I suppose, of people we can call on if there are crises or specialist matters that we can't deal with.... We've got a special connection with a firm called [A.B.]. Actually because I used to play squash with one of the partners, and that sort of built into a personal relationship and expanded into a business relationship. They are a very large firm and if we need specialist tax advice, perhaps somebody wants to do something peculiar, we would refer more often than not to that firm (Acc/7).

It is evident that reference to experts has two features in common with mentorship and with consultations with colleagues, namely that it normally involves referring to a single individual or organization, and that the reference is made on an *ad hoc* basis for help with a specific problem. A different but related type of interpersonal activity consists in being a member of a fairly stable, relatively small group in which general issues are discussed and common interests shared. Confusingly, this process is also commonly designated as networking: here, simply to avoid ambiguity, it will be labelled more ponderously as professional interaction.

Professional interaction can serve a variety of purposes and take a variety of forms. Sometimes the constituency is limited to the members of a single, reasonably sized organization. Thus, for example, Owen et al. (1989) found in their interview study of 96 GPs that practice-based educational meetings were common, and that these received a high rating from the participants in the research. Horder et al. (1989) in a study of ways of influencing the behavior of GPs, also singled out teamwork and peer group contact. One respondent, an engineer (E/17), described two different types of interaction which took place within his medium-sized firm. One was designed as a collective means of keeping up with the literature without actually reading it: the more junior members of staff were asked to review current research in a particular field and give a presentation on it, leading to a general discussion. The other was meant to keep the partners and associates in the picture about each others' activities: it comprised "a lot of people around a big table talking about a whole wide variety of things…and just keeping your eyes and ears open rather than just getting your head burrowed in the actual project work you're doing."

Many of the interpersonal activities described by respondents, however, involved some fairly regular contact between members of different practices. A number took the form of carefully organized groups, though with a relatively open agenda. The consultant dermatologist quoted above contrasted the nationally-based meetings of her main professional association with the bi-monthly regional get-togethers with her fellow-specialists. The former tend "to be a showpiece in the sense that you bring along very rare cases and very complex cases that you've worked out." However, "in the local group you'll bring up your half-baked cases…and open [them] up to debate…interestingly enough that's often more instructive" (M/2).

A GP, on the other hand, saw the function of her group as being as much sociopolitical—in forming a "better relationship between the hospitals and the GPs"—as informative:

> We have what we call a flying circus which we've organised ourselves—we and several of the other practices in the area. We invite all the [local] GPs and we have a lunchtime meeting, we get sponsorship, and we invite one of the consultants and we talk about issues that are affecting them and us. Whether they be clinical, new treatments or whether they be management issues, whatever comes up, it's very informal but it's actually quite useful and it gives you a better relationship between the hospitals and the GPs I think. I think it's very important (M/7).

Another example of professional interaction was concerned less with the acquisition of ideas than with the "sharing of experience" in a context of mutual trust (though that too allows for learning, albeit of an organizational rather than a technical kind):

> There is a network that we have which is called the gang of five, which is a great name for the five architectural practices of similar mind who meet probably every month or 6 weeks, and the agenda is something we decide from meeting to meeting. We've had some very, very interesting sharing of experience and that might be on our relative incomes or it might be on how we deal with the pressure to go into agreements with clients of a particular sort. So that's tremendously useful to have conversations in which you are not necessarily having to be guarded, it's not competitive exposure, but it's a sympathetic kind of exposure…it's absolutely riveting really to see how differently we might approach things and it just helps a lot to have that comparison (Arc/7).

There are also groups which offer professional support particularly to those working as sole practitioners or in relatively small partnerships. One of my informants, a chartered accountant in a three-partner practice (Acc/1), referred to a confederation of seven or eight firms across the country whose members—about a dozen people—met a couple times a year in a chosen location, beginning with a pleasant social dinner and spending the whole of the next day in intensive discussion—partly in reviewing problems brought along by members and partly in more general debate. Between meetings, the members kept in touch, providing mutual advice for which a charge was made only if a substantial amount of work was involved. Another consortium, this time of small engineering firms, operates as a source of advanced technical know-how. All the members work in a highly specialized field, and the consortium, which runs on a "learning by applying" basis, keeps them collectively in touch with frontline research (E/7).

A further self-help group, described by an interviewee (P/4), had a distinctive profile in pharmacy. It grew up around the need for women community pharmacists, returning to the profession after raising a family, to get back in touch with current developments and bring themselves up-to-date with new products. The eight members met on Saturday mornings in each others' houses to exchange ideas and knowledge. They chose a topic, looked at the relevant products, pooled what they knew, discussed how to deal with any issues arising, and decided what questions had to be asked of the client. As in a number of other professional interactions, the social aspects—and particularly the benefits of mutual support—appeared to be as important as the professional gains.

In the array of different forms of interaction, professional committees must be said to occupy a marginal position. Their memberships are not characteristically comprised of people who wish to learn, and their agendas are not usually dictated by considerations of professional development. Nevertheless, a number of respondents—mainly, it should be said, in the construction industry—spoke of the potentialities of committees as useful sources of technical as well as commercial and political information.

For the most part, those in other professions who had joined committees had done so for reasons less evidently connected with professional, as against personal, interest or advancement. The few exceptions included a chartered accountant (Acc/14) who used his participation in committee work for his Institute to ensure that he was in touch with where the profession was going and what was the current state of the market, and a consultant surgeon (M/4) whose membership of a number of committees in his local health authority had helped him to know what was happening in health service politics and management.

Viewed as a whole, professional interaction, along with other forms of interpersonal learning, can be seen as providing an effective counterpart or supplement to resource-based, practice-based, and practice-related activities. Each approach has its characteristic strengths, and each its enthusiastic advocates. What remains to be discussed is how far the various learning modes co-exist.

Characteristics of Informal Learning

The exposition of aspects of informal learning has, up to this point, had the elements of a fiction, albeit an artifactual rather than a totally artificial one. In order clearly to characterize the various approaches, they have been presented atomistically, as if each in practice existed independently and in isolation from the rest. In reality, of course, learning in the professions is a much more holistic affair, in which different strategies are blended together in seeking the effective pursuit of a particular developmental need.

As an architect, in talking about the types of support on which he and his colleagues might draw, observed:

> You do a lot of referencing [of written and visual sources] and you would be using materials that you would have to check out with the representatives and the technical advisers, and you would be picking up from other people within the department what they had used before, but also what you could use in the future. You would be using magazines and other people to learn from. It's very much an ongoing situation, keeping up to date with what's available (Arc/10).

A hospital pharmacist (P/13), working in a very different environment, spoke of her "big learning curve" in joining the intensive care unit at a London teaching hospital. She began by undertaking a systematic search for review articles on the subject and did a great deal of other relevant reading, to a point at which she was able to put together a coherent conceptual framework (this had to be done in her own time). She was also able to accompany the ward rounds on three days each week, picking up points from nursing staff, junior doctors, and consultants, all of whom she found to be very helpful. Once she had the concepts clear in her head, she found it much easier to understand what was going on.

Other respondents similarly made it plain that they were ready to employ more than one strategy whenever it came to having to extend and develop their capabilities. The particular combinations of techniques were liable to vary with the nature of the requirement, though not in a rigidly mechanical way.

It is understandable enough why the formal approaches discussed in chapter 6 should offer a different kind of enhancement of professional competence from the informal ones reviewed in this chapter, in that they are geared towards providing longer-term, more general support. As the earlier survey of structured CPD activities indicated, courses can among other things serve the purpose of helping participants work towards further qualifications, catch up with new developments in a particular field, and—no less importantly—develop expertise in contextual skills, such as management, client relations, and computing, while conferences may offer a less focused form of updating, but also consolidate existing contacts, initiate new ones and, in some cases, help to promote professional reputations. Formal provision is however less effective in promoting the tacit knowledge underpinning appropriate ways of talking and behaving, in meeting specific problem-solving needs, or in developing certain kinds of practical skills. In contrast, informal approaches have particular strengths in helping practitioners to tackle short-term, fairly circumscribed problems, and to learn key skills on the job. They do, however, presuppose a facility in learning how to learn, and in knowing whom to ask, what to observe, or where to look things up.

Underlying these common characteristics, interesting contrasts can be seen to emerge between different professions and—recalling the findings by Bucher and Strauss (1961)—even within an individual profession. As noted earlier, the processual professions in my sample—medicine, architecture, and engineering—gave a particular emphasis to writing in a reflective way about their subject matter, while those relying on a predominantly technical knowledge base—medicine and engineering again, and to a lesser extent pharmacy and architecture—tended to be oriented towards research and hence to develop fairly close links with cognate university departments.

The traditional reliance in medicine on an apprenticeship style of training—encapsulated in the slogan "see one, do one, teach one"—seems to be more a product of social than of cognitive factors, in that U.S. medical training can be seen to adopt a more tightly structured, formal approach. The emphasis in law and accountancy on networking, coupled with a guardedness against giving away commercially useful information to competitors, also appears to be a product of social considerations, exacerbated by the move from professional to business values. However, the examples cited in this chapter, especially from solicitors (though other evidence relates to barristers as well) of "boning up" on issues on a short-term basis clearly reflects the accretive and particulate aspects of legal knowledge. Again, at an intraprofessional level, it is evident that the greater emphasis given by insolvency practitioners than by auditors to interpersonal skills (see chapter 2) reflects the intrinsic differences between the sub-professions, rather than being a consequence of convention.

Other idiosyncrasies referred to earlier in this chapter include the reliance of architects on looking at existing buildings—related to Cuff's (1991) account of architectural knowledge as generalizing from one problem to the next—and the penchant of engineers for developing codes of practice (which could reasonably be designated as a cognitive requirement, in that it involves working out safe and manageable technical procedures) and for sitting on committees (whose justification would seem to be mainly social).

The picture then is a complex one, involving the interplay of different learning approaches, diverse presenting of problems and needs, and the varying characteristics, social and cognitive, of different professions and specialisms. What is most evidently in common is the ready use, by all the individuals involved in this enquiry, regardless of their particular fields of expertise, of both formal and informal learning approaches, insofar as they can be seen as enhancing professional reputations and capabilities, and as helping to meet the challenges which arise in the course of a professional career.

The types of informal learning activity considered here are not generally recognized as acceptable modes of continuing professional development, in that they are neither easily visible nor amenable to quantification. However, since in reality they play a significant part in the enhancement of professional capability, to fail to acknowledge their importance is considerably to underrate the extent to which practitioners maintain the quality of their work. It is partly the resulting underestimation of the range and extent of professional development which has given rise to the wide-ranging political pressure for accountability measures and quality assurance procedures—a phenomenon to which the next chapter will be addressed.

Notes

1. They somewhat confusingly add "and even attendances at traditional CME courses." Allowing that the boundary between the formal and the informal may at times become blurred, it is not easy to see how such courses can comprise, in their own terms, "informal self-directed learning."

2. For example, Geertsma et al. (1982) found that among a sample of 66 practicing physicians in Rochester, New York, "journals and colleague communication were by far the most frequent agencies" (p. 757); formal CME accounted for less than 10 percent of identifiable change. A survey of the CME activities of 2,173 practicing physicians in Canada, conducted by Curry and Putnam (1981) in 1979–80, found that 73.3 percent used reading to update their knowledge and a surprising 55.7 percent to enhance their skills: the corresponding figures for formal courses were 9.3 percent and 17.1 percent. A small-scale study of 30 young U.S. graduate engineers found that their main resources for vocationally related learning were printed materials, peers, and experts: courses played only a small part (Rymell, 1981). Somewhat comparable findings emerged from a study by Cervero et al. (1986) of 471 practicing engineers in Illinois. Ninety-four percent claimed to read engineering periodicals; 88 percent would, in a typical month, need to take expert advice; 53 percent rated colleague discussions "very useful." Course attendance was given less prominence, though significantly more than in the other three studies cited: within the time frame of the enquiry 36.9 percent had attended in-house courses and 18.5 percent (mostly younger engineers) had been on university-sponsored credit courses.

3. References directly relevant to this perspective on change include Bailey (1973) pp. 13–14; Elmore (1979) pp. 604–611; Marris (1975) pp. 156–57; Weatherley and Lipsky (1977) pp. 172–196.

4. From a very different perspective, theory as the rhetorical ideal is contrasted with practice as the rumpled reality. An entertaining example is given in Laffin and Young (1990), quoting an interview with a borough treasurer: "One of the things I'm really involved in is creative accounting which really means cooking the books. I have to be prepared to bend my pure accounting principles to the need of the particular authority" (p. 61).

5. They were, of course, writing at a time when everyone, save in exceptional circumstances, was assumed to be of masculine gender.

6. It is, however, contradicted in a large-scale questionnaire-based study of 1,523 general practitioners in Western Scotland carried out in 1991. The results showed a high participation rate in postgraduate education activities, with lectures as the most popular format and distance- and practice-based learning as the least popular (Kelly and Murray, 1994). This is so out of line with the other comparable research findings cited in chapters 6 and 7 that one may be given to wonder how far the amelioration of the isolated working context of many respondents was a motivating factor for attendance at group events.

7. However, she goes on to add that "it need not be the only means to gain expertise…continuing education is the best opportunity for specialized training" (Cuff, 1991, pp. 258–59).

8. Current reforms in Britain, based on the Calman Report (1993), are expected to change the emphasis to approximate more closely the U.S. system, with its tighter structure, its more formalized approach, and its earlier specialization.

9. There are other side effects as well, as Allery et al. (1991) found in their interviews with 99 GPs, 33 of whom were currently responsible for training:

> Trainers are significantly more likely than non-trainers to be organizing their own continuing medical education, to be using their day-to-day work as a basis for continuing medical education, and to be involving other members of the primary health care team in their continuing medical education activities.

10. There is an interesting divergence here from the findings of research into the micro-level, psychological aspects of professional learning (see chapter 1), where

the existence of the phenomenon is noticed only very tangentially, if at all. For example, in the widely ranging and well-regarded work by Eraut (1994) there are only two entries under "networking" in the index, one leading back to two brief sentences in the text and the other to a single entry in a table in the appendix.

8

Questions of Quality

Accountability and Quality Maintenance

Trust is a rare commodity, as hardly gained as it is readily lost. Insofar as the professions in general once enjoyed its possession, the second half of the twentieth century saw its steady decline. Chapter 2 touched on a variety of reasons: the irresponsibility of some practitioners, the misconduct of others, and the increased media coverage given to both; a better-informed and more sceptical public, giving rise to a discernable shift in client attitudes; and a general move towards commercial values and practices, spurred in part by the growth in size of many practices. If these were among the causes of the change in credibility, the consequences could be seen in terms of the growing demands for practitioners to demonstrate their capability and for their professional bodies to answer for their conduct.

The form in which such demands tended to be couched in the later 1970s and early 1980s was in terms of accountability. One analysis (Becher et al., 1981) distinguished three variants: contractual accountability, arising in organizational settings and calling for conformity with official requirements or legal regulations; professional accountability, denoting collegial relationships within the professional community and a requirement not to draw one's profession itself into disrepute; and moral accountability, owed to one's clients and others in some way dependent on one's professionalism. Prominent among the examples of contractual accountability are the legislative or quasi-legislative demands introduced to govern professional conduct (see the section on "The Effects of Legislation and National Policy" in chapter 3). Professional accountability is illustrated by the ethical codes of the main professional bodies, together with the formal procedures for arraignment in cases of professional misconduct. Moral accountability is exemplified by the reference in chapter 3 to the "service oriented quality sys-

FIGURE 8.1
The Quality Maintenance Tree

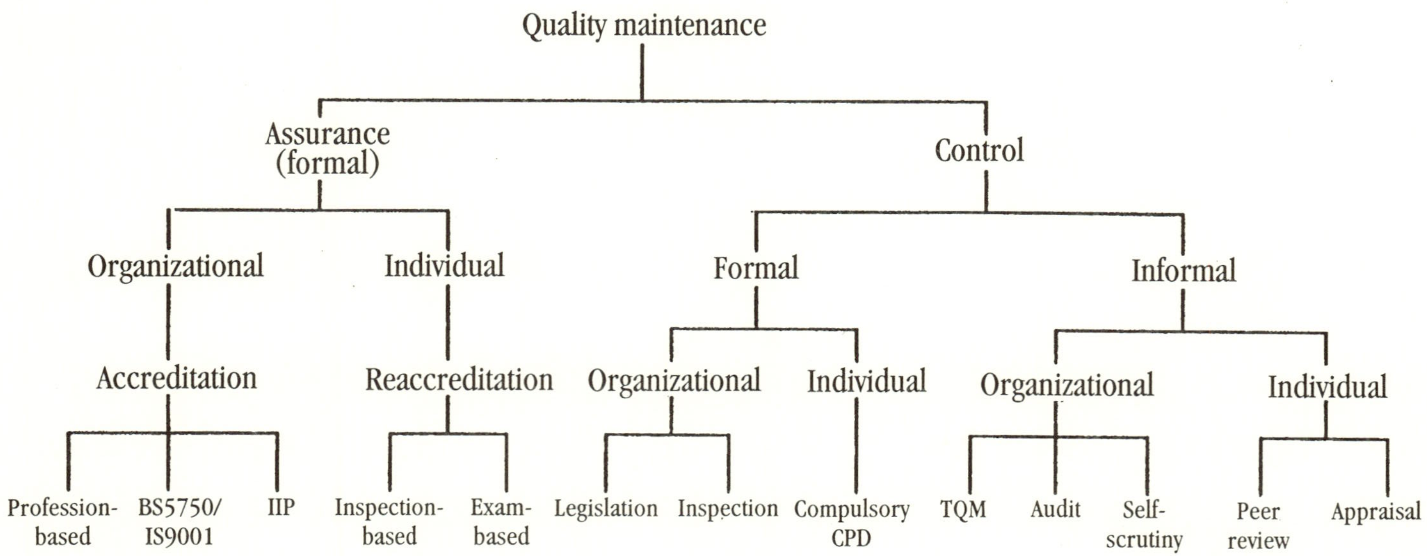

tem" introduced in a hospital pharmacy in response to the earlier complaint that it treated clients "like second class citizens" (P/16).[1]

Johnson (1972) sees a distinction between these forms of accountability in terms of the extent to which the profession concerned is bureaucratized and its associated "differences in the types of knowledge and ideologies espoused":

> Where a colleague system...still largely controls the system of practice, as is the case with medicine in Britain today, the ethical and community [alias moral and professional] functions of the association remain important. The various branches of social work on the other hand enjoy little autonomy in determining the content of practice, and social work ethics are largely encompassed in the rules of the agencies which employ them [contractual accountability] (p. 82).

While this contention may have been valid in the early 1970s, it seems less plausible today. No one could say that accountancy or engineering, for instance, are bureaucratized professions, or that they have little autonomy in determining the content of practice: and yet both are subject to numerous procedural rules and restrictions.

The increase in legislative constraints over recent decades is not the only significant change since Johnson's (1972) study. New departures in terminology can be significant in signalling alterations in intellectual climate: the move from occasional talk of accountability to more insistent references to quality is one such departure. The origins of what one respondent (E/4) ruefully termed "a quality culture" can be traced back to advanced industrial practice in the early 1920s. Joss and Kogan (1995) give a brief but informative account of its subsequent progress, notably through the work of Deming and Juran in rebuilding industry in postwar Japan to the subsequent emergence of the concept of Total Quality Management (TQM). The slow infiltration of the notion of quality from commercial into professional life began in the 1980s and has continued to gather momentum over the intervening years. Its impact has been significantly greater on medicine than on any of the other professions here considered: in consequence most of the references below are to activities and practices in that field.

The general reaction to quality demands among those interviewed, both inside and outside medicine, was by no means obstructive. Few respondents wished to sidestep the requirement that they should be able to demonstrate their ability effectively to carry out their professional duties. A number were nonetheless dubious about the way in which this expectation was expressed. One problem was seen to lie in the inflexibility of the mechanisms for quality assurance and their uneven relevance to professionals in different fields and contexts. As one GP (M/7) put it, "there's a tendency for politicians to go for uniform solutions, even when that is not the best answer." A preference among those devising quality assessment procedures for "hard quantitative information" (Arc/13) was held to rule out much of the really important evidence about professional capability and to focus instead on easily measured but shallow and misleading data. Another concern related to the "vast amounts of time and paper" (P/16) involved in most accountability exercises, often consuming the very resources that might otherwise have been spent on improving the quality of the provision under scrutiny: "you can't just do the job, you have to show that you have done it" (E/4). The doctors and pharmacists working in the public sector tended towards the pessimistic view that, even given their best efforts, a combination of dwindling resources and increasing workloads was bound to affect quality for the worse: even so, the pharmacist just quoted (P/16) acknowledged that "the patients have a right to complain, and should be encouraged to do so."

Against a rising tide of external demand for formal and systematic demonstration of professional competence, there were occasional protests that such demonstrations were inappropriate and uncalled for. One line of argument was that specialization itself—an increasingly widespread phenomenon—guaranteed a greater measure of expertise, and therefore of quality of provision, than existed in former times. Another claim, advanced independently by both an architect and a structural engineer, was that quality assurance was antipathetic to good design in the constraints it placed on creativity: "designers have to feel free, not tied down by quality measures" (Arc/16); "engineering design doesn't flourish in straitjackets, because it's a creative process" (E/30). In any case, "the maintenance of quality is built in by tradition—the systems are there but not formalized. If they were, the clients would have to pay more to help meet the extra costs" (Arc/16).

A barrister (L/17)—it might seem characteristically—also argued strongly in favor of informal monitoring procedures, on the grounds that "the market is the most effective judge: there are certainly bad barristers, but they are found out by the inadequate work they do. In the face of cut-throat competition, it isn't possible to conceal poor performance." A related point, made by a number of respondents, was that it is common knowledge who is good and who is bad—that professional quality is generally quite easy to judge.

This comfortable contention was sharply contradicted by a consultant physician (M/15), who took the view that "patients don't know how to judge quality [in relation to hospital doctors], and nor do GPs—they are impressed by a good bedside manner rather than by whether the treatment itself is reliable." He nevertheless had some reservations about the move towards the systematic testing of competence, and the grounds on which it was justified: "the whole business seems to have started with a vague feeling among politicians that the medical system isn't satisfactory, and needs to be put right."

The domination of the quality debate by the medical profession can be explained, at least in part, by the greater penalties for failure in the field of health care. Human life can be much more evidently at stake in the context of faulty diagnosis, inadequate testing, or incompetent surgery—and, by extension, in the careless dispensing of a prescription—than it is in the poor conduct of a court case, the failure to spot an irregularity in a set of accounts, or even the dangerously inadequate design of a building. Medics have by long tradition emphasized their internal vigilance over professional conduct, harking back to the ancient Greek model set by Hippocrates. They are accordingly readier than most other callings to respond to proposals that they should justify their actions and demonstrate their abilities. As one respondent (M/2) observed, referring to her specialism:

> Because it is a slightly esoteric subject, virtually no one at the hospital knows anything about it at all. It's very easy to stop asking yourself questions, and nobody else will question you…which is actually quite dangerous.

Another medical interviewee (M/20), currently working for a professional body, raised as "the perennial problem" the issue of what to do with poorly performing doctors. The General Medical Council, he observed, "started by keeping out quacks, went on to try to eliminate crooks, and then attempted to cope with unprofessional conduct—but it hasn't come up with an effective way of identifying and dealing with poor performance."

Rotten Apples and Whistle Blowing

The notion that a dramatic increase in quality could be achieved in any given profession by "weeding out the incompetents" has all the engaging simplicity to render it attractive to civil servants and politicians. Thus, for example, in the 1990s successive British governments sought to empower the national inspectors of schools to identify and cause to be dismissed those teachers whom they judged as performing significantly below acceptable standards. The policy could scarcely be deemed a success since, in a period of over-sized classes, school governors were reluctant to risk understaffing their schools; because, moreover, a clear definition could not be articulated of substandard performance; and because employment legislation made it difficult to dismiss staff on what could not clearly be established as reasonable grounds.

Nonetheless, the debate about incompetent professional performance continues unabated, particularly but not exclusively in relation to medicine. The size and significance of the problem is largely a matter of guesswork. It is of interest that Rosenthal (1995), who devotes a whole book to the subject, notes on the basis of her interviews with GPs that "estimates consistently ranged between 3 percent and 5 percent...it is difficult to assess the accuracy of such estimates" (p. 94); while Houle (1980), writing more than a decade earlier about the professions in general, estimates the "laggards" as forming some 5 percent of each professional population. Since neither author says anything about how incompetence is to be identified, one cannot put much weight on the five percent figure, beyond saying, perhaps, that it is the kind of intelligent guess one might pluck out of the air when confronted with the question.

There is also an issue about the sources of incompetence. Here Armytage (1996) comes up with an intriguing comment in relation to the legal profession:

> An analysis of professional indemnity suits against practising lawyers...tends to suggest that carelessness, poor communication, stress and overwork—rather than ignorance of information or techniques—are the major causes of professional incompetence. Yet an observation of practice reveals that mandatory legal education is predominantly concerned with transmitting substantive information, as though ignorance was the cause of the problem (p. 174).

Since formally organized continuing professional development programs in other professions share this predominant concern with information-giving (see chapter 6), their claim to make a major contribution towards eliminating incompetence may equally deserve to be called into question.

The professional bodies, who make it their responsibility to determine the requirements for continuing professional development, generally also perform another and longer-established function in the maintenance of quality. In all six of the professions considered here, either the professional body itself or a statutory agency with strong professional representation sits in judgment on cases of irregularity or misconduct.

A brief illustrative reference to the process was given by a pharmacist (P/20), who noted that in community pharmacy disciplinary procedures usually stem from a particular complaint, which is likely to be followed up by a visit from a team of inspectors. If the complaint is upheld, procedures are set up for investigating legal infringement. A serious offense would be reported to the law department of the Society, and then referred to the legal infringement or ethics committee, depending on the nature of the case. Where there is a question of striking a member off the register, this is referred to a separate statutory committee.[2]

There is an understandable tendency for professional bodies to adopt a reactive stance towards the identification of unsatisfactory performance: while they see an obligation to respond to complaints, they do not in general take positive steps to preempt them. A high-level administrator in the leading professional body in accountancy was frank enough to acknowledge that "as far as I am aware, most professional bodies have not instituted inspection procedures actually to find the bad eggs and do something about them. That has become more and more a weakness of our activities" (Swinson, 1991, p. 16). He later hinted at a probable reason for this reluctance: "a major disciplinary case can cost, very quickly indeed, very considerably more than £100,000 to run and very often up to £250,000."

Instead, it is common practice to put the onus for reporting inadequacy on the miscreant's professional colleagues: "Members of the profession," explained one interviewee (Acc/22), "have a duty to report colleagues who break the rules—often because they are reluctant to ask advice. This requirement is clearly laid down in the Institute's ethics guide." Hunt (1995) similarly urges hospital doctors to meet their obligation to disclose malpractice, while also arguing for more systematic self-regulation. Along similar lines, a senior member of the medical profession (M/27) directly concerned with questions of professional conduct argued that it was better for the responsibility for "whistleblowing" to rest within the medical fraternity than it would be to "accept external coercion through some contractual arrangement," such as regular independent inspection.[3] Birley (1996) in his turn stresses the responsibility of doctors to the community, and emphasizes that they have a prime duty to the safety of their patients, whether their own or those put at risk by the sub-standard care of colleagues.

Despite such exhortations, individual members of the profession appear obdurately to echo the reaction of schoolchildren to the cognate practice of "sneaking" or "telling tales." One informant (M/25) said bluntly, "people won't do it—though they may take the disastrous colleague on one side." Another (M/10) acknowledged that

> Of course there are people who don't carry weight and people who are plain incompetent. They just have to be carried along. Surgery is a bit like piano playing—your skill is very evident. Most people are safe enough, but you can't make all surgeons as good as the best. Unsafe surgeons tend to be steered off the big operations and to become specialised in a minor field.

Kopelow (1994), commenting on this phenomenon, observes that "Physicians...are remarkably cautious about anything that documents or records a physician's competence or performance, primarily because the information may not be accurate" (p. 165). Freidson (1994) acknowledges that

> Indeed, one should be reluctant to judge the work of a colleague when one lacks direct experience with the case and its circumstances. "There, but for the grace of God, go I," "Who am I to judge" or "It may be my turn next" may be heard said to explain the suspension of condemnatory judgement (p. 203),

but he goes on to add:

> This etiquette expresses an important part of the ideal-typical spirit of professionalism—namely, collegiality...But because it tends to prevent the use of adequate regulatory procedures which protect the public, it violates the profession's implicit contract with the state and the public. There may be an intrinsic conflict between the profession's efforts to maintain the solidarity of its members and its fiduciary relationship with society (pp. 203–204).[4]

If one accepts that there is a genuine moral dilemma here, it is less easy to condone the victimization of those who follow their social consciences by breaking the embargo and reporting an unacceptably low level of performance. That such victimization can occur is confirmed by Eraut (1994), who cites

> two separate cases in which Australian engineers, who publicly complained about unprofessional behavior by colleagues which threatened the local environment, were subsequently arraigned by their professional body for bringing their profession into disrepute (p. 227).

Coming nearer to home, one of my medical interviewees (M/29) referred to an incident directly known to her in which an anesthetist reported a consultant surgeon whose incompetence had caused a significant number of fatalities. In consequence, her account ran, the anesthetist was relieved of his post, while the surgeon was allowed to pursue his lethal career.

There were those among the interview sample who questioned the whole basis of an approach to sustaining quality in the professions through a concentration on eliminating incompetent practitioners. One moderately couched expression of doubt came from a respondent (M/26) whose job it was to audit quality across a wide front:

> The whole problem with quality assurance of any kind is that there's an awful lot of wasted effort just to get a bit of benefit, so there are going to be a lot of perfectly competent doctors who do all the things like being re-assessed and re-accredited and getting resentful because of it. It's like getting into a long queue at an airport, going through a security check: you know it's right and proper but you know very well you haven't got a bomb in your case, so why shouldn't you go through? It is desirable—yes, of course—to prevent incompetences and bad practice, but you need to pay very careful attention to making sure that it isn't heavy-handed.

A more direct repudiation of "a concentration on the 'rotten apples' in the profession as a punitive element" came from a medical member of staff of a professional association (M/20). In his view, the main effort should be directed towards

> trying to encourage everyone to do better. In any case, people may not agree on who the rotten apples are. What's needed is an approach that will tackle both collective and individual improvement.... Overall, there's a need for a non-threatening creative atmosphere, based on the contention that there are bad systems rather than bad people.

A variation on the same theme was put forward by a leading academic currently in a key administrative post (M/30), who identified two competing processes: the first, "raising quality through a framework for personal development, which assumes that most people are committed"; the second "identifying the 'dangerous minority' and applying sanctions to them so as to allay public anxiety." He considered each process to be valid, but deplored the confusion between them. There was, he maintained, a need for "a mechanism to weed out the bad minority of 5 percent or less rotten apples," but this needed to be clearly separated from the more important need to improve the performance of the majority. The latter was an educational process, but the former was not.

Berwick (1989) expresses a strong preference for the educative stance. He contrasts the dubious "Theory of Bad Apples," based on quality by inspection, with the desirable "Theory of Continuous Improvement," enhancing quality through sound and supportive organization, and emphasizing processes as much as outcomes. His central contention is that "we can best begin by freeing ourselves from the fear, accusation, defensiveness and naiveté of an empty search for improvement through inspection and discipline" (p. 56). In the real world, however, inspection and similar devices comprise one of the main stocks in trade of those who lay down the rules of the quality game.

Modes of Procedure

Before reviewing the various common mechanisms related to quality, and the ways in which they impinge on professional activity, it may be useful to have in mind some broad distinctions between different kinds of procedure for safeguarding or enhancing professional standards. There would be no great virtue in embarking on an elaborate taxonomic exercise, but an awareness of some basic categories is relevant to a clearer appreciation of what is going on when claims to competence are made or when professional performance is called into question. Four different elements will be briefly identified as comprising a simple typology: the sources of the procedure; the contrast between formal and informal mechanisms; whether the concern is with professional organizations and practices or with individuals; and whether the purpose is directed at assurance or control.

The first of these distinctions is straightforward. Quality mechanisms can be—and in certain cases are—imposed by government, usually in the form of rules or regulations. In chapter 2, mention was made of underpinning national legislation such as the various Parliamentary Acts governing accountancy practice and the Health and Safety Acts conditioning the work of architects and structural engineers, as well as the numerous *ad hoc* rulings imposed by the Department of Health on community pharmacists. More pervasive, however, are the demands made on their members by the professional bodies, often with the proclaimed purpose of fending off government or other external intervention. A third source is in its nature less visible, namely the individual activities of practices and practitioners to meet their self-imposed quality standards. There is here, as elsewhere, no neat correspondence of sets of responsibilities with types of procedure: for example, inspection—though generally a prerogative of professional bodies—may be taken on by a government agency; while peer review—though also a mechanism commonly used by professional bodies—may in turn be initiated by an individual practice as part of its own quest for improvement.

The distinction between formality and informality of procedure loosely follows that between government and professional bodies on the one hand and individual practices and practitioners on the other.

Formal procedures are those which are, at least in some degree, expected to carry public credibility, because they are instigated—and their outcomes established—by supposedly disinterested agencies independent of the person or organization which is subject to the quality judgment in question.[5] The findings of formal procedures are usually publicly announced, or at least made available to enquirers. The same is not necessarily true of informal procedures, which are usually set up for the purpose of private enlightenment. Thus the staff appraisal schemes adopted in a number of the larger practices, especially in law and accountancy, which are designed to help individuals to identify their weaknesses and to take steps to remedy them, are essentially domestic exercises depending for honest participation on a promise of confidentiality. Although they may be the subject of internal negotiation and may depend on standardized procedures, they are not formal in the sense attributable to the public procedures typically deployed by government and professional bodies.

The third distinction—that between mechanisms relating to individuals and those concerned with organizations—needs little gloss. The latter are understandably more recent in their development and adoption than the former, in that the traditional form of professional practice was that of the sole practitioner: standards of quality were first established at the level of the individual, rather than being attributable to a collectivity. Organizationally based arrangements are not sharply to be distinguished from individually based ones—practices, whether large or small, consist of individuals, and have to be judged mainly in terms of the performance of their members. However, the examination of organizational quality normally involves questions of efficient management and corporate coherence as well as of overall competence in the performance of professional duties, while the confirmation of personal capability calls for the closer scrutiny of how a given practitioner functions.

Finally, there is a contrast to be drawn between quality assurance and quality control. The first denotes those practices which lead to a kind of external guarantee or certification, while the second relates to some form of monitoring of how well required tasks are being carried out. To put it another way, assurance is a matter of judging the outcomes of a special performance-testing exercise while control focuses on the processes of everyday practice. Assurance is retrospective, in the sense that it looks back on an achievement (though it may have a deliberately limited validity and be subject to periodic renewal); control is to the contrary prospective, in that it points forward to the expectation of further improvement.

Another difference between quality control and quality assurance may be of importance in determining peoples' attitudes towards the procedures in question. With the exception of the compulsory periodic accreditation of practices or the regularly renewable certification of practitioners, most quality assurance mechanisms are voluntary. That is to say, organizations or individuals can opt when and whether to submit themselves to the test, and if they fail can usually have more than one chance to repeat the exercise. There may of course be strong competitive or peer pressure to seek quality assurance, but it is significant in psychological terms that the professionals concerned have a direct say in whether or not to participate. Quality control typically lacks any such voluntaristic element, because its credibility depends on the compulsory and impartial application of its measures to all who are subject to them. For this reason, among others, forms of quality control are generally regarded as undesirable impositions in a way that quality assurance mechanisms are not.

Having marked these different categories at a somewhat general and abstract level, it remains to put them to work in the context of the interview data and the associated research literature on quality issues in the professions. As will become evident—if the discussions in earlier chapters have not already made it so—the different professional groups each have their own characteristic patterns of practices and requirements, though between them they span the whole range of possibilities. Medicine, as noted above, is subject to the greatest concern, less because of inadequate general standards than because of the serious consequences of failure on the part of individual practitioners. The review of quality mechanisms which follows is divided, for convenience, into separate sections, the first two dealing with quality assurance and the second two with quality control.

Organizationally Based Quality Assurance

The jargon associated with quality issues is far from tidy and precise: people are inclined to use the same terms to mean different things and different terms to mean the same things. However, among the varieties of quality assurance, accreditation commonly denotes some formalized and usually periodic procedure for certifying the fitness of a professional organization to carry out its work. Its common characteristics, as enumerated by Scrivens (1995), include voluntary participation, standards against which operations can be assessed, compliance checked by independent assessors, and an outcome which denotes a pass, fail, or specified grade. In medicine, particularly close attention is given to the contexts in which initial practical training and experience are acquired. A number of the Royal Colleges therefore arrange for training sites to be regularly accredited—typically once every five years or so. The Royal College of General Practitioners, for example, requires all training practices to undergo periodic inspection and all trainers to attend regular in-service programs (see chapter 7). The possibility of extending this kind of scrutiny to all hospital consultancies and all general practices was being widely discussed during the period in which the fieldwork was being conducted. A number of respondents were dubious about the amount of time, effort, and organization that would be involved in extending the arrangements to cover such a large constituency—particularly if, in surgical contexts, it might call for a direct assessment of the professional skills of the individual surgeons concerned. Scrivens (1995), after a lengthy discussion, comes to the conclusion that accreditation in medicine is "an imprecise science. It is perhaps best to view it as a management consultancy approach to dealing with the problems faced by managers rather than a tool for measuring the performance of the health services" (p. 148).

A different and only distantly related instance of accreditation—which may also be denoted as validation—is to be found in academic departments which provide initial professional training. In University Schools of Pharmacy, for example, the content of degree courses is scrutinized every five years, in a process which involves not only extensive documentation but also a visit of inspection by a group involving experienced practitioners as well as senior academics. Similar arrangements exist, among other professions, in architecture and engineering. In all such cases, it is the relevant professional body that organizes and oversees the accreditation exercise, as a manifestation of its concern to safeguard professional standards.

There are other accreditation procedures, however, which operate independently of the professions themselves, being designed to certify the satisfactory adoption of quality maintenance practices in virtually any kind of organization. The most widely recognized—BS5750 and ISO9000—are promulgated respectively by the British Standards Institute and the International Standards Organization: both involve closely similar demands. The main requirements in each are for the systematic specification of organizational aims and objectives, the determination of specific quality performance targets, the provision of arrangements directed at determining the extent to which these targets are being met, the development of feedback mechanisms to enable any necessary remedial action to be taken, and—not least—the compilation of documents which spell out all aspects of the process in detail and manuals which set out the performance expectations at every level in the system. The final stage is a visit from external assessors, which is repeated periodically. These complex processes appeared on the basis of the interview data to be largely confined to architecture and engineering (only one respondent outside these professions mentioned that his relatively small solicitor's practice was currently applying for BS5750 accreditation). The reason soon became evident: all government agencies contracting for construction work, and a growing number of private ones, now only accept tenders from practices which have the necessary BS or ISO kitemark. Many of the engineers whose firms had acquired this recognition thought the exercise had been worthwhile: "it helps to keep costs down and to encourage efficiency" (E/12); "it makes us do the things we should do in terms of structure and management" (E/29). The sceptics commented that even if the documentation might be necessary to improve quality, "it generates an awful lot of paper" (E/24) and presupposes extensive commitment: "it's not easy to win people's hearts and minds" (E/19). The architects were in general less enthusiastic: a typical response was that "BS5750 formalizes one's operating procedures—that doesn't do any harm, but it's not of much use, and it costs a lot." The Latham Report (1994), quoting a large-scale survey of experiences with BS5750 in the construction industry, confirmed this ambivalence of reaction, in terms of "mixed results and responses from the firms surveyed" (§7.43).

A less widely adopted accreditation system, as far as the professions are concerned, carries the title Investors in People (IIP). This is less to do with functions and procedures than are BS5750 and ISO9000, and focuses instead mainly on staff development, appraisal, and working relations. As with the other approaches, its origins lay in industry and commerce and its incursion into the professional world is relatively recent. In my sample, a hospital pharmacist (P/16) at senior management level had decided to apply on behalf of his pharmaceutical services organization for IIP certification, and an accountant (Acc/14) mentioned that his firm had already gained accreditation. There were no other references to this particular form of organizational recognition: a possible explanation may be that staff training in the professions is already considered to be catered for by continuing professional development programs devised by the appropriate professional bodies.

Individually Based Quality Assurance

The main individual counterpart to organizationally based accreditation can also take a variety of forms. One straightforward distinction relates to whether the individual concerned is seeking professional status or has already acquired it. It is an essential feature of any profession that entry is only accessible to those who have earned an appropriate initial qualification. This typically involves both a series of qualifying examinations and a period of practical experience. Once qualified, however, it has been standard policy to allow members of the profession to continue in practice without further tests or qualification procedures until they retire. That policy has changed in two main respects. First, it is increasingly the case that entry into a specialist field within a profession now calls for some formal demonstration of appropriate competence, usually in the form of an examination. Tax advisers and insolvency practitioners are well-established examples of the trend. But second, the argument—originally advanced a generation or so ago—that the rate of change requires that professional licenses should not remain indefinitely valid, but should be subject to periodic renewal, has very gradually begun to be taken seriously, and even more tentatively to be put into practice in some sectors of the medical profession.

Reaccreditation, as this process is commonly called, has developed to a more advanced stage in the U.S. than in Britain. Since about the mid-1990s, however, a number of the medical Royal Colleges have begun to require their members to undergo some form of validation of their continuing capability. The tendency has been to take the easy way out, and to accept the accumulation of a required number of CME (Continuing Medical Education) points (see chapter 6) as sufficient evidence of being professionally up-to-date. This contrasts sharply with the decision of, for example, the Royal College of General Practitioners in 1988 to award its Fellowship "by assessment and on the basis of the doctor's clinical work with patients in the setting of his/her own practice" (RCGP 1990, p. 38). At around the same time, Newble et al. (1991) were able to report that 16 of the 23 specialty boards in the U.S. (examining boards in medicine) either had instituted or had plans to institute regular recertification by written examination, performance evaluation, or CME participation with a time limit, in most cases, of ten years. Benson (1991), writing specifically about the American Board of Internal Medicine (ABIM), draws the distinction signalled earlier in this chapter between compulsory relicensure, designed to "get the dangerous drivers off the road," and the ABIM's voluntary "continuing improvement model" of recertification, which "will offer a carrot, not yield a stick" (p. 241). Equally ambitiously, the Ontario medical system has, according to Davis (1990), adopted a joint Peer Assessment Program, involving a half-day visit by two unknown peers, and a Physician Enhancement Program resulting in evaluation, remediation, and assessment.

Those of my medical respondents who were not so already, expected before long to be subject to reaccreditation, but were uncertain of the form it might take. A minority thought it would follow the inspection-based model of accreditation of GP training practices, but most expected it to be exam-based. A standard reaction was negative: "they would need to be very specialized for senior consultants" (M/0); "people in their thirties would object to even more exams—they've already taken so many" (M/2); "the U.S. schemes based on assessment don't really work, and take time away from patients—having to retake examinations at the age of fifty would only encourage people to leave medicine" (M/24); "it might be a nice challenge to do an exam, but unfortunately exams aren't always an accurate test" (M/15). More generally, there was a concern that "there are certainly some areas where standards are not good, but reaccreditation won't achieve much" (M/7); "there's a risk that it could become an empty bureaucracy" (M/20). A medic in an administrative post (M/23), while considering individual reaccreditation to be "a worthwhile thing to do," commented that it was focused on less significant issues than was organizationally based accreditation, with its concern for the whole context. It was clear from the interview responses as a whole that none of the other five professions had reached a point at which the issue of reaccreditation loomed large: the question of quality assurance at the individual level continued to depend on the informal criteria of reputation with one's peers and acceptability to one's clients.

Organizationally Based Quality Control

There is no sharp distinction between quality assurance and quality control. Although they serve different purposes in terms of accountability, the same basic procedures—peer group review and observation of practice, submission and scrutiny of documentary evidence—are invoked in each. The balance of emphasis in quality control, however, is less exclusively tilted in the direction of the medical profession, except in the case of Total Quality Management and of a specific form of audit, to be discussed briefly below.

One of the commonly adopted forms of control—concerned with the promotion rather than the demonstration of quality—has already been touched on in chapter 3 and referred to again earlier in this chapter, namely legislation and regulation. In its organizational, as opposed to individual, mode its main impact falls on pharmacies and firms of accountants, architects, and structural engineers. Pharmacies—the first of these—are subject to numerous procedural requirements, including the need for pharmacy superintendents to lay down standard protocols and procedures for all qualified and non-qualified staff; to provide information leaflets on individual drugs and their consequences; and to notify the Medicines Control Agency of any problems which occur in relation to prescriptions. The accountants' firms are subject to a wide range of regulatory procedures, stemming for the most part from the Companies Act and the Insolvency Act, and are required to maintain the operational standards laid down by the Accountancy Standards Board: as one respondent (Acc/9) commented, "carrying out these requirements becomes ever more onerous." The main comparable burdens on firms of architects and structural engineers derive from the official Building Regulations (which are frequently amended and extended), U.K. Health and Safety Regulations, and the Construction Design and Maintenance specifications promulgated by the European Commission. The engineering practices are in addition subject on an informal basis to their own profession's Codes of Practice.

Another main control procedure—designed to ensure conformity with aspects of sound professional practice, rather than merely to specify it—is widely understood. Inspection, involving either specially appointed (and sometimes specially trained) people, or one or more knowledgeable peers, is now an established part of professional life for pharmacists and accountancy partnerships. Industrial pharmacies are open to visitations by the Medicines Inspectorate and community pharmacists to the inspectors working for the Pharmaceutical Society as well as to occasional drugs checks from the police. Accountancy—in recognition of its significant responsibilities for general financial practice—is subject to random visits of inspection by the Joint Monitoring Unit (set up collectively by the six professional bodies) to check on compliance with the relevant standards.

While both regulation and inspection are in the category of formal quality control procedures, designed to be credible to the public, two other types of control—Total Quality Management and audit—may be designated as informal, in that they are primarily designed to satisfy internal professional requirements. The central concern of Total Quality Management (TQM) is with improving day-to-day operations rather than with ensuring conformity with documented procedures. The study by Joss and Kogan (1995), focusing on its application to the health professions, defines TQM as "an integrated, corporately led program of organizational change, designed to engender and sustain a culture of continuous improvement based on customer-oriented definitions of quality" (p. 13). Its essential feature is the commitment of all participants in the totality of the organization's activities to a shared concern to improve the quality of its products and services. The approach was strongly promoted in British medicine by the Department of Health, but Joss and Kogan conclude that "the outcomes of the TQM experiments in the [National Health Service] were disappointing" (p. 167). It did not feature at all significantly in my medical respondents' comments, and there was only one other reference—by an accountant—to a professional practice which had adopted it.

In contrast, the application of the techniques of what is termed medical audit seems to have been fairly extensive within both hospital medicine and general practice.[6] The word 'audit' is confusing here, in that there is no insistence, as in financial audit, on rigorous independent scrutiny of formally presented accounts. As Kogan and Redfern (1995) explain, it is as an aspect of controlling quality that calls for some systematic (usually quantitative) information relevant to improving the existing standards of care, with particular reference to possible improvements in the interest of patients. Rosenthal (1995) identifies four distinct approaches: a review of case notes; routinely collected service data; population-based epidemiological studies; and the analysis of the appropriate use of investigations and therapies. The specific activities to be selected for scrutiny are a matter for the decision of the group of doctors concerned, and there is no requirement for outsiders to be involved. There is therefore little cumulative and independently validated information: and even in quite sizeable exercises in systematic data collection, the number of cases is rarely large enough to offer statistically reliable results (Lockyer and Harrison, 1994).

But despite the "very disparate understanding of what audit is" (M/ 6), and the perception that its quality is "very variable" (M/15), it has been heavily endorsed by hospital managements. Not to be outdone, the Royal College of General Practitioners (1990) rates it as "a very high priority" (p. 12) and maintains that it "should be incorporated as part of everyday general practice" (p. 35). Estimates of the actual incidence at around the period of that pronouncement are somewhat inconsistent: Owen et al. (1989) found that just over half the practices in which they conducted interviews (51 out of 96) had adopted medical audit, while Derry et al. (1991) identified as many as two participating practices in every three in their contemporary survey in Oxfordshire.

The medical audit process has attracted a great deal more negative than positive comment. The "audit of audits" by Derry et al. (1991) disclosed considerable deficiencies in the conduct of practice audits, while Lord and Littlejohns (1996) found, from their large-scale questionnaire survey of audit in U.K. hospitals and community health care providers, that even after some years of experience many medical staff remain sceptical about its value. My respondents offered a number of critical comments: "audit is low gear stuff—it can change people's practice marginally, but it's an expensive way of doing so" (M/10); "there's always a problem of translating audit into action—and at present the monitoring of the quality of services is pretty poor" (M/21); "the kind of audit I'm involved in [scrutinizing the results of treatment of four and a half thousand patients over ten years] takes an enormous amount of time to run, and doesn't seem likely to make any scientific difference" (M/24). Horder et al. (1986) confirm this reaction, tracing little evidence that audit findings influence practitioners' behavior. Pollitt (1993) sees it as "particularly weak with respect to public accountability" (p. 24), while Wergin et al. (1988) deem the review of notes on patients—termed "chart review" in the US—to be an ineffective evaluation instrument, because of inaccuracies and inconsistencies in data recording, insensitivity to subtle changes in patient management, and restrictions in the scope of behaviors to those that can be easily recorded.

Even the positive assessments tend to be guarded. A medic in an administrative post (M/23) noted a recent research study as showing audit to be a waste of money, and detected "a backlash against it." She considered that audit should avoid following a medical research model, and should "ideally be much softer," though conceding that the medical profession "is driven by numbers and tends to be sniffy about qualitative research." Lockyer and Harrison (1994) allow that, despite its disadvantages, audit may be of some use "in identifying extreme deficiencies and deviations" (p. 176); Derry et al. (1991) see its positive benefit in providing evidence of the quality of care, rather than in enabling practitioners to improve; while Batstone (1990), in an apparently contradictory comment, regards it as "essentially an educational rather than a managerial tool."

The case for devoting some degree of attention to a form of quality control that is in the first place profession-specific, and in the second generally held to be of dubious value, lies not as much in the features of that process itself as in the light it can throw on more general exercises in informal organizationally based self-scrutiny. Most of these are even less tightly designed than medical audit programs, but share the same overall purpose of providing the members of a practice group or firm with evidence to help enhance the quality of their collective activities. As examples of the genre, they share the same weaknesses of being time-consuming, non-cumulative, and haphazard in operation and outcome: they also lack public credibility, but that is because they are not designed with such a purpose in view. Architecture as a profession employs a variety of such procedures, none of them unduly costly or sophisticated, including—in smaller practices—scrutiny of all incoming and outgoing mail by a single partner,[7] to ensure the coherence of the firm's activities and the consistency of its interactions with clients; some practices also organize formal critiques of specific designs and reviews of overall projects carried out internally by senior staff at appropriate intervals. In other professional settings, collective self-scrutiny is largely *ad hoc*, arising from particular operational problems which need to be sorted out by some form of internal investigation.

Individually Based Quality Control

The individual counterpart to regulation, as a formal mode of organizational quality control, is compulsory continuing professional development (CPD). Enough has already been said in chapter 6 about this particular set of procedures to make further discussion unnecessary. There are no unique labels for the other two main types of individual quality control, but peer review and appraisal are the most commonly used; both are commonly adopted as informal processes, although the first may be formalized into a variant of inspection. It involves direct observation of a practitioner at work by one or more knowledgeable colleagues, resulting in feedback designed to improve deficiencies in performance and to signal satisfactory achievement. The second does not normally call for first-hand scrutiny of practice but tends instead to rely on reports on professional performance by close colleagues, or on self-assessments of perceived strengths and weaknesses. The impact of both peer review and appraisal is weakened by the absence of effective sanctions: as one respondent (M/19) pointed out, "Striking people off the register isn't easy to do when there aren't enough others with the same specialism in the system: even if they're only deemed to need retraining, who will retrain them; and who will pay for the training?"

Writing in the context of medicine in the U.S., Ramsey (1993) notes that "peer ratings provide a practical method to assess clinical performance in areas such as humanistic qualities and communication skills that are difficult to assess with other measures [such as examinations]" (p. 1655). His concern is with quality assurance rather than quality control: in that connection he reports that peer rating proved acceptable to 84 percent of his survey sample (314 physicians in three different states) as a means of recertification.[8] The reaction to peer review in the U.K. medical fraternity is considerably more mixed. While two of my respondents welcomed its non-threatening adoption as a form of voluntary quality assurance, there were concerns about its possible employment for compulsory quality control, including the question of whether the peers concerned should be colleagues or people from a comparable workplace and the problem of how to discount the personal biases of the reviewers. The emphasis, moreover, as one respondent (M/27) pointed out, would inevitably be on the quality of a particular performance rather than on the overall competence of the individual being reviewed.

Peer review was not widely adopted, or contemplated for possible adoption, outside medicine. What is undoubtedly the best-established peer review procedure takes place within a branch of the legal system, namely the Independent Tribunal Service, where both full-time and part-time chairpersons are closely monitored during their probationary first year, and the large majority who survive the process with the help of remedial advice and training are subject to further observation by experienced colleagues at least once every three years. It seemed all the more remarkable, in light of this example, that judges—who carry a greater responsibility—were at the time of the fieldwork subject to no kind of performance review. One of those interviewed (L/15) said he would welcome a critique of his performance, but another (L/8) merely commented that by long tradition no judge, other than one undergoing training, would enter another's court.

Across the professions, appraisal is a more widely adopted mode of quality control. Although its main function is to identify, usually on an annual basis, the requirements of individual practitioners for staff development and training, it also tends to be used for other purposes, such as the renewal or otherwise of employment contracts, promotion, or the improvement of service delivery. It is more relevant in the context of large practices, where staff members may not be known personally to senior managers, than in small ones. In many firms, the intended link between appraisal and subsequent training is surprisingly inadequate, almost to the point of non-existence. Various reasons were put forward for this: "people should choose what training they have" (L/20); "it would be wrong to impose a rigid approach" (E/10); "there isn't a close enough relationship between training and appraisal, because the resources are too limited to meet the demands" (Acc/11). In the case of a large engineering firm, organizational politics got in the way of the connection: the training department did not control the training budget; individual departments were responsible for meeting the costs of courses and other provision, but were not always prepared to do so, because of "a conflict of resources" (E/19). One of the few examples of an apparently effective appraisal process was described by a senior architect working for a local authority (Arc/20): "There is a formal system, with targets set and performance evaluated each year. There are also continuing appraisals throughout the year, linked to training programs. New staff have a probationary period to identify their strengths and weaknesses. And I make it my business to vet all the courses people are sent on." A summary of the general position was provided by a disenchanted training manager in an accountancy firm (Acc/23): "The professional institutes and the profession itself seem to be coming away from an emphasis on marketing products to an emphasis on people, and in most firms managements agree that people are their most important assets, but they still don't do anything about it [spending money on systematic staff development]."

Quality and Professional Life

The considerations advanced in this chapter leave little room for doubt that quality assurance and quality control have become significant elements in professional practice. Although the incidence of the various measures differs substantially from one profession to another, none remains untouched by quality requirements. The changes in peoples' working lives induced by this relatively recent phenomenon must be added to the catalogue of other external and internal pressures enumerated in chapter 3. It is understandable enough that most respondents, while accepting the inevitability of the consequent demands, and showing a conditional readiness to accede to them, nevertheless view them as burdensome, costly, and time-consuming.

Of the three main sources of quality maintenance procedures mentioned earlier—government, professional bodies, and individual practices and practitioners—it is evident that the second has played the most active role. New demands are commonly introduced on the contention that it is vital for the profession itself to safeguard and guarantee its standards, rather than ceding the responsibility to political control. This claim being more or less readily granted by the practitioners, their corporate representatives are liable to set about instituting quality measures with what then seems, to those affected by them, an excess of zeal. As one cynical commentator (M/19) remarked, "The government hasn't really pressurized them [the professional bodies] about quality assurance: they're only too ready to take on the flavor of the day. The government is very happy about the move towards accreditation because it doesn't have to pay a penny—all the costs fall on the profession itself. The only thing the politicians really care about is how much public money is involved."

Whether or not one agrees with this analysis, it may be appropriate for some purposes to see quality issues as an essentially political phenomenon, designed to contain what might otherwise be represented as the unbridled power of professional groups. In this light, quality could indeed be labelled as a creature of political fashion—"the flavor of the day": and, like all fashions, expect to enjoy only a limited life. The verdict of one interviewee (E/30) that "quality assurance was all the rage until two or three years ago, but has fortunately now taken a back seat" nevertheless seems unduly optimistic. Its demise must, on the argument with which this chapter opened, await the restoration of a greater measure than now exists of public trust.[9] There seems no evident alternative but for the professions to continue to implement quality assurance and quality control procedures until they have achieved that elusive purpose.

Notes

1. Joss and Kogan (1995) identify three closely comparable "dimensions of quality": systemic (related to operating systems and processes); technical (concerned with

professional content); and generic (involving inter-personal aspects, including standards of conduct to others).

2. Personnel problems in hospital pharmacy are, in contrast, dealt with on a local basis. Another respondent (P/16) gave the instance of a female pharmacist who made several errors in dispensing radiopharmaceuticals. It turned out that she had had inadequate pre-registration training (there was no checking system in place to detect this). She was given a redesigned training program and closely monitored afterwards. The same respondent went on to explain that, in cases where people develop a drink problem, they are counselled through the hospital's occupational health system. In other instances of inadequate performance, they may be moved around in their jobs until they find one with which they can cope. A markedly less lenient attitude exists towards anyone showing an inadequate control over the provision of drugs: the defaulter would be first suspended and, if the problem repeated itself, dismissed.

3. See, however, chapter 3, note 1.

4. That is, in the categories identified earlier in the chapter, between professional and moral accountability.

5. The credibility is not automatically earned by the procedure, since the impartiality of the agency concerned may be suspect. Official enquiries by the police force on apparently unprofessional conduct by its members so frequently find them free of blame that they are commonly seen by a sceptical public as "whitewash"—a meaningless but costly ritual.

6. A variant on the same basic process, known as clinical audit, concerns itself primarily with the evaluation of facilities and services outside the directly medical aspects. An example offered by a hospital pharmacist (P/13) centered on an expensive treatment for chest cases which did not need to be administered more than once every six hours: the audit found that many prescriptions called for more frequent dosages. As a result, consultants were persuaded to avoid over-prescription, and significant savings were made.

7. An analagous procedure is adopted, as an informal, individually based method of quality control, in relation to the work of probationers in some of the larger legal and accountancy firms.

8. The practical relevance of the procedure is cast into considerable doubt by his revelation that separate ratings from eleven peer physicians were needed to provide a reliable assessment of the individual.

9. The relationship between trust and accountability is lucidly explored, in the context of higher education, in Trow (1996).

Part 5

Retrospect

9

Conclusion

The Rationale in Retrospect

To a very large extent, the structure as well as the content of this book has been determined by the testimony of the 190 respondents spread across the six professions under review. Where possible, that testimony has been matched against the independent findings of other researchers: but the evidence from this source, whether corroborative or questioning, has not been sufficient to justify a claim to objectivity in the assertions made or the conclusions reached. If, as is clearly the case, the internalist perspective adopted here is biased towards the largely favorable representations of their activities by the professionals themselves, it is no less evident, as postmodernism has taught us, that outright objectivity is equally contentious a claim for those sociological studies of the professions that have chosen a more detached, externalist framework. Indeed, many of them, as indicated in chapter 1, can be seen to reflect the prevailing theoretical stances of their day, and accordingly begin to lose their persuasiveness as those theories become outmoded by others.

Insofar as what has been said in the preceding chapters is seen as an impressionistic narrative rather than a documentary deposition, the twin tests of its acceptability must lie in whether it rings true and hangs together. To further that consideration on the part of the reader, a brief review will be offered here of the main underlying themes and the conclusions that arise from them.

There is good evidence to support the claim that the phenomenon of change has been a particularly significant feature of professional life over recent years. Chapter 3 outlined a range of social and cognitive factors which have impinged to greater or lesser degrees on the six professions under study (and arguably on many others as well). Change can also be seen as of growing significance in professional careers (chapter 4), particularly with the advent of specialization and the move towards large practices with hierarchical promotion structures. And as noted in chapter 8, quality demands have also given rise to a variety of new requirements in working practice.

To survive changes of this magnitude and extent calls for a considerable degree of commitment, of both a general and a more specific kind. The general form involves a readiness to cope with the continuing demands of a professional setting. Those who are unwilling or unable to do so include some people who have chosen to make their careers outside mainstream practices, others who have taken the opportunity for early retirement, and others still who have resigned, or have been required to withdraw from their profession, because of stress, lack of motivation, or some evidence of serious inadequacy (see chapter 4). By far the majority of respondents, however, can be seen to display a close identification with their careers to a point at which, for many, professional activity becomes an integral part of their personalities, not to be distinguished from the rest of their lives.

The more specific form of commitment involves the need to sustain professional capability in the face of a succession of imperatives which existing knowledge and experience are unable satisfactorily to meet. The main incentive to do so appears to stem from the desire to achieve a sound reputation among colleagues in the first instance and clients in the second. At a less immediate level, the collective requirement to enhance the status of the profession as a whole also emerges as being of some significance.

Where reputation and status serve as the basis for continuing to maintain capability, the means of doing so can be seen to lie in the coping strategies deployed to acquire new knowledge and to develop new skills. As the accounts in chapters 6 and 7 make plain, there is a wide variety of such strategies, ranging from participation in highly structured formal courses to informal interactions with colleagues. A number of other researchers, notably Gear et al. (1994) and Eraut et al. (1998), endorse the conclusion that informal learning plays the major role, though largely ignored in the schemes devised by professional bodies for continuing professional development.

One of the significant features of the contemporary scene invokes simultaneously the three themes—change, commitment, and capability—whose complex interrelationship has been briefly discussed above. The current political concern with quality control and quality assurance (chapter 8) can be traced back to two main sources. The first is the perception, from outside the professions themselves, of an excessive degree of self-interest and a corresponding lack of attention to clients' concerns: at best, an inability effectively to communicate with lay persons, and at worst a deliberate mystification, often used as a vehicle for charging excessive fees. In recent years this accusation—whether or not accepted as valid—has been met by serious attempts among practitioners in all six professions to adopt a more explicitly client-centered approach, although as often happens the external impression has lagged behind the internal actuality.

The second basis for the imposition of quality measures rests on the phenomenon that the medics colorfully term the "bad apples." As one respondent, quoted in chapter 8, pointed out, "you can't make all surgeons as good as the best" (M/10). Any attempt systematically to identify and weed out the bottom five percent (say) in any professional group would be a self-perpetuating exercise, in that once they were removed from the scene another set of individuals would automatically qualify as the next cohort of least effective practitioners. Nevertheless, there is a strong case for preventing those known to be incompetent from continuing in normal practice: so some means of recognition of lack of capability—whether formal or informal—is a reasonable requirement, as is the existence of measures to deal with the problem once it is identified. It is here that implicit professional norms of collegiality serve to weaken public confidence, as serious cases remain unreported or are perceived to be dealt with in an ineffective way, while the occasional "whistle-blower" is penalized for disloyalty rather than praised for his or her public spirit.

It would perhaps be as well, as a number of respondents and researchers have argued, to separate the organizational problem of dealing with professional inadequacy from the educational problem of promoting allround improvements in performance. Most quality control measures are geared towards the first of these objectives, while quality assurance procedures are on the whole concerned with the second. But whether they are categorized as formal or informal, there is little doubt that the advent of quality demands has given rise to significant changes in attitudes and practice, has heightened the concern with enhancing capability, and has put further strains on the maintenance of professional commitment.

Variations and Similarities

It is sometimes claimed by casual observers of white Caucasian origin that all Chinese look alike: no doubt the converse would also be true.

But to those in that vast ethnic group, it is evident that all Chinese look different. The former observation rests on a general similarity of feature as viewed from a cultural distance, and the latter on a close scrutiny that takes the similarities for granted, and goes beyond them to a more subtle and culturally sensitive awareness of the distinctions. The study of the professions is not greatly different. Those who view them from a distance, treating them as a coherent social phenomenon, are apt to stress their homogeneity; those who seek to explore them from a closer vantage point cannot long ignore their manifold differences.

In the present study, the pattern of correlations and contrasts between and within the six professions has transpired to be extraordinarily complex: so much so that it defeats any straightforward analysis. Even within the same general family the main branches diverge in significant ways, and may themselves subdivide in different directions. Sometimes unexpected connections can be found between apparently quite disparate fields, while sharp discontinuities can occur between what seem to be closely related activities. Classification becomes an elusive pursuit: for every generalization one is tempted to make, an important exception is liable to become apparent. In illustration of these points, Bucher and Strauss (1961) remark on "the great diversity of enterprise and endeavor that mark the profession; the cleavages that exist along with the division of labor; and the intellectual and specialist movements that occur...." (p. 326). As quoted in chapter 2 above, they go on to add that "One branch of a profession may have more in common with elements of a neighboring occupation than with their own fellow professionals" (p. 330). Although they were writing specifically about medicine, what they have to say is of direct relevance to other professions as well.

In chapter 1, it was suggested that aspects of professional cultures could be illuminated through a study of the procedures used to maintain capability in the face of change. In the event, a variety of cultural features of the six professions could be identified from the scrutiny of particular aspects of practice. For example, the tendency for medics, pharmacists, and engineers to have recourse to academic specialists in seeking solutions to particularly intractable problems helps to underpin the distinction between technically based and non-technical professions, as does—on the other side of the divide—the greater openness of lawyers, accountants, and architects to consult members of professions other than their own.[1] Similarly, the stronger reliance on mentorship arrangements among medics, architects, and structural engineers throws light on the concept of processually based professions, while the notion of procedurally based ones is supported by the stronger reliance on documentary sources among pharmacists, lawyers, and accountants.[2]

But as one begins to understand more about professional practices and values, the inverse relationship becomes possible, enabling a growing cultural understanding to throw light on otherwise puzzling strategies for maintaining capability. It is, for instance, by recognizing the determinedly independent—or, as earlier suggested, anarchic—social features of both the barristers' fraternity and the architects' community that an understanding can be reached of their marginal involvement in formal CPD arrangements. Similarly, it is by becoming aware of the social phenomenon of their lack of direct commercial relationships with their clients—in Britain at least—that one can make sense of the fact that doctors, pharmacists, and barristers remain less interested than solicitors, architects, and structural engineers in enhancing their presentation skills. On the cognitive side, the particular enthusiasm shown by hospital doctors for attending international conferences is given a clearer perspective by the recognition that theirs is both a specialized and an academicized field; similarly, the relative absence of specialization among architects and structural engineers can be seen as a function of a cognitively homogeneous knowledge domain.

It is important, however, to recognize the tentative and contingent nature of these correlations. To speak of "law" is to homogenize three significantly different sub-professions—barristers, solicitors, and the judiciary—each of which has its own complex of internal distinctions. The same is true of most of the other professions under review: and even the apparent exceptions—architecture and structural engineering— have their occasional experts in conservation, airport design, and the like. So every claim made about a profession as a whole runs the risk of failing to take into account the exceptions. And of course at the individual level no two professionals are identical. One striking difference stems, as noted in chapter 4, from the contextual contrasts between working in large firms and small practices. Even within such categories, the members may display radically differing views and values: such common features as they have will be largely a product of their broadly comparable inductions into professional life. To say this is not to deny the possibility of making general statements, which have the important virtue of bringing out significant features of the collectivity: it is rather to make it clear that what is allowable at one stratum of generality may be subject to question from a closer standpoint, yielding a more detailed view. But much the same limitations, one may note, are evident in any ethnographic account.

Some Potential Implications

From Knowles (1970) onwards, many of those who have written about adult and continuing education have emphasized the importance of giving the initiative to the learner and avoiding a didactic approach. Yet by a curious paradox of the pedagogues, they are liable to address their own audience of fellow-educators in highly directive terms, issuing firm instructions on what is and what is not to be done. Houle (1981) and his followers concerned with the more specific field of continuing professional education offer few departures from this tradition. However, since consistency with the established principles of adult learning demands the need for the readers of this book to make up their own minds and draw their own conclusions, the now-usual neat summary, firing a rapid series of bullet-points for action, seems oddly inappropriate.

Nevertheless, it may be useful to draw the discussion to a close by reminding the various prospective audiences identified in chapter 1 of some of the key points which are potentially relevant to their respective interests, beginning with those trainers in professional bodies and other agencies whose role it is to provide the organized resources for continuing professional development. For them, perhaps the most significant issues may be found in chapters 6 and 7, where the respondents and the research literature together suggest some of the limitations as well as some of the advantages of formal courses, and illustrate the wide range of strategies which enable useful learning to take place. A clearer knowledge of these, and a better understanding of the rationales behind them, might well suggest some useful ways in which such strategies could be supported and underpinned, rather than being seen as unwelcome ways of detracting from carefully planned contributions to continuing professional development. Some of the findings reported in other parts of the book may suggest further reasons for, and possibilities of, adapting learning opportunities to the particular needs and circumstances of intended recipients, given the potential variety of those needs and circumstances and their likely inability to be fitted into a simple formula.

Those in the professional bodies responsible for the development and implementation of general CPD policy—as against specific course provision—seem in many cases surprisingly out of tune with their members. To have such members' complex and sometimes conflicting views on the subject set out, as in Chapter 6, might give cause for reconsideration of some of the more crudely mechanistic schemes, and perhaps strengthen the case for an open and flexible arrangement which allows appropriate credence to the many informal approaches, explored in chapter 7, to updating knowledge, enhancing capabilities and coping with intractable professional problems. By the same token, the members of the relevant professional bodies responsible for laying down and invigilating standards of quality control and approaches to quality assurance might find, in the discussion of the issue in chapter 8, some reasons to review current requirements and to build more firmly on the existing values and practices of the practitioners who are expected to conform to them. It may be worth a reminder, in this connection, of the now firmly established finding that formal policies made from the top down suffer innumerable distortions in the process of implementation unless they also accord reasonably closely with the cultural perspectives of those at the receiving end.

The main implications for the initial training of professionals are likely to be somewhat different from those for both continuing professional development and quality procedures. In many professions, the first stage in one's career takes place in a university or other academic setting, in which the emphasis tends to fall almost exclusively on inculcating the technical aspects of professional knowledge. As a result, quite a few of those first encountering their professions in action have some difficulty in transmuting their knowledge of theory into the realities of practice. A number of respondents' comments on this problem are noted in chapters 4 and 7. They serve to underline a more general issue which arises in a number of places in the text, namely the considerable but often-overlooked importance of contextual knowledge—not only an acknowledgment of the rules of acceptable behavior and appropriate values and beliefs current in any given profession, but also some forewarning of the nature of organizational politics, an awareness of how to present oneself and how to relate to clients, and a recognition of the eventual need for management skills. Aldridge (1994) makes the point in relation to engineering, but his comments seem equally pertinent to other professions:

> In the past, a new engineer was only expected to be on top of the technology and be capable of working within a specific technical domain. Competition, economics and organization were the kinds of topics that were to be learned through experience.... Today such topics are increasingly important to new and practising engi-

neers and should be considered for possible inclusion in the curricula of traditional engineering courses (p. 231).

It does not necessarily follow that a large proportion of time need be spent in preparing prospective professionals for "real life"; as against equipping them with the technical knowledge base they are likely to require. However, it may be suggested that some key elements at least of contextual awareness could usefully be built in to the teaching of conventional topics. Moreover, the pressure on initial academic programs to span the relevant professional knowledge field in both breadth and depth[3] may deserve to be resisted in light of the strong evidence from respondents that they are able on their own initiative to learn much of what they need as they go along.

Those members of the six professions which have formed the subject of the study, alongside other professionals interested in reflecting about their working lives and the impact of the changes to which they are subject, may find issues to interest them in most of the preceding chapters. It was noticeable in the course of conducting the interviews how limited was the respondents' knowledge about, and how lively their interest in, the views and activities of fellow-professionals in other fields, and similarly how marked the wish to know about others' ways of coping with problems comparable to their own. This suggests a particular emphasis, for them, on chapters 2, 3, 4 and 5: though the topics of formal and informal learning and quality should also serve both to reinforce what they already know and to raise new issues for consideration.

A further group of potential readers identified in the introductory chapter comprise those who have an academic or scholarly interest in professionalism as a field of enquiry in its own right. As noted in chapter 1, this study differs from most in its internalist approach, offering a contrast to the more usual exploration of issues on a macro scale relating to political and organizational concerns, and often bracketing several different professions together for the purpose of overall generalization. It can also be clearly differentiated from studies focusing on the micro processes shaping the ways in which professionals learn, and from the wide variety of other writings on professions, whether viewed individually or collectively. Some of the evidence put forward on how members of the six occupational groups under study think, feel, and act, and what are their contextual constraints and working conditions, may nevertheless be of interest and relevance to fellow-researchers in the social sciences and the field of higher education.

A book intended for a lay audience, or even for those at the point in their education at which they might be considering professional careers, would need to have been written differently from this one, with a less insistent resort to supporting evidence and a greater highlighting of the more noteworthy findings. Nevertheless, if any member of such an audience happens by chance to stray into this apparently alien territory, it must be hoped that he or she will find at least some source of entertainment, some new and interesting knowledge, and some material food for thought.

What seems to emerge above all from the welter of different considerations raised in this enquiry is the need for both demystification and disaggregation. One of the many achievements of Bronislaw Malinowski as a founding father of social anthropology was to show that the practices of the Melanesians he studied, though apparently exotic and arcane, could be seen to derive from thoughts and feelings closely comparable with those of his Western readers—that their social conduct was governed by "a rational appreciation of cause and effect," combined with "personal sentiments such as ambition, vanity, pride, desire of self-enhancement by display and also attachment, friendship and devotion" (Malinowski, 1926, p. 58). In its own way, the present study too should have "show[n] the familiar in the apparently strange,"[4] making it apparent that professionals, too, are not alien and mysterious forms of life, but that they share with other people a wide range of human feelings and concerns. Being able in part to see the world through their eyes—to know not only the considerations that guide them in what they do but also the reasons which lie behind what they think—one can begin to make better sense of the variety of activities in which they engage and the reasons for their responses to some of the pressures put upon them from the outside.

A closer understanding along these lines also makes it easier to see the absurdity of some of the wide generalizations made about professionalization, especially as one begins to recognize the multiplicity of internal distinctions between and within individual professions. It should in particular have become evident that professionals cannot be indiscriminately lumped together and treated as a homogeneous mass possessed of clearly identifiable common properties. They are neither collectively given to high-flown claims about altruism, as represented in some of the earlier writings on the professions, nor uniformly subject to grossly avaricious or power-seeking motives, as some of their later critics have maintained. Like other groups of people, they are a mixed bunch, with a scattering of common features. Among these, as the evidence presented here suggests, one may number a lively intelligence, an openness to questioning, a strong concern to carry out their jobs to the best of their ability, and a general willingness to enhance that ability over time and to sustain it in a context of unremitting change.

Notes

1. The connections here may not be immediately obvious. Difficult technical problems are likely to call for reference to fellow-professionals with highly specialized expertise; non-technical knowledge domains are less sharply bounded, and open to contributions from differing perspectives.
2. By way of elaboration, mentoring is particularly important when learning to conduct new processes ("see one, do one" under tutelage; then "teach one" as a mentor in turn); procedures are more readily picked up from texts and other written materials.
3. Professional bodies are themselves in some cases the occasion for such pressure, in their often highly conservative attitudes to the validation of initial training courses.
4. Hammersley and Atkinson (1995, p. 207).

Postscript
The Role of the Universities

One of Sherlock Holmes' ingenious solutions to a crime rested on the phenomenon of the dog that did not bark. In Britain, the higher education system, like the canine in the detective story, has remained strangely silent and inert. Yet the official statistics provided by the Universities and Colleges Admissions Service (UCAS, 1998, table 1) show that, in 1996, just under 40 percent of applicants to higher education opted for vocationally or professionally oriented courses. Across the years, the universities have become overwhelmingly the main source of initial training for the professions: but their role in support of continuing professional learning has been, and still remains, negligible.[1]

There is admittedly a certain amount of interchange at the level of the individual. As noted in chapter 7, practicing members of the technically based professions—medicine, pharmacy, and engineering—tend to seek the advice of their academic counterparts in solving difficult and unfamiliar problems,[2] while architects—and to a lesser extent lawyers and pharmacists—may be drawn as practitioners into teaching on initial training courses. In his extensive review of the relationships between academic and professional lawyers, Partington (1988) documents, among other activities, the involvement of individual academics in training programs for the judiciary and courses for members of tribunals, but offers no suggestion that university law departments might take a collective role in continuing professional development.

In 1991, Vaughan observed that "the actual number of [professional] bodies which are collaborating with Higher Education over provision of modularised award-bearing courses for CPD is still small.... All that is certain is that [the market] will grow." At more or less the same time, the Royal College of General Practitioners (1990), in setting its future priorities, commented regretfully that "Only about 1 per cent of general practitioners in the College hold doctorates," and expressed the hope that "about 100 general practitioners a year during the 1990s will obtain [them]" (p. 50). That there has indeed been some increase in the

245

numbers of practitioners who find it worthwhile to acquire higher academic qualifications is suggested by the review in chapter 4 of respondents who had taken this step; an observation supported, in relation to lawyers, by Partington (1992): "for this reason [demonstrating competence in a specialism], numbers of practitioners do now seek further qualifications in new subject areas—often in the form of modules from taught Masters' programmes" (p. 86).

The limitations on the take-up of such courses are partly self-imposed. As a solicitor (L/30) noted "the London LlM course puts on a broad range of options, but it isn't marketed to practitioners. In any case, the pressures of time and money prevent most junior solicitors from enrolling." A structural engineer (E/19) confirmed that "There are relatively few university-based CPD courses because universities don't know how to sell their wares—they go to the operating level rather than to the top people. Commercial firms are much more persistent in their sales techniques." On the other side of the fence, an academic engineer (E/1) acknowledged that "our strategy here, and in other universities, is a bit hit and miss—we don't tie up the loose ends."

When it comes to the contribution of universities to programs designed specifically for non-specialist practitioners, as against those on advanced topics to which a limited number of specialists might be attracted, the picture is even more bleak. As Coulson-Thomas (1991) observed in reviewing the future of the professions, "It is surprising that more professional associations are not entering into joint ventures and various forms of arrangements with universities." One of my respondents (L/22) remarked, along similar lines, "It's puzzling why university law schools don't figure much in CPD—perhaps academic lawyers regard themselves as being above vocational training."

Two academic accountants provided different but complementary explanations of this apparently strange state of affairs. The first (Acc/21) argued that universities could well feature more prominently in CPD provision if it did not take away useful time and resources from research: so "we tend to keep it in the locker that we can do it". The second (Acc/22) contended that there was so little university involvement with CPD because it was primarily targeted at practical knowledge, involving the application of rules in subject areas in which the universities have no special advantage. He added that "anyway, CPD courses tend to be expensive to organize and market." Twining (1994b) writes for more than the legal profession when he remarks that "there is a certain amount of opportunism and entrepreneurship by some universities, but almost no serious analysis (at least in public) of what the university community might appropriately contribute to this developing field [of CPD programmes]" (p. 96). Even though the scale of academic involvement in the U.S. is very considerably greater,[3] Stern (1987), from his perspective as Dean of University Extension in the University of California, Berkeley, took the view that

> So far American universities in this field have been exploitative, have regarded continuing education essentially as an extractive industry auxiliary to the enterprise, which is meant to produce, in order of importance, research and then to provide graduate students and undergraduate students with degrees (p. 55).

Others have been ready to endorse his subsequent comment that, nonetheless, "universities are important to the organized future of continuing professional education" (p. 55). A senior engineer in a research organization (E/27) was emphatic in his observation that "industry and the academic world together can fulfill the need to be professional about CPD better than either can alone." The Lord Chancellor's Advisory Committee (1997) in its turn "believes that the universities could make a much more significant contribution to the needs of the profession by adapting and developing courses which would enable practitioners to meet and to exceed the requirements of the professional bodies' formal schemes," postulating the need to "facilitate cooperation between the universities and the professional bodies to further this development" (para 3.10).

If a more active involvement in CPD were to be seen as a worthwhile activity for academic institutions, they would find no shortage of advice on where their priorities should lie. In general terms, Twining (1994b) suggests the need to fill a conspicuous gap:

> In Great Britain CLE [Continuing Legal Education] tends to veer between two extremes: minimalist provision of "top-up" and "crash" courses lasting from a few hours to not more than a week and academic courses lasting at least an academic year. There are a few exceptions, but by and large there is something of a vacuum between get-skilled-quick and get-wise-slow provision (p. 96).

Gear et al. (1994) recommend universities, amongst other things, "to make available their expertise for formal professional education and informal professional learning alike, through courses, consultancies, data bases and personal contacts. Here, they are likely often to collaborate with professional bodies and employing organizations in assessing what needs to be provided, and in evaluating the benefits" (p. 79). Reinforcing the theme of partnership between "higher-education institutions and professional communities," Eraut (1994) proposes

> collaborative research projects into the acquisition and development of important areas of professional knowledge and know-how;
>
> problem-oriented seminars for groups of researchers and mid-career professionals...;
>
> a jointly-planned programme of continuing education opportunities for mid-career professionals which assists them: to reflect on their experience, make it more explicit through having to share it, interpret it and recognize it as a basis for future learning; and to escape from their experience in the sense of challenging traditional assumptions and acquiring new perspectives (p. 57).

There is, it would seem, less difficulty in writing an attractive prospectus for universities to follow than there is in persuading them to adopt a more active stance in the first place. The main current disincentive is likely to stem from the academics' own professional demands and pressures: a need both to excel competitively to earn research funding and at the same time to meet exacting requirements for quality in teaching. It is only insofar as continuing professional development can, firstly, be seen as a worthwhile exercise and, secondly, be fitted somehow into this tight existing framework, that substantial progress may be made. The provision of research and consultancy on a collective rather than an individual basis, for large organizations or consortia of small ones—as advocated by Gear et al. (1994) and Eraut (1994)—may form one starting-point for future growth, as may an extension of award-bearing and other courses along the lines suggested by Twining (1994b).

But in the end, it could well be circumstance—the large-scale reduction of research budgets, or a sizeable decline in the undergraduate population—not exhortation, that brings about a significant change in the level of the universities' participation in the enterprise. And if and when it does, one may be sure that the academic groups concerned will settle for their own interpretation of their role, rather than following the prescriptions of their well-wishers. It is only to be hoped that they will trouble themselves beforehand to acquire a clear understanding of the social contexts and cultural values within which they decide to operate, along the lines that this book has—subject to the limits set out in chapter 1—been concerned to portray.

Notes

1. To say this is to set aside the contributions to the subject by a number of departments of adult and continuing education and a handful of specialist researchers

into higher education. However, such contributions—as in the case of the present one—necessarily deal with general issues and strategic problems rather than with the specific learning needs of particular professional groups.

2. Dowlatshaki (1996), on the basis of a survey of 378 engineering firms in the U.S. mid-west, records that "only 24 percent" of the respondents expressed a preference for asking for help from university professors in solving business-related problems. This seems quite a high percentage in relation to British practice, serving to emphasize the more active involvement of American academics in continuing professional development.

3. Abbott (1988) offers a particularly interesting series of arguments about why this should be so, reaching back into the early days of professionalization. He cites J.S. Mill's much-quoted remark that "Men are men before they are lawyers, or physicians, or merchants, or manufacturers; and if you make them capable and sensible men, they will make themselves capable and sensible lawyers or physicians," and argues that in Britain this antipathy to professional education persisted "well into the twentieth century" (p. 203). In contrast, though he is sceptical about the role of U.S. universities in continuing professional education, he notes that by 1980 they were spending a sizeable part of their corporate expenditure budget—of some $64 billion a year—on its provision.

Appendix
Methodological Issues

The Purpose in View

The doctrine of accountability, when applied to social enquiry, calls on the researcher or researchers concerned to offer some indication of how the relevant work was carried out. The fact that few members of the intended audience are likely to be interested in such details does not discharge that obligation. The purpose of this appendix is accordingly to take the minority of readers concerned with such issues behind the scenes, exposing to view the mechanics of the backstage and understage activities which made the final presentation possible. In doing so, it will follow a chronological sequence from the initial process of planning the program to its possible implications for future research.

Setting Up the Study

The origins of the investigation are sketched out in the preface. The notion of concentrating on six professions, and within that frame of focusing on the responses of their members to change, evolved gradually—as did the subsequent aim to carry out some thirty interviews in each field. To achieve this intention as a single researcher over a limited period of time, and to help cover the associated costs of teaching replacement, travel, and the like, it was clearly necessary to apply for financial support. In the first instance, pilot interviews were carried out with one or two contacts in each profession to confirm the feasibility of the exercise and to pinpoint some of the main issues for initial exploration; the key items in the relevant research literature were also reviewed. This initial work formed the basis of a successful grant application to the Economic and Social Research Council (ESRC). As a result, the detailed planning of the fieldwork began in the autumn of 1993.

The strategy for identifying the respondents and the procedure for carrying out the interviews are outlined in chapter 1. The selection of potential respondents from those named by previous interviewees was based on what Cohen and Manion (1994) term "purposive sampling," which amounts to nothing more complex than making deliberate choices according to current need. A key stage in the process was the initial contact, which involved a personal letter mentioning the name of the colleague who had made the recommendation, an accompanying background note explaining the nature and purpose of the enquiry, and a list of possible themes for discussion under five main headings: the nature and sources of recent challenges; the attractions and problems of developing new expertise; the availability and relevance of formal training; the nature and sources of informal support; and a review of the coping process. It was emphasized that "the agenda will in practice be a matter for individual negotiation." A few respondents followed the checklist systematically, item by item; the large majority used it, as intended, as a springboard for a discussion of their own current concerns (the extent of their collective deviation will be evident from comparing the original themes with those covered in the chapters of this book). Unfortunately, no systematic record was kept of the percentage of refusals to participate among those approached, though it was certainly less than 30 percent. Quite a sizeable proportion of eventual respondents needed however to be sent reminders, and in some cases second reminders, before accepting the invitation to collaborate in the study.

Data Collection and Recording

The deliberate intention to avoid prejudging the central issues, allowing them to be defined to a large extent by the respondents themselves, meant that the interviews were not consistent in their coverage. The study could therefore in no sense be seen as a small-scale social survey, allowing for statistically based information on a closely defined set of topics: rather, it took a form analogous with a detective investigation, in which new clues could be followed up and emergent findings checked with subsequent respondents. New topics were readily added to the agenda and issues already resolved were deleted as the interviews proceeded: those later in the sequence became more closely focused than the earlier ones as the opportunity was taken to seek corroboration of significant features of the profession concerned.

The interviews were carried out on a part-time basis between October 1993 and the summer of 1996. They varied in length from half an hour to more than two hours, with the large majority lasting for just over an hour.

In all but a few cases, the interviewees readily gave permission for the proceedings to be recorded: in addition, however, written notes were taken throughout the discussion. These were transcribed alongside the interview recordings, providing a manageably brief summary, normally of three to four typed pages per interview, and pinpointing key passages likely to merit verbatim quotation. The resulting material provided one of the two main data sources, the other being the literature review.

The latter, as noted in chapter 1, served both as a check on the interview findings and as a means of confirming the relevance of many of them to the North American and Australian context. The main work of tracking down the relevant references, scattered across a considerable range of publications, was undertaken during a three-month Visiting Associateship in the spring and early summer of 1997 at the University of California, Berkeley, whose excellent library houses an extensive collection of the relevant materials. This previously unplanned but invaluable visit was made possible by the ESRC's agreement to my using under-spent funds for the purpose.

Analyzing and Cross-Checking the Data

The first stage of data analysis involved allocating a summary of each significant statement in each interview under the appropriate classificatory heading for the profession in question. The headings, although broadly similar across the six professions, embodied variations reflecting the idiosyncrasies of each: they included up to twenty main themes, such as specialist areas, course provision, information sources, and career development, some with three or more subdivisions. This detailed and time-consuming exercise—carried out mainly in the second half of 1996—resulted in a data base which made it possible to locate under one heading all the comments on a particular issue made by respondents in any given profession.

The itemized data base compiled along these lines was supplemented by an annotated list of research publications, each incorporating brief notes on relevant items of content, short quotations, and cross-references to photocopied extracts of key passages. This product of the literature search yielded some 250 items: not all of them proved to be relevant to the final writing-up.

The two data bases—one arising from the interviews and the other from the review of the research literature—were then combined in a third, synoptic compilation whose headings, though derived from the original analysis, evolved into the main and subsidiary themes which provided the detailed contents for the resulting book. The overall process of analyzing the data was informed by a number of the texts on research methodology, especially those published over the years by Anselm Strauss and his various co-authors: Glaser and Strauss (1967), Schatzman and Strauss (1973), and Strauss and Corbin (1990).

Shaping, Testing, and Presenting the Findings

A lively interest was evinced in learning about the outcome of the enquiry by several of the early respondents. As it was clear that the final publication would be unlikely to appear for at least five years from the period of the initial interviews, an interim report was prepared after about one-third of the interviews had been completed in each profession, and was sent to all those who had by that time contributed to the research. It was also made available to subsequent interviewees who expressed a similar interest; and a version was published in an appropriate scholarly journal (Becher, 1996).

As the process of data analysis proceeded—some preliminary aspects having marched in parallel with the program of interviews—the opportunity was taken to try out a number of the emergent ideas on academic colleagues, mainly in the format of seminars. The bulk of these took place between 1995 and 1997: within Britain, in the Universities of London, Reading, Sheffield, and Sussex; in Australia in Armidale, Brisbane, Canberra, Lismore, and Sydney; and in the U.S. in Berkeley. More formal conference papers were given in London and at an international Conference of Higher Education Researchers in Rome. A number of these events were of value in suggesting new interpretations of the data or in raising hitherto unconsidered questions.

Various friends and colleagues have been kind enough to offer critical comments on parts, and in some cases the whole, of the draft text: their contributions have been acknowledged in the preface. They comprised another helpful source of improvement, as did the officials in the professional bodies cited in chapter 2 who supplied up-to-date statistics on membership, checked the relevant factual information, and corrected it where necessary.

Future Avenues of Research

As noted in chapter 1, an approach to the study of the professions along the ethnographic lines adopted in the present study is relatively novel. Insofar as its findings are considered to be of interest and relevance, a wide range of future research possibilities accordingly lies ahead. In the first place, it might be productive to study one or more individual professions in greater depth, using participant observation techniques where feasible, or to undertake a similar set of comparative case studies of some of the many professions not included in the sample covered here: perhaps particularly those which are less well-established or whose boundaries are less clearly drawn. Possible examples might include banking and insurance work, surveying, nursing, and social work (teaching is relatively well-documented).

A further possibility would be to explore some particular topics in greater depth, such as quality issues or the varied patterns of professional careers. Another potentially interesting line of enquiry might involve a study of professions within the significantly different context of continental Europe, and perhaps—more ambitiously—a comparison between them and their Anglo-American-Australian counterparts.

It is at least to be hoped that some of the findings, hypotheses, and explanations offered in the course of this book might be tested, elaborated, and extended in a number of different directions. One of its central concerns has after all been to demonstrate the possibilities of a relatively new approach, rather than to foreclose a potentially lively debate: definitive survey maps are not the stock-in-trade of those who aspire to opening up a little-explored area of territory.

Notes on Respondents Referred to in the Text

Accountants

Acc/0 Male chartered accountant, late career, in university department in large town.

Acc/1 Male chartered accountant, late career, partner in three-partner firm in small provincial town.

Acc/2 Male chartered accountant, mid-career, in green-fields university finance office.

Acc/3 Male management accountant, mid-career, in privatized public utility, semi-rural setting.

Acc/4 Female management accountant, early career, in large manufacturing company in small town.

Acc/5 Female chartered accountant, early career, in regional branch of large accountancy firm.

Acc/6 Female insolvency practitioner, mid-career, partner in London office of medium-large accountancy firm.

Acc/7 Male chartered accountant, late career, partner in four-partner provincial firm.

Acc/10 Female insolvency practitioner, early career, in regional branch of medium-large accountancy firm.

Acc/11 Male chartered accountant, late career, partner in large London accountancy firm.

Acc/12 Male chartered accountant, mid-career, in regional branch of large accountancy firm.

Acc/13 Female auditor, early career, in regional branch of large accountancy firm.

Acc/14 Male chartered accountant, late career, partner in medium-sized suburban accountancy firm.

Acc/15 Male chartered accountant, mid-career, partner in large London accountancy firm.

Acc/16 Male chartered accountant, early career, in London branch of large European banking firm.

Acc/17 Male tax accountant, late career, in London branch of large international technology company.

Acc/19 Male chartered accountant, early/mid-career, in large London accountancy firm.

Acc/20 Male chartered accountant, early career, in London office of medium-large accountancy firm.

Acc/21 Male management accountant, late career, London-based university department.

Acc/22 Male chartered accountant, late/mid-career, in provincial university department.

Acc/23 Male chartered accountant, early/mid-career, in London branch of medium-sized accountancy firm.

Acc/24 Male certified accountant, late career, partner in three-partner firm in provincial town.

Acc/25 Male tax accountant, late career, partner in small suburban accountancy firm.

Acc/26 Male corporate finance specialist, mid-career, in small London-based corporate finance organization.

Acc/28 Male chartered accountant, mid-career, in corporate management department of large London legal firm.

Acc/29 Male chartered accountant, early/mid-career, financial controller in small provincial manufacturing company.

Acc/30 Male chartered accountant, late career, partner in large London accounting firm.

Architects

Arc/1   Male, late career, senior partner in medium-sized London firm.
Arc/2   Male, late career, senior partner in small London firm.
Arc/3   Male, mid-career, partner in two-partner London firm.
Arc/4   Male, late career, partner in small provincial firm.
Arc/5   Male, late career, partner in medium-large suburban firm.
Arc/6   Male, late mid-career partner in provincial office of large multisite firm.
Arc/7   Female, mid-career, partner in medium-sized London firm.
Arc/8   Female, mid-career, director of large metropolitan firm of housing developers.
Arc/9   Female, mid-career, in building design department of London borough.
Arc/10 Female, mid-career, partner in two-partner semi-rural firm.
Arc/11 Female, late/mid-career, partner in two-partner London firm.
Arc/12 Male, mid-career, partner in medium-sized provincial firm.
Arc/13 Male, late career, senior partner in two-partner London firm.
Arc/14 Male, late career, partner in two-partner provincial firm.
Arc/15 Male, late career, partner in London office of large multinational firm.
Arc/16 Male, late career, director of medium-sized subsidiary of large London firm.
Arc/17 Male, late career, partner in large multidisciplinary London firm.

Arc/18   Male, mid-career, managing director of large multidisciplinary provincial firm.
Arc/19   Male, early-mid career, planning officer in London borough.
Arc/20   Male, late career, chief officer in provincial borough council.
Arc/21   Male, mid-career, partner in large London firm.
Arc/22   Male, late career, partner in three-partner provincial firm.
Arc/23   Male, late career, partner in small provincial firm.
Arc/24   Male, mid-career, partner in London office of large multisite consultancy firm.
Arc/25   Male, late career, managing director of medium-large multidisciplinary London firm.
Arc/26   Male, late career, partner in large multidisciplinary London firm.
Arc/27   Male, early/mid-career, head of construction and development in London headquarters of large multinational oil company.
Arc/28   Male, late career, sole partner in provincial practice.
Arc/29   Male, mid-career, partner in small-medium provincial firm.
Arc/30   Male, late career, senior partner in medium-large London firm.

Engineers

E/0   Male structural engineer, retired, retired academic.
E/1   Male civil engineer, late/mid-career, in senior academic post in metropolitan university.
E/2   Male structural engineer, late career, senior staff member of professional organization.
E/3   Male, mid-career, associate partner in London office of medium-large firm of consulting engineers.
E/4   Male, late/mid-career, in London office of large firm of consulting engineers.
E/6   Female, mid-career, in small-medium provincial firm of contracting engineers.
E/7   Male, mid-career, in medium-sized, provincially based testing agency for the construction industry.
E/8   Male, late/mid-career, senior partner in four-partner London firm of consulting engineers.
E/9   Male, early career, in large London firm of consulting engineers.
E/10   Male, late career, in large London firm of consulting engineers.
E/11   Male structural engineer, early career, sole partner in provincial consultancy firm.
E/12   Male, mid-career, in medium-sized provincial firm of consulting engineers.
E/13   Male structural engineer, late career, in senior post in County Architects Department.

E/14   Male, late/mid-career, partner in medium-sized provincial firm of consulting engineers.

E/15   Male, early/mid-career, managing partner in small-medium London firm of consulting engineers.

E/16   Male, mid-career, partner in large suburban firm of consulting engineers.

E/17   Male, mid-career, in large provincial firm of contracting engineers.

E/18   Male, mid-career, project manager in small provincial firm of contracting engineers.

E/19   Male, mid-career, in provincial office of large firm of contracting engineers.

E/21   Male, late career, senior partner in six-partner London firm of consulting engineers.

E/23   Male, late career, senior partner in semi-rural two-partner firm of geotechnical consultants.

E/24   Male, mid-career, in provincial office of large firm of contracting engineers.

E/25   Male, late career, managing partner in small-medium London firm of consultant engineers.

E/26   Male, late career, partner in large London firm of consulting engineers.

E/27   Male civil engineer, late career, senior staff member of engineering-based research organization.

E/28   Male, late career, partner in London office of large firm of contracting engineers.

E/29   Male, late career, managing partner of small-medium London firm of consulting engineers.

E/30   Male, late career, partner in London office of small-medium firm of contracting engineers.

Lawyers

L/0   Male, mid-career, academic in green fields university department.

L/0'   Male, mid-career, senior academic in London-based university department.

L/1   Male solicitor, late career, senior partner in large provincial firm.

L/2   Male barrister, late career, in London chambers.

L/3   Female, late career, high court judge.

L/4   Female solicitor, early/mid-career, in large provincial firm.

L/5   Female solicitor, mid-career, partner in small-medium London firm.

L/6   Female barrister, mid-career, in London chambers.

L/7   Male Queen's Counsel, mid-career, in London chambers.

L/8   Male, late career, county court judge.

L/9   Female solicitor, early career, in medium-large London firm.

L/10   Female solicitor, mid-career, partner in three-partner provincial firm.
L/11   Female solicitor, mid-career, partner in small London firm.
L/13   Male barrister, mid-career, in London chambers.
L/14   Male barrister, early career, in London chambers.
L/15   Male, late career, county court judge.
L/16   Male, late career, senior officer in Independent Tribunal Service.
L/17   Male barrister, early career, in London chambers.
L/19   Male non-practicing barrister, mid-career, in small London firm.
L/20   Female solicitor, early/mid-career, partner in large City firm.
L/21   Male solicitor, late/mid-career, partner in large London firm.
L/22   Male solicitor, late/mid-career, head of legal department in large international oil company.
L/23   Male solicitor, late/mid-career, in large London firm.
L/24   Female barrister, mid-career, partner in specialist section of large London accountancy firm.
L/25   Male solicitor, late/mid-career, partner in large London firm.
L/26   Male solicitor, late/mid-career, senior officer in legal department of London borough.
L/27   Male solicitor, mid-career, head of London-based legal department of national bank.
L/28   Male solicitor, early career, in medium-large provincial firm.
L/30   Male solicitor, mid-career, partner in large London firm.
L/32   Male barrister, mid-career, in London chambers.

Medics

M/0   Male academic, mid-career, in provincial university medical research unit.
M/1   Male consultant pathologist, mid-career, in large provincial hospital trust.
M/2   Female consultant dermatologist, mid-career, in large provincial hospital trust.
M/3   Female GP, mid-career, in small semi-rural practice.
M/4   Male consultant surgeon, late career, in large provincial hospital trust.
M/5   Female GP, mid-career, in large suburban practice.
M/6   Female GP, early career, involved part-time in GP training in large London hospital.
M/7   Female GP, early/mid-career, in small semi-rural practice.
M/8   Female consultant surgeon, early/mid-career, in London hospital trust.
M/9   Female consultant urologist, early/mid-career, in provincial hospital trust.
M/10   Male consultant surgeon, late career, in provincial hospital trust.
M/11   Male GP, mid-career, in small London practice.
M/12   Male GP, mid-career, sole partner in London practice.

M/13   Male consultant neurologist, mid-career, in large provincial hospital trust.

M/14   Female consultant obstetrician, mid-career, in London teaching hospital.

M/15   Male consultant endocrinologist, early/mid-career, in large provincial hospital trust.

M/16   Female consultant gynecologist, mid-career, in London teaching hospital.

M/17   Female qualified doctor, mid-career, senior staff member of professional organization.

M/18   Male consultant renal physician, early/mid-career, in London teaching hospital.

M/19   Male consultant anesthetist, mid-career, in London teaching hospital.

M/20   Male qualified doctor, senior staff member of professional organization.

M/21   Male retired consultant physician, former chairman of suburban hospital trust.

M/22   Male academic, late career, in provincial university medical school.

M/23   Female consultant physician, mid-career, in senior post in London regional health authority.

M/24   Male consultant physician, early/mid-career, in London teaching hospital.

M/25   Male consultant gynecologist, mid-career, in provincial hospital trust.

M/26   Male qualified doctor, mid-career, senior staff member in national quality agency.

M/27   Male qualified doctor, late career, senior staff member of professional organization.

M/28   Male academic, late career, in provincial university medical school.

M/29   Female qualified doctor, mid-career, full-time senior officer in professional association.

M/30   Male consultant pathologist, late career, in senior post in London health authority.

Pharmacists

P/1   Female community pharmacist, late career, with part-time teaching post in provincial university.

P/2   Female hospital pharmacist, mid-career, in large provincial hospital trust.

P/3   Male academic pharmacist, late career, in provincial university.

P/4   Female community pharmacist, late/mid-career, in two-partner provincial practice.

P/5   Male community pharmacist, late/mid-career, sole partner in provincial practice.

P/6   Male hospital pharmacist, mid-career, principal pharmacist in large provincial hospital trust.

P/7   Female industrial pharmacist, early career, in provincial plant of large international pharmaceutical company.

P/8   Female community pharmacist, mid-career, in semi-rural health center practice.

P/9   Female industrial pharmacist, early/mid-career, in provincial plant of large international pharmaceutical company.

P/10   Male community pharmacist, late career, sole partner in provincial practice.

P/11   Male community pharmacist, mid-career, sole partner in provincial practice.

P/12   Male community pharmacist, late career, senior manager in large multiple pharmacy.

P/13   Female hospital pharmacist, early/mid-career, in large London teaching hospital.

P/14   Male community pharmacist, late/mid-career, superintendent pharmacy manager in supermarket chain.

P/16   Male hospital pharmacist, mid-career, director of services in large provincial hospital trust.

P/17   Male community pharmacist, mid-career, sole partner in provincial practice.

P/18   Male hospital pharmacist, early career, pharmacy adviser in London health authority.

P/19   Male community pharmacist, mid-career, manager of small chain of four provincial pharmacies.

P/20   Female hospital pharmacist, late career, senior office-holder in professional organization.

P/21   Female industrial pharmacist, late career, senior manager in large international pharmaceutical company.

P/23   Male academic pharmacist, late/mid-career, in London medical school.

P/24   Female hospital pharmacist, mid-career, chief pharmacist in small semi-rural hospital trust.

P/26   Female hospital pharmacist, late/mid-career, pharmaceutical manager in London community health service trust.

P/27   Female qualified pharmacist, mid-career, officer in professional organization.

P/28   Male community pharmacist, retired from sole partnership in provincial practice.

P/29   Female qualified pharmacist, late/mid-career, self-employed consultant and part-time academic teacher.

P/30   Male hospital pharmacist, mid-career, senior manager in London teaching hospital.

References

Abbott, A. (1981) Stakes and status strain in the professions *American Journal of Sociology* 86, 819–35.

Abbott, A. (1988) *The System of Professions*. Chicago: University of Chicago Press.

Abernethy, D. (1994) Britain leads continuing medical education—whither America? *Postgraduate Medical Journal* 70, 643–45.

Acheson, H.W.K. (1974) Continuing education in general practice in England and Wales *Journal of the Royal College of General Practitioners* 24, 643–47.

Addis, W. (1990) *Structural Engineering*. New York: Ellis Horwood.

Addis, W. (1994) *The Art of the Structural Engineer*. London: Artemis.

Aldridge, M.D. (1994) Professional practice: a topic for engineering research and instruction *Engineering Education* 83, 3, 231–35.

Allaker, J. and Shapland, J. (1995) *Organising UK Professions: Information about the Professions*. Sheffield: University of Sheffield Institute for the Study of the Legal Profession.

Allen, I. (1994) *Doctors and their Careers*. London: Policy Studies Institute.

Allery, L. et al. (1991) Differences in continuing medical education activities and attitudes between trainers and non-trainers in general practice *Postgraduate Education for General Practice* 2, 176–82.

Al-Shehri, A., Stanley, I. and Thomas, P. (1993) Continuing education for general practice *British Journal of General Practice* 43, 249–53.

Anderson, L.J. (1989) Practice management *Professional Negligence*. Nov/Dec 1989.

Architects Registration Council (1996) *Annual Report and Accounts 1995–96*. London: ARCUK.

Armytage, L. (1996) *Educating Judges*. The Hague: Kluwer.

Atkinson, P. and Delamont, S. (1990) Professions and powerlessness *Sociology Review* 38, 1, 90–110.

Austen, J. (1818) *Persuasion*. New York: Bantam Books Edition.

Bailey, F.G. (1973) *Debate and Compromise*. Oxford: Blackwell.

Bainbridge, D. (1991) IT and the practice of law, in Lee, G.L. (ed) *The Changing Professions*. Birmingham: Aston Business School.

Barnes, M. (1997) Self-regulation and complaints handling, in Hanlon, G. and Halpern, S. (eds) *Liberating Professions, Shifting Boundaries*. Sheffield: University of Sheffield Institute for the Study of the Legal Profession.

Barnett, R., Becher, T. and Cork, M. (1987) Models of professional preparation, *Studies in Higher Education* 12, 1, 51–63.

Bashook, P.G. (1993) Clinical competence and continuing medical education, in Coles, C. and Holm, H.A. (eds) *Learning in Medicine*. Oslo: Scandinavian University Press.

Batstone, G.F. (1990) Educational aspects of medical audit *British Medical Journal* 301, 326–28.

Becher, T. (1989) *Academic Tribes and Territories*. Milton Keynes: Open University Press.

Becher, T. (1990) Professional education in a comparative context, in Torstendahl, R. and Burrage, M. (eds) *The Formation of the Professions*. London: Sage.

Becher, T. (ed) (1994) *Governments and Professional Education*. Buckingham: Open University Press.

Becher, T. (1996) The learning professions *Studies in Higher Education* 21, 1, 43–55.

Becher, T., Eraut, M. and Knight, J. (1981) *Policies for Educational Accountability*. London: Heinemann.

Becker, H.S. (1970) *Sociological Work*. Chicago: Aldine.

Bennett, N.L. and Hotvedt, M.O. (1989) Stage of career, in Fox, R.D., Mazmanian, P.E. and Putnam, R.W. (eds) *Changing and Learning in the Lives of Physicians*. New York: Praeger.

Benson, J.A. Jr. (1991) Certification and recertification *Annals of Internal Medicine* 114, 238–42.

Berkeley, E.P. (ed) (1989) *Architecture: A Place for Women*. Washington: Smithsonian Institute Press.

Berwick, D.M. (1989) Continuous improvement as an ideal in health care *New England Journal of Medicine* 320, 1, 53–56.

Betz, M. and O'Connell, L. (1983) Changing doctor-patient relationships *Social Problems* 31, 84–95.

Birenbaum, R. (1982) Reprofessionalisation in pharmacy *Social Science and Medicine* 16, 871–78.

Birks, P. (ed) (1994) *Reviewing Legal Education*. Oxford: Oxford University Press.

Birley, J.T. (1996) Whistle-blowing—the National Health Service as an open society *Journal of the Royal Society of Medicine* 89, 10, 541–42.

Boreham, N.C. (1989) Modelling medical decision-making under uncertainty *British Journal of Educational Psychology* 59, 187–99.

Brown, D.S. (1989) Room at the top, in Berkeley, E.P. (ed) *Architecture: A place for Women*. Washington D.C.: Smithsonian Institute Press.

Brown, R. (1982) Work histories, career strategies and class structure, in Geddes, A. and Mackenzie, G. (eds) *Social Class and the Division of Labour*. Cambridge: Cambridge University Press.

Brown, S.L. and Klein, R.H. (1982) Woman-power in the medical hierarchy *Journal of the American Medical Women's Association* 37, 6, 155-64.

Bucher, R. and Strauss, A. (1961) Professions in process *American Journal of Sociology* 66, 4, 325–34.

Burchell, S., Clubb, C. and Hopwood, A.G. (1985) Accounting in its social context *Accounting Organizations and Society* 10, 381–413.

Burrage, M. (1992) *Mrs Thatcher against Deep Structures*. Berkeley, California: University of California Institute of Governmental Studies. Working Paper 92–11.

Burrage, M., Jarausch, K. and Siegrist, H. (1990) An actor-based framework for the study of the professions, in Burrage, M. and Torstendahl, R. (eds) *Professions in Theory and History*. London: Sage.

Burrage, M. and Torstendahl, R. (eds) (1990) *Professions in Theory and History*. London, Sage.

Calman Report (1993) Department of Health: *Hospital Doctors—Training for the Future*. Heywood, Lancs: Health Publications Unit.

Carr-Saunders, A.M. and Wilson, P.A. (1933) *The Professions*. Oxford: Clarendon Press.

Carter, R. and Kirkup, G. (1990) *Women in Engineering*. Basingstoke: Macmillan Education.

Cartwright, L.K. (1987) Occupational stress in women physicians, in Payne, R. and Firth-Cozens, I. (eds) *Stress in Health Professionals*. Chichester: Wiley.

Céreq (1997) School-to-work transition and after *Training and Employment*, 28. Marseille: Centre d'Etudes et de Recherches sur les Qualifications.

Cevero, R.M. (1988) *Effective Continuing Education for Professionals.* San Francisco: Jossey-Bass.

Cevero, R.M. (1992) Professional practice, learning and continuing education *International Journal of Lifelong Education* 11, 2, 91–101.

Cervero, R.M., Miller, J.D. and Dimmock, K.H. (1986) The formal and informal learning activities of practising engineers *Engineering Education* 77, 2, 112–14.

Cherniss, C. (1980) *Professional Burnout in Human Services Organizations.* New York: Praeger.

Christakis, N.A., Jacobs, J.A. and Messikomer, C.M. (1994) Change in definition from specialist to generalist in a national sample of physicians *Annals of Internal Medicine* 121, 9, 669–75.

Clyne, S. (ed) (1995) *Continuing Professional Development.* London: Kogan Page.

Cohen, L. and Manion, L.(1994) *Research Methods in Education*, Fourth Edition. London: Routledge.

Collier, J. (1993) Post-qualification specialism—the way forward? *Accountancy* 112, 1199, 71–72.

Collins, R. (1979) *The Credential Society.* Orlando, Florida: Academic Press.

Coulson-Thomas, C. (1991) The future of the professions, in Lee, G.L. (ed) *The Changing Professions.* Birmingham: Aston Business School.

Crandall, S.J.S. (1990) The role of continuing medical education in change and learning *Journal of Continuing Education in the Health Professions* 10, 4, 339–48.

Crinson, M. and Lubbock, J. (1994) *Architecture: Art or Profession?* Manchester: Manchester University Press.

Crompton, R. (1987) Gender and accountancy *Accounting, Organizations and Society* 12, 103–10.

Crompton, R. and Sanderson, K. (1986) Credentials and careers *Sociology* 20, 1, 25–42.

Crompton, R. and Sanderson, K. (1989) *Gendered Jobs and Social Change.* London: Unwin Hyman.

Cross, K.P. (1981) *Adults as Learners.* San Francisco: Jossey-Bass.

Cuff, D. (1991) *Architecture: The Story of Practice.* Cambridge, MA: MIT Press.

Curry, L. and Putnam, W.R. (1981) Continuing medical education in maritime Canada *Canadian Medical Association Journal* 249, 563–66.

Curry, L., Wergin, J.F. and Associates (1993) *Educating Professionals.* San Francisco: Jossey-Bass.

Darke, M. (1996) *Research Awards funded under the Architects Registration Acts, 1970–1995.* London: ARCUK.

Davies, M. (1994) Solicitors' negligence *International Journal of the Legal Profession* 1, 3, 387–95.

Davis, D.A. et al. (1990) Attempting to ensure physician competence *Journal of the American Medical Association* 263, 15, 2041–2.

Davis, D.A. and Fox, R.D. (eds)(1994) *The Physician as Learner.* Chicago: American Medical Association.

Davis, D., Lindsay, E. and Mazmanian, P. (1994) The effectiveness of CME intervention, in Davis, D. and Fox, R.D. (eds) *The Physician as Learner.* Chicago: American Medical Association.

Davis, D.A. et al. (1995) Changing physician performance *Journal of the American Medical Association* 274, 9, 700–706.

Dawson, S. (1994) Changes in the distance: professionals reappraise the meaning of management *Journal of General Management* 20, 1, 1–21.

Department of Health (1995) *Hospital Doctors: Training for the Future*. Supplementary Report by the Working Group Commissioned to Consider the Implications for Academic and Research Medicine. London: NHS Executive.

Derber, C., Schwartz, W.A. and Magrass, Y. (1990) *Power in the Highest Degree: Professionals in the Rise of a New Mandarin Order*. New York: Oxford University Press.

Derry, J. et al. (1991) Auditing audits *British Medical Journal* 303, 1247–9.

Dingwall, R. and Lewis, P. (eds) (1983) *The Sociology of the Professions*. London: Macmillan.

Dowlatshaki, S. (1996) An empirical assessment of continuing education needs *Journal of Management in Engineering* 12, 5, 37–45.

Eaton, G. and Webb, B. (1979) Boundary encroachment: pharmacists in the clinical setting *Sociology of Health and Illness* 1, 69–89.

Elmore, R.F. (1979) Backward mapping: implementation research and policy decisions *Political Science Quarterly* 94, 4, 601–16.

Elston, M.A. (1991) The politics of professional power, in Gabe, Jetal (eds) *The Sociology of the Health Service*. London, Routledge.

Elston, M.A. (1993) Women doctors in a changing profession, in Riska, E and Wegar, K. (eds) *Gender, Work and Medicine*. London: Sage.

Eraut, M. (1994) *Developing Professional Knowledge and Competence*. London: Falmer Press.

Eraut, M., Alderton, J., Cole, G. and Senker, P. (1998) *Development of Knowledge and Skills in Employment*. Research Report No. 5. Brighton: University of Sussex Institute of Education.

Etzioni, A. (ed) (1969) *The Semi-Professions and their Organization*. New York: Free Press.

Evans, A.D. (1985) Can mandatory continuing education be justified? *Journal of Professional and Legal Education* 3, 1, 35–46.

Fox, R.D., Mazmanian, P.E. and Putnam, R.W. (eds) (1989) *Changing and Learning in the Lives of Physicians*. New York: Praeger.

Freedman, J. and Power, M. (1992) Law and accounting: transition and transformation, in Freedman, J. and Power, M. (eds) *Law and Accountancy*. London: Paul Chapman.

Freidson, E. (1986) *Professional Powers*. Chicago: University of Chicago Press.

Freidson, E. (1994) *Professionalism Reborn*. Cambridge: Polity Press.

Freudenberger, H.J. and Richardson, B. (1980) *Burnout: The High Cost of High Achievement*. Garden City NY: Anchor.

Gear, J., McIntosh, A. and Squires, G. (1994) *Informal Learning in the Professions*. Hull: University of Hull Department of Adult Education.

Geddes, A. and Mackenzie, G. (eds) (1982) *Social Class and the Division of Labour*. Cambridge: Cambridge University Press.

Geertsma, K.H., Parker, R.C. and Whitbourne, S.K. (1982) How physicians view the process of change in their practice behavior *Journal of Medical Education* 57, 10, 752–61.

Gerholm, T. (1990) On tacit knowledge in academia *European Journal of Education* 25, 3, 263–72.

Glaser, B.G. and Strauss, A. (1967) *The Discovery of Grounded Theory*. New York: Aldine.

Glazer, N. (1974) The schools of the minor professions *Minerva* 12, 3, 346–63.

Goodlad, S.J. (ed) (1984) *Education for the Professions*. Guildford: Society for Research into Higher Education.

Gordon, D.E. (1987) The ins and outs of specialization *Architecture* 76, 10, 95–8.

Gouldner, A.W. (1957) Cosmopolitans and locals *Administrative Science Quarterly* 2, 281–306 and 444–80.

Griffith, D.E. (1983) Professional continuing education in engineering, in Stern, M.R. (ed) *Power and Conflict in Continuing Professional Education*. Belmont, CA: Wadsworth.

Guardian (1996) Think big and go far, *On Line* p. 2, May 23.

Hafferty, F.W. and McKinlay, J.B. (eds) (1993) *The Changing Medical Profession*. New York: Oxford University Press.

Hammersley, M. and Atkinson, P. (1995) *Ethnography: Principles in Practice*. Second edition. London: Routledge.

Hanlon, G. (1994) *The Commercialisation of Accountancy*. Basingstoke: Macmillan.

Hanlon, G. and Halpern, S. (eds) (1997) *Liberating Professions, Shifting Boundaries*. Sheffield: University of Sheffield Institute for the Study of the Legal Profession.

Hanson, A.L. and De Muth, J.E. (1991) Facilitators and barriers to pharmacists' participation in lifelong learning *American Journal of Pharmaceutical Education* 55, 20–29.

Harris, S. and Rymer, D. (1983) *Case Studies in CPD*. Research Paper 22. York: Institute of Advanced Architectural Studies.

Hirschman, A.O. (1970) *Exit, Voice, and Loyalty*. Cambridge MA: Harvard University Press.

Hopkins, A., Solomon, J. and Abelson, J. (1996) Shifting boundaries in professional care *Journal of the Royal Society of Medicine* 89, 7, 364–71.

Horder, J., Bosanquet, N. and Stocking, B. (1986) Ways of influencing the behaviour of general practitioners *Journal of the Royal College of General Practitioners* 36, 517–21.

Houle, C.O. (1980) *Continuing Learning in the Professions*. San Francisco: Jossey-Bass.

Huberman, M. (1983) Recipes for busy kitchens *Knowledge: Creation, Diffusion, Utilisation* 4, 478–510.

Hughes, A.K. (1994) *Developing European Professions*. Bristol: University of Bristol Department of Continuing Education.

Hughes, N. (1995) The rabbits and lettuces: the dual role of professional bodies, in Clyne, S. (ed) *Continuing Professional Development*. London: Kogan Page.

Hunt, G. (ed) (1995) *Whistle Blowing in the Health Service*. London: Edward Arnold.

Illich, I. et al. (1977) *Disabling Professions*. London: Marion Boyars.

Jackson, J.A. (ed) (1970) *Professions and Professionalisation*. Cambridge: Cambridge University Press.

James, J. (1991) Whistling against the wind, in Lee, G.L. (ed) *The Changing Professions*. Birmingham: Aston Business School.

Jamous, H. and Peloille, B. (1970) Professions or self–perpetuating systems?, in Jackson, J.A. (ed) *Professions and Professionalisation*. Cambridge: Cambridge University Press.

Jenkins, J. (1994) Practice management *International Journal of the Legal Profession* 1, 2, 223–36.

Jennett, P. et al. (1994) The characteristics of self-directed learning, in Davis, D.A. and Fox, R.D. (eds) *The Physician as Learner*. Chicago: American Medical Association.

Jewell, D. (1991) The future of general practice *British Medical Journal* 303, 510–2.

Johnson, H.J. and Kaplan, R.S. (1987) *Relevance Lost: The Rise and Fall of Management Accountancy*. Cambridge MA: Harvard Business School Press.

Johnson, M. (1983) Professional careers and biographies, in Dingwall, R. and Lewis, P. (eds) *The Sociology of the Professions*. London: Macmillan.

Johnson, T.J. (1972) *Professions and Power*. London: Macmillan.

Joss, R. and Kogan, M. (1995) *Advancing Quality*. Buckingham: Open University Press.

Kelly, M.H. and Murray, T.S. (1994) General practitioners' views on continuing medical education *British Journal of General Practice* 44, 387, 469–71.

Kelly, M.H. and Murray, T.S. (1996) Motivation of general practitioners attending postgraduate education *British Journal of General Practice* 46, 407, 353–56.

Knowles, M.S. (1970) *The Modern Practice of Adult Education*. Chicago: Follett.

Kogan, M. and Redfern, S. (1995) *Making Use of Clinical Audit*. Buckingham: Open University Press.

Kopelow, M. (1994) Competency based assessment, in Davis, D.A. and Fox, R.D. (eds) *The Physician as Learner*. Chicago: American Medical Association.

Laffin, M. and Young, K. (1990) *Professionalism in Local Government*. Harlow: Longman.

Lambert, T.W. et al. (1996) Career preferences of doctors *British Medical Journal* 313, 7048, 19–24.

Larson, M.S. (1977) *The Rise of Professionalism*. Berkeley: University of California Press.

Latham Report (1994) *Constructing the Team*. London: HMSO.

Lee, G.L. (1991) *The Changing Professions: Accountancy and Law*. Birmingham: Aston Business School.

Levi-Strauss, C. (1978) *Myth and Meaning*. London: Routledge.

Lockyer, J. and Harrison, V. (1994) Performance assessment, in Davis, D.A. and Fox R.D. (eds) *The Physician as Learner*. Chicago: American Medical Association.

Lorber, J. (1984) *Women Physicians: Careers, Status and Power*. London: Tavistock.

Lord, J. and Littlejohns, P. (1996) Impact of hospital and community provider based clinical audit programmes *International Journal for Quality in Health Care* 8, 6, 527–35.

Lord Chancellor's Advisory Committee (1996a) *First Report on Legal Education and Training*. London: Lord Chancellor's Office.

Lord Chancellor's Advisory Committee (1996b) *Conference on the First Report on Legal Education and Training*. London: Lord Chancellor's Office.

Lord Chancellor's Advisory Committee (1996c) *Consultative Conference on Continuing Professional Development*. London: Lord Chancellor's Office.

Lord Chancellor's Advisory Committee (1997) *Continuing Professional Development for Solicitors and Barristers*. London: Lord Chancellor's Office.

Madden, C.A. and Mitchell, V.A. (1993) *Professions, Standards and Competence*. Bristol: University of Bristol.

Malinowski, B. (1926) *Crime and Custom in Savage Society*. London: Routledge.

Marlach, C. and Schaufeli, W.B. (1993) Historical and conceptual development of burnout, in Schaufeli, W.B. et al., *Professional Burnout*. Washington D.C.: Taylor and Francis.

Marre (Lady) Report of the Committee on the Future of the Legal Profession (the Marre Report) (1988) *A Time for Change*. Bar Council and Law Society.

Marris, P. (1975) *Loss and Change*. London: Routledge.

Marsick, V.J. (ed) (1987) *Learning in the Workplace*. London: Croom Helm.

Marsick, V.J. and Watkins, K.E. (1990) *Informal and Incidental Learning in the Workplace*. London: Routledge.

Martin, R. (1989) Out of marginality, in Berkeley, E.P. (ed) *Architecture: A Place for Women*. Washington D.C.: Smithsonian Institute Press.

Maupin, R.J. (1993) We've come a long way, maybe: gender differences in career and family expectations of accountancy graduates *Ohio CPA Journal* 51, 4, 15–17.

McIlwee, J.S. and Robinson, J.G. (1992) *Women in Engineering*. Albany: SUNY Press.

McKee, B. (1997) Continuing education—scholarship or scam? *Architecture* 1997, 86, 3, 98–101.

McKeen, C.A. and Bujaki, M.L. (1994) Taking women into account *CA Magazine* 127, 2, 29–35.

Merton, R. (1967) *On Theoretical Sociology*. New York: Free Press.

Mills, C. W. (1951) *White Collar*. New York: Oxford University Press.

Monopolies Commission (1970) *Professional Services*. HMSO Cmnd 4463–1.

Morison, J. and Leith, P. (1992) *The Barrister's World*. Milton Keynes: Open University Press.

Muzzin, L.J., Brown, G.P. and Hornosty, R.W. (1994) Consequences of feminisation of a profession *Women and Health* 21, 2–3, 39–56.

Myers, I.B. (1980) *Gifts Differing*. Palo Alto: Psychologists Press.

Neale, P. (1994) Professional responses to the European challenge, in Neale, P. (ed) *Creating European Professionals*. Leeds: University of Leeds Department of Continuing Professional Education.

Neale, P. (ed) (1994) *Creating European Professionals*. Leeds: University of Leeds Department of Continuing Professional Education.

Newble, D., Jolly, B. and Wakeford, R. (1994) *The Certification and Recertification of Doctors*. Cambridge: Cambridge University Press.

Nicholas, S. (1994) 'Mobility of doctors—the theory and the practice', in Neale, P. (ed) *Creating European Professionals*. Leeds: University of Leeds Department of Continuing Professional Education.

Nicholls, M.W.N. and Hind, C.R.K. (eds) (1996) Continuing Medical Education in Europe *Postgraduate Medical Journal* Vol. 72, Supplement 1.

Nowlen, P.M. (1988) *A New Approach to Continuing Education for Business and the Professions*. New York: Macmillan.

Ormrod Report (1971) *Report of the Committee on Legal Education* Cmnd 4595. London: HMSO.

Owen, P.A. et al. (1989) General practitioners' continuing medical education within and outside their practice. *British Medical Journal* 299, 238–40.

Partington, M. (1988) Academic lawyers and "legal practice" in Britain *Journal of Law and Society* 15, 4, 374–91.

Partington, M. (1992) Academic lawyers and legal practice in England *Legal Education Review* 3, 1, 75–93.

Partington, M. (1994) Training the judiciary in England and Wales *Civil Justice Quarterly* 13, 319–36.

Paterson, A. (1983) Becoming a judge, in Dingwall, R. and Lewis, P. (eds) *The Sociology of the Professions*. London: Macmillan.

Payne, R. and Firth-Cozens, J. (eds) (1987) *Stress in Health Professionals*. Chichester: Wiley.

Phillips, L.E. (1983) Trends in State licensature, in Stern, M.R. (ed) *Power and Conflict in Continuing Professional Education*. Belmont, CA: Wadsworth.

Phillips, L.E. (1987) Is mandatory continuing education working? *Möbius* 1, 57–64.

Pitts, J. and Vincent, S. (1994) General practitioners' reasons for not attending a higher professional education course *British Journal of General Practice* 44, 383, 271–73.

Polanyi, M. (1967) *The Tacit Dimension*. New York: Doubleday.

Pollitt, C. (1993) The politics of medical quality *Health Services Market Research* 6, 1, 24–34.

Powell, J.P. and Banks, P.L. (1989) Learning during a professional career *International Journal of Career Management* 1, 1, 35–40.

Powell, M. (1985) Developments in the regulation of lawyers *Sociological Forces* 64, 281–305.

Pritchard, J. (1995) *The Legal 500*. London: Legalese.

Pugh, M.D. and Wahrman, R. (1983) Neutralising sexism in mixed-sex groups: do women have to be better than men? *American Journal of Sociology* 88, 746-62.

Putnam R.W. and Campbell, M.D. (1989) Competence, in Fox, R.D., Mazmanian, P.E. and Putnam, R.W. (eds) *Changing and Learning in the Lives of Physicians*. New York: Praeger.

Ramsey, P.G. et al. (1993) Use of peer ratings to evaluate physician performance *Journal of the American Medical Association* 269, 1655–60.

Reid, G., Acker, B.T. and Jancura, E.G. (1987) An historical perspective on women in accounting *Journal of Accountancy*, Centennial Issue, May 163, 5, 338–55.

Rice, P. (1994) *An Engineer Imagines*. London: Artemis.

Riska, E. and Wegar, K. (eds) (1993) *Gender, Work and Medicine*. London: Sage.

Roberts, J. and Coutts, J.A. (1992) Feminisation and professionalisation *Accounting, Organizations and Society* 17, 3/4, 379–95.

Rosenthal, M.M. (1995) *The Incompetent Doctor*. Buckingham: Open University Press.

Roslender, R. (1992) *Sociological Perspectives on Modern Accountancy*. London: Routledge.

Rothman, R.A. (1984) Deprofessionalisation: the case of law in America *Work and Occupations* 11, 2, 183–206.

Royal College of General Practitioners (1990) *A College Plan: Priorities for the Future*. Occasional Paper 49. London: Royal College of General Practitioners.

Ryle, G. (1949) *The Concept of Mind*. London: Hutchinson.

Rymell, R.G. (1981) How much time do engineers spend learning? *Engineering Education* 72, 2, 172–74.

Schatzman, L. and Strauss, A.L. (1973) *Field Research*. Englewood Cliffs: Prentice-Hall.

Schaufeli, W.B. et al. (1993) *Professional Burnout*. Washington D.C.: Taylor and Francis.

Schön, D. (1983) *The Reflective Practitioner*. New York: Basic Books.

Schön, D. (1987) *Educating the Reflective Practitioner*. San Francisco: Jossey-Bass.

Schreiber, S.C. (1987) Stress in physicians, in Payne, R. and Firth-Cozens, J. (eds) *Stress in Health Professionals*. Chichester: Wiley.

Scotland, J. (1998) *The Implications of Power and Gender for Contemporary Nurse Education*. Unpublished D.Phil. Thesis, University of Sussex.

Scrivens, E. (1995) *Accreditation*. Buckingham: Open University Press.

Shapland, J. and Sorsby, A. (1994) *Starting Practice: Work and Training at the Junior Bar*. Sheffield: University of Sheffield Institute for the Study of the Legal Profession.

Shaw, G.B. (1932) *The Doctor's Dilemma*. Standard Edition. London: Constable.

Sherr, A. (1993) *Solicitors and their Skills*. London: Law Society.

Skordaki, E. (1997) The growth of the corporate adviser, in Hanlon, G. and Halpern, S. (eds) *Liberating Professions, Shifting Boundaries*. Sheffield: University of Sheffield Institute for the Study of the Legal Profession.

Sparkes, J. (1984) Continuing education in engineering, in Goodlad, S.J. (ed) *Education for the Professions*. Guildford: Society for Research into Higher Education

Spencer, A. and Podmore, D. (eds) (1987) *In a Man's World: Essays on Women in Male-dominated Professions*. London: Tavistock.

Spurr, S.J. (1990) Sex discrimination in the legal profession *Industrial and Labor Relations Review* 43, 4, 406–17.

Squires, G. (in press) *Teaching as a Professional Discipline*. London: Falmer.

Stern, M.R. (ed) (1983) *Power and Conflict in Continuing Professional Education.* Belmont, CA: Wadsworth.

Stern, M.R. (1987) CPE: The learning landscape *Möbius* 7, 1, 48–56.

Strauss, A.L. and Corbin, J. (1990) *Basics of Qualitative Research.* Newbury Park: Sage.

Swinson, C. (1991) The professions and 1992, in Lee, G.L. (ed) *The Changing Professions.* Birmingham: Aston Business School.

Symes, M., Eley, J. and Seidel, A.D. (1995) *Architects and their Practices.* Oxford: Butterworth Architecture.

Thomas, P.A. (1992) Thatcher's will *Journal of Law and Sociology* 19, 1, 1–12.

Thornton, M. (1996) *Dissonance and Distrust: Women in the Legal Profession.* Melbourne: Oxford University Press.

Torstendahl, R. (1990) Introduction: promotion and strategies of knowledge-based groups, in Torstendahl, R. and Burrage, M. (eds) *The Formation of the Professions.* London: Sage.

Torstendahl, R. and Burrage, M. (eds) (1990) *The Formation of the Professions.* London: Sage.

Tough, A. (1971) *The Adult's Learning Projects.* Toronto: Ontario Institute for Studies in Education.

Trow, M. (1996) Trust, markets and accountability in higher education *Higher Education Policy* 9, 4, 309–24.

Turner, B.S. (1987) *Medical Power and Social Knowledge.* London: Sage.

Twining, W. (1994a) *Blackstone's Tower: The English Law School.* London: Sweet & Maxwell.

Twining, W. (1994b) Postgraduate legal studies, in Birks, P. (ed) *Reviewing Legal Education.* Oxford: Oxford University Press.

UCAS (1988) *A Statistical Bulletin of Subject Trends, 1996 Entry.* Cheltenham: Universities and Colleges Admissions Service.

U.K. Inter-professional Group (1994) *Survey of CPD.* London: U.K. Inter-professional Group.

U.K. Inter-professional Group (n.d.) *Professional Careers for Women.* London: U.K. Inter-professional Group.

Vaughan, P. (1991) *Maintaining Professional Competence.* Hull: University of Hull Department of Adult Education.

Vytlačil, A. (1989) The studio experience, in Berkeley, E.P. (ed) *Architecture: A Place for Women.* Washington D.C.: Smithsonian Institute Press.

Watkins, J., Drury, L. and Preddy, D. (1992) *From Evolution to Revolution: The Pressures on Professional Life in the 1990s.* Bristol: University of Bristol.

Watkins, J., Drury, L. and Bray, S. (1996) *The Future of UK Professional Associations.* Cheltenham: Cheltenham Strategic Publications.

Weatherley, R. and Lipsky, M. (1977) Street-level bureaucrats and institutional innovation *Harvard Educational Review*, 27, 2, 171–97.

Wergin, J.F. et al. (1988) CME and change in practice *Journal of Continuing Education in the Health Professions* 8, 147–59.

Wescott, S.H. and Seiler, E.E. (1986) *Women in the Accounting Profession.* New York: Markus Wiener.

Wessells, D.T. et al. (eds) (1989) *Professional Burnout in Medicine and the Helping Professions.* New York: Haworth Press.

Wilmott, H. (1986) Organizing the profession *Accounting Organizations and Society* 11, 6, 555–80.

Wood, A. (1994) The solicitor in Europe, in Neale, P. (ed) *Creating European Professionals.* Leeds: University of Leeds Department of Continuing Professional Education.

Wood, R.G., Corcoran, M.E. and Courant, P.N. (1993) Pay differences among the highly paid *Journal of Labor Economics* 11, 3, 417–41.
Woodward, S. (1990) Education for life *Professional Lawyer* 1, 3, 11–13.
Zoltan, E. and Chapanis, A. (1982) What do professional persons think about computers? *Behavior and Information Technology* 1982, 1, 55–68.

Index

Abbott, A., 7, 8, 41, 47, 48, 79, 80, 99, 249
Abernethy, D., 146
Academic Tribes and Territories, ix
accountancy respondents, Acc/1, 65, 167, 202; Acc/2, 53; Acc/3, 91, 157, 178; Acc/4, 159, 162; Acc/5, 98, 198; Acc/6, 52, 121, 127, 128, 130, 187; Acc/7, 156, 184, 200; Acc/9, 225; Acc/10, 65, 177; Acc/11, 83, 155, 177, 188, 230; Acc/12, 71, 111, 119, 125; Acc/13, 119, 120; Acc/14, 73, 91, 162, 202, 222; Acc/15, 73, 96, 119, 159; Acc/16, 98; Acc/17, 92, 126; Acc/19, 72, 102, 103; Acc/20, 187; Acc/21, 47, 143, 246; Acc/22, 35, 47, 53, 65, 215, 246; Acc/23, 95, 102, 230; Acc/24, 112; Acc/25, 73, 74, 76, 87, 107, 112, 116; Acc/28, 95; Acc/29, 35, 177, 180, 198; Acc/30, 53, 58n., 74, 103, 191, 199
accountants and accountancy, 5, 16, 17, 19, 26, 33–36, 37, 42, 43, 44, 45, 50, 51, 53, 57n., 58n., 61, 65, 67, 68, 71, 72, 80, 83, 84, 88n., 94, 95, 96, 98, 100–101, 102, 103, 104, 105, 107, 108, 110, 111, 112, 113n., 116, 117, 119, 120, 121, 122, 123, 125, 128, 129, 130, 131, 132, 133, 148, 154, 156, 157, 162, 165, 166, 170, 171, 181, 198, 204, 225, 238, 239; academic accountants, 65, 246; auditing, 34, 35, 47, 103; certified accountants, 35; chartered accountants, 35, 98, 105; management accountants, 35, 47, 65, 84, 101
Accounting Standards Board, 65
Accounting Organizations and Society, 36
Acheson, H.W.K., 141
Addis, W., 8, 40, 42
advanced qualifications, 103–4, 156, 195, 246

Aldridge, M.D., 241
Allaker, J., 57n.
Allen, I., 91, 113, 115, 117, 118, 125, 127
Allery, L., 206n.
Al-Shehri, A., 153
American Accountancy Association, 33
American Board of Internal Medicine, 224
American Medical Association, 146
Anderson, L.J., 84, 160
Architects Journal, 38
Architects Registration Board (earlier Council), 37, 116
Architectural Association, 37
architects and architecture, 4, 5, 16, 17, 19, 36–38, 39, 40, 42, 43, 44, 45, 46, 53, 54, 55, 58n., 65–66, 67, 68–69, 70, 71, 72, 80, 82, 83, 84, 85, 86, 88n., 94, 95, 96, 98, 99, 101, 102, 104, 105, 107, 108, 109, 110, 112, 116, 121, 122, 123, 127, 128, 130, 131, 132, 133, 148, 152, 153, 156, 162, 163, 165, 166, 167, 170, 181, 189, 198, 205, 212, 218, 222, 225, 228, 238, 239, 245
architecture respondents, Arc/1, 72, 118, 121, 163, 167; Arc/2, 54, 107, 185, 189, 192; Arc/3, 43, 53, 76, 80, 86, 164, 189; Arc/4, 38, 80, 102, 108, 187, 193, 198; Arc/5, 74, 192, 194; Arc/6, 53, 163; Arc/7, 55, 73, 76, 80, 118, 185, 193, 201; Arc/8, 37; Arc/9, 127; Arc/10, 55, 65, 152, 203; Arc/11, 55, 72, 80, 122, 124, 154; Arc/12, 74, 86, 162, 194; Arc/13, 69, 121, 123, 163, 212; Arc/14, 104, 105, 120; Arc/15, 43, 53, 54, 82, 180; Arc/16, 99, 152, 162, 166, 212; Arc/17, 71, 85, 96, 98, 101, 166, 194; Arc/18, 66, 99, 143, 144, 185; Arc/19, 87, 107, 110, 159; Arc/20, 95, 153, 230;